Pascal Sigg
Mediating the Real

Contemporary Literature | Volume 27

Pascal Sigg, born in 1983, works as a journalist in Switzerland covering media, technology and democracy for various outlets. He studied English, German and comparative literature at the Universities of Bern and Zurich. He was a visiting researcher at Boston College in 2018 and holds a BA in Journalism and Communication from the Zürcher Hochschule für Angewandte Wissenschaften.

Pascal Sigg
Mediating the Real
Self-Reflection in Recent American Reportage

[transcript]

This work was accepted as a PhD thesis by the Faculty of Arts and Social Sciences, University of Zurich in the spring semester 2023 on the recommendation of the Doctoral Committee: Prof. Dr. Martin Heusser (main supervisor) and Prof. Dr. Michael C. Frank.

The Open Access edition is published with the support of the Swiss National Science Foundation.

Bibliographic information published by the Deutsche Nationalbibliothek
The Deutsche Nationalbibliothek lists this publication in the Deutsche Nationalbibliografie; detailed bibliographic data are available in the Internet at https://dnb.dnb.de/

This work is licensed under the Creative Commons Attribution 4.0 (BY) license, which means that the text may be remixed, transformed and built upon and be copied and redistributed in any medium or format even commercially, provided credit is given to the author.
https://creativecommons.org/licenses/by/4.0/
Creative Commons license terms for re-use do not apply to any content (such as graphs, figures, photos, excerpts, etc.) not original to the Open Access publication and further permission may be required from the rights holder. The obligation to research and clear permission lies solely with the party re-using the material.

First published in 2024 by transcript Verlag, Bielefeld
© Pascal Sigg

Cover layout: Maria Arndt, Bielefeld
Copy-editing: Anna Tomasulo, Chad Jorgenson and Sean O'Dubhghaill
Proofread: Alexandra Cox, Dortmund
Printed by: Majuskel Medienproduktion GmbH, Wetzlar
https://doi.org/10.14361/9783839473269
Print-ISBN: 978-3-8376-7326-5
PDF-ISBN: 978-3-8394-7326-9
ISSN of series: 2701-9470
eISSN of series: 2703-0474

Printed on permanent acid-free text paper.

Contents

Acknowledgments 7

Introduction

Mediating Mediatized Realities 11

1 Reportage and Mediation

1.1 The Complications of 'Literary Journalism' 43

1.2 The Human Qualities of Reportage 55

1.3 The Human Medium Inspecting Itself 71

2 On Real Communing: Mediating Coordinated Experience

2.1 Authenticity and Uncertainty in Touristic Experience 83

2.2 The Desperate Medium in David Foster Wallace's "A Supposedly Fun Thing I'll Never Do Again" (1997) 89

2.3 The Believing Medium in George Saunders's "The New Mecca" (2005) 115

2.4 The Incapable Medium in John Jeremiah Sullivan's "Upon This Rock" (2012) 133

2.5 Uncertainties and the Negotiation of Trust in Communing 149

3 On Real Bodies: Mediating Other Human Media

3.1 Reflexive Subjectivities and Their Differences 153

3.2 The Mysterious Medium in George Saunders's "Buddha Boy" (2007) 159

3.3 Aware Media in John Jeremiah Sullivan's
    "Getting Down to What is Really Real" (2011) 175

3.4 Different Media in Mac McClelland's
    "Delusion is the Thing With Feathers" (2017) 191

3.5 The Possibilities of Reflexivity 209

4 On Real Fragmentation: Mediating Violence

4.1 Material and Symbolic Violence 213

4.2 The Fractured Medium in George Saunders's "Tent City, U.S.A." (2009) 219

4.3 The Atoning Medium in Michael Paterniti's
    "Should We Get Used To Mass Shootings?" (2016) 237

4.4 The Resilient Medium in Rachel Kaadzi Ghansah's "A Most American
    Terrorist" (2017) 253

4.5 The Reflexivity of Violence 271

Conclusion

The Possibilities of Human Media 275

Bibliography 287

Acknowledgments[1]

This book is itself the result of countless acts of mediation that transcend various limits. I am highly grateful for the different acts of collaboration that I have gotten to experience along the way.

First and foremost, this book would never have exited the printing presses without the favorable conditions of my private life.

Jeanne Jaros has encouraged this wild project from start to finish. She also provided financial security for our young family throughout the process and raised two kids on the side.

My parents always stood for unconditional support despite their marginal understanding of the academic world.

My two employers during the affected time, Sportamt der Stadt Zürich (Manuela Schläpfer and Stephan Wild-Eck) and Infosperber (Urs P. Gasche) provided highly flexible, worker- and research-friendly conditions for me to continually sustain this project with part-time work.

Academically, my primary supervisor Prof. Martin Heusser put me on track by injecting the right thought in my mind at the right time and providing critical feedback as well as institutional support when needed.

---

1 Parts of this book have been previously published in the following papers:
Sigg, Pascal. "The Disclosure of Difference." In *The Routledge Companion to American Literary Journalism*, edited by William Dow and Roberta Maguire, 498–508. New York: Routledge, 2020.
Sigg, Pascal. "Witnessing and the Theorization of Reportage." In *Literary Journalism and Social Justice*, edited by Robert Alexander and Willa McDonald, 69–82. Cham: Palgrave Macmillan, 2022.

The fresh eyes, guidance and critical yet always constructive feedback of Prof. Michael C. Frank, my second supervisor, were instrumental to the book's finalization. The regularly held discussions with Frank, Olivia Tjon-a-Meeuw and Alan Mattli at the University of Zurich's English Department helped finetune my argument and sharpen entire paragraphs.

Josh Roiland helped in the very early stages by simply normalizing the possibility of the project. Chris Wilson at Boston College stood for much needed time of deep focus and reflection as he invited me to spend the spring term 2018 in Chestnut Hill. His dear support was perfectly complemented by the dearest possible hospitality of Kit Kilbourn and Scott Shear in Jamaica Plain. The stay itself was only made possible by the generous financial aid of the Emil-Boral-Foundation, which covered living expenses.

In addition, two trips to conferences in Halifax and Vienna as well as two short retreats to Mailly in France were paid for by the University of Zurich.

Anna Tomasulo, Chad Jorgenson and Sean O'Dubhghaill turned my written English into readable prose at various stages of the process.

Further thanks go to the entire community of the International Association of Literary Journalism Studies, which has provided a fertile environment for my research interests and definitely knows how to address social needs.

Finally, I would like to thank the Swiss Science Foundation (SNF) for financing the open access publication of this book, which the team at transcript competently turned into a simply delightful thing.

Introduction

Mediating Mediatized Realities

In 2007, the writer David Foster Wallace edited an annual compilation entitled *Best American Essays*.[1] In his foreword, Wallace reflected on the criteria used in the selection of the essays. As part of his reasoning, Wallace described contemporary US culture as "a culture and volume of info and spin and rhetoric that I know I'm not alone in finding too much to even absorb, much less to try to make sense of." In Wallace's view, this culture was marked by a permanent mediation that was particularly consequential for nonfiction writers:

> Part of our emergency is that it's so tempting ... to retreat to narrow arrogance, pre-formed positions, rigid filters, the 'moral clarity' of the immature. The alternative is dealing with massive, high-entropy amounts of info and ambiguity and conflict and flux; it's continually discovering new areas of personal ignorance and delusion. In sum, to really try to be informed and literate today is to feel stupid nearly all the time, and to need help. That's about as clearly as I can put it.[2]

Wallace argued that this state of social and cultural reality poses an acute, endless challenge to any human self that tries to make sense of reality, not least to a writer like himself. In his opinion, this reality craved both humility and a willingness to cooperate.

Wallace's position essentially combines two strains of argumentation; he perceives a general change in a cultural reality that is somehow decisively shaped by the very ways in which reality itself is mediated. This argument is identical, by and large, with the scholarly discourse surrounding mediatiza-

---

1   Foster Wallace, *The Best American Essays 2007*.
2   Foster Wallace, "Deciderization 2007 – A Special Report," xxiii.

tion, "a meta-process that is grounded in the modification of communication as the basic practice of how people construct the social and cultural world".[3]

This process, per definition, cannot be neutral. Typically, it has been conceived of as being driven by waves of technological innovation, each of which increased the role played by technical media in its respective culture. Many thinkers have pointed out that mediatization thus affects social interaction by causing a kind of separation, or even alienation, because it more clearly separates a physical entity from its symbolic meaning. The German media scholar Friedrich Krotz, for instance, has argued that "mediatization must be understood to be a dismantling process, as the growing role of media separates the unity of every instrumental action into a communicative and an instrumental action."[4]

Wallace claims that it is imperative that the authorial communication of reality be reinvented in order to live up to the ways in which communication affects reality in general, even while mediatization plays a central role in changes being made to the social and cultural world—and even as it is decisively driven by technology. In other words, writers have to come up with ways to describe and make palpable how technological mediation affects the very reality that they themselves write about. Most importantly, they must do so in a more engaging way than classic realism had, which he primarily associates with entertaining visuality. Classic realism, Wallace has claimed, is "soothing, familiar and anesthetic; it drops us right into spectation."[5] But what might this updated realism look like? In his poetological comment, Wallace only vaguely suggested that it would have to include an intensified self-reflection that resulted in both a sense of either weakness or humility and in a need for human collaboration.

Analyzing the practical answers to the task outlined by Wallace is this study's main objective. It explores how writers of reportage, such as Mac McClelland,[6] Rachel Kaadzi Ghansah, George Saunders, or David Foster Wallace himself, have taken on this complex challenge by way of emphasizing their

---

3   Krotz, "Mediatization: A Concept With Which to Grasp Media and Societal Change," 26.
4   Krotz, "Media, Mediatization and Mediatized Worlds: A Discussion of the Basic Concepts," 83.
5   McCaffery, "An Interview with David Foster Wallace," 138.
6   In 2018, McClelland underwent sex reassignment therapy and, consequently, identified himself as the male reporter Gabriel Mac. I herein stick to Gabriel Mac's former female identity, Mac McClelland, because it is highly significant for the analysis of his text and because, in fact, the text analyzed was published under his previous female name. Mac, "The End of Straight"; Mac, "About."

own existential humanity (as media manifested in various acts of self-reflection). First, the writers exhibit their own specific acts of mediation throughout their texts in four key domains. Thus, they anchor both material and symbolic acts of sensemaking in their bodies and assert the specific qualities of human mediation and aesthetic experience. Second, the writers demonstrate how their subjective sensemaking corresponds to the larger world, and how sensemaking is affected by a mediatization that occupies the core of the very real topics they write about: communing, subjectivity, and violence. In this way, these writers pit their specific human mediality against the larger processes of technological mediation that similarly shape social and cultural reality.

More to the point, I argue that these writers' self-reflective texts signify the human medium's response to technical media's commodification, spatialization, and anestheticization of human experience. The texts represent a specific way of a coming to consciousness as a medium within journalism's commercial context. Just like artists, to use Fredric Jameson's argument, reporters act "within a mediatic system in which their own internal production also constitutes a symbolic message and the taking of position on the status of the medium in question."[7] This kind of awakening, as a human subject within technologically mediated culture, involves a foregrounding of sensual perception, feeling, imagination, and memory in order to provide an epistemological depth by way of self-reflection that technical media alone cannot muster. On a larger level, as I argue in the conclusion, these texts amount to a human reclamation of agency by way of an intensification of critique that necessitates scrutinizing mediation itself.

This theoretical frame most obviously applies to a specific kind of realist writing in which the concepts of author and narrator—which are kept apart in the study of fictional literature for good reasons—converge. A specific portion of such writing has been theorized as literary journalism. As Josh Roiland has suggested:

> literary journalism is a form of nonfiction writing that adheres to all of the reportorial and truth-telling covenants of conventional journalism, while employing rhetorical and storytelling techniques more commonly associated with fiction. In short, it is journalism as literature.[8]

---

7   Jameson, *Postmodernism, or, The Cultural Logic of Late Capitalism*, 162.
8   Roiland, "By Any Other Name: The Case for Literary Journalism," 71.

Following Roiland's definition, then, literary journalism is the product of a narrowly defined kind of work that includes both reporting and writing. Literary journalism is infused with a clear intentionality to carry out a particular professional assignment. Writers of literary journalism are required to research a pre-determined topic and are expected to convey their findings in artful prose that tells a story. Hence, all of the texts analyzed in this study were originally conceived within this professional framework. The three texts by George Saunders, for instance, were contracted by GQ magazine, which sent Saunders to Dubai, Nepal, and Fresno, in order to experience a predetermined material aspect of contemporary reality first-hand. In Dubai, he experienced the emerging megacity as a global community. In Nepal, he investigated the reality of a Buddhist boy who had supposedly been meditating for an extended period. Finally, he literally exposed himself to homelessness by living in a camp in Fresno, all while pretending to be homeless.

The assignment's context also usually provides an indicator as to where these texts were originally published. These pieces were all first published in American periodical print magazines that commission this kind of reporting, even though they were occasionally compiled in essay collections or made available online thereafter. Another indicator of their connection to a specific branch of publishing, which focuses on magazine journalism, is their occasional acknowledgment of the industry itself. Some of the nine texts, which are analyzed in the chapters that follow, were nominated for a National Magazine Award in Feature Writing, and one of them won a Pulitzer Prize in Feature Writing. Finally, scholars like myself have explicitly categorized the texts written by David Foster Wallace, George Saunders, John Jeremiah Sullivan, and Mac McClelland as literary journalism.[9]

Importantly, I do not mean to imply that I view the challenge formulated by Wallace or the writers' responses thereto as new. Instead, I identify the contemporary configuration of an older less explicit, albeit still very modern, authorial stance that views communicative potential in the writer's self-reflection as a living human medium. Still, this synchronic study of nine exemplary texts (each selected for their extensive display of self-reflection published with and after David Foster Wallace) seeks to identify an intensification of authorial consciousness in reportage since the New Journalism of the 1960s and 1970s.

---

9   Roiland, "Derivative Sport: The Journalistic Legacy of David Foster Wallace"; Sigg, "The Disclosure of Difference."

Crucially, this intensification corresponds to a comparative increase in mediatization. The writers' motivations, broadly canonized under New Journalism, can be tied to concerns with mediation generally, concerns that were similar to (but not yet as pervasive as) those of the contemporary writers analyzed throughout this study. Many scholars share the view that New Journalism's emphasis on language or style was mainly a response to a media business, the primary mode of representation of which was an industry-driven objectivity more akin to images than texts. In Chris Anderson's view, for instance, the New Journalists' style and their very use of language was typified by a stubborn "belief in the power of language to order and create" and was itself the argument.[10] Jason Mosser has claimed that written language in works by New Journalists could attain a rhetorical power that could generate a sense of presence.[11] New Journalism has generally been credited with undermining "the authoritative versions of reality created by conventional journalism."[12] However, the writers of such experimental texts, from the 1960s and 1970s, mainly highlighted the impossibility of directly accessing meaning in a culture and society increasingly perceived of as fantastic, given that they primarily questioned communication itself.[13] These writers only began to reflect upon their own role as media in response to media technology's development, as the existing analyses of New Journalism suggest.

David Eason, for instance, has argued that the American New Journalism, of the 1960s and 1970s in particular, should primarily be read as a response to the ubiquity of visual mediation in a new mass-produced image-world that failed to account for social and cultural diversity. Most importantly, Eason also identified a modernist mode, in contradistinction to what he termed a realist approach in which reader and writer "are joined in an act of observing which assures that conventional ways of understanding still apply."[14] This approach

---

10   Anderson, *Style as Argument: Contemporary American Nonfiction*, 180; Hellmann, *Fables of Fact: The New Journalism as New Fiction*; Mosser, *The Participatory Journalism of Michael Herr, Norman Mailer, Hunter S. Thompson, and Joan Didion: Creating New Reporting Styles*, 33–42.
11   Mosser, *The Participatory Journalism of Michael Herr, Norman Mailer, Hunter S. Thompson, and Joan Didion: Creating New Reporting Styles*, 44; Winterowd, *The Rhetoric of the "Other" Literature*, 32.
12   Mosser, *The Participatory Journalism of Michael Herr, Norman Mailer, Hunter S. Thompson, and Joan Didion: Creating New Reporting Styles*, 54.
13   Eason, "The New Journalism and the Image-World," 192.
14   Eason, 192.

engages, according to Eason, in a "multilayered questioning of communication, including that between writer and reader, as a way of making a common world",[15] as is evident in the writings of Hunter S. Thompson, Norman Mailer, or Joan Didion. In other words, the experimentation undertaken by these writers mainly serves to emphasize communication's inconvenient aspects, which they perceive to be repressed in other forms of communication, such as the image-world that is manufactured by the mass media. I would suggest that, overall, the texts analyzed in my study take such concerns with communication or mediation one step further, even though I cannot deliver evidence by way of a synchronic analysis and there may be exceptions too.

A Postmodern Approach

It appears tempting, at first glance, to categorize my undertaking as the unearthing of a humanist post-postmodern turn in nonfictional literature, and particularly from a narrower literary studies perspective. David Foster Wallace's nonfiction has already been classified as post-postmodern, after all.[16] However, rather than departing from postmodern thought, I understand the texts that have been analyzed, as well as my own analysis thereof, as the very expression of postmodern ideas of knowledge and literature itself. Similar to certain postmodern ideas, the texts are concerned with countering realism on a larger level. For instance, Linda Hutcheon has argued, with regard to postmodern fiction, that it "asks its readers to question the process by which we represent our selves and our world to ourselves and to become aware of the means by which we *make* sense of and *construct* order out of experience in our particular culture."[17] More particularly then, this study aims to stake out the ways in which this claim might apply to recent literary journalism, an explicitly realist field of literature.

My approach relies on the work of French philosopher Jean-François Lyotard, who understood the postmodern as a tripartite structure. In his 1985 essay "Note on the Meaning of 'Post-'", Lyotard identifies three conflicting and contradictory versions of the postmodern: the first version marks the sense of succession in "post-" that signifies a new direction, compared to that taken by

---

15 Eason, 192.
16 Hoffmann, *Postirony: The Nonfictional Literature of David Foster Wallace and Dave Eggers*.
17 Hutcheon, "Telling Stories: Fiction and History," 235.

the modern.[18] The second version simultaneously suggests that this sense of succession ought not to be equated with a sense of progress in Western societies. This is because progress, as Lyotard writes, "seems to proceed of its own accord, with a force, an autonomous motoricity that is independent of us."[19] The third version points to a kind of critical self-reflection that Lyotard sees at work in postmodern thought, "a working through... performed by modernity on its own meaning."[20] For Lyotard, then, the postmodern combines a particular analysis of the modern western social world, as disrupted or disaggregated by forces of capitalism, with a continuous critical self-reflection that itself resists the possibility of taking any idea of continuity for granted.

My aim is to perform an analysis of contemporary literary journalism that takes Lyotard's three versions of the postmodern and his understanding of art as intervention into account and that expands the possible ways to present human experience.[21] Literary journalism and reportage, as discourse and genre, are at the very intersection of art and journalism—an explicitly realist practice and business—and appear particularly promising for a reevaluative postmodern study. Such an approach seeks to find what is different, and potentially new, in the texts that have been analyzed, while at the same time it scrutinizes the pre-existing categories of analysis of literary journalism and reportage as typically modern genres; in this way, it involves performing a self-reflection of modernity in ways similar to the writers themselves in their actual works of reportage.

Consequently, at the core of such an undertaking resides an updated and specific understanding of the key concepts of realist representation and hence genre, including the authorial self, reality, and their interrelations. This updating requires certain theoretical groundwork, the results of which are deployed throughout different areas of this study. As a primarily literary analysis, it places a premium on a critical analysis of the field of literary journalism and the genre of reportage.

Detailed discussions of genre and specifically the theoretical disentangling of literary journalism and reportage are presented in the following theoretical chapter titled "Reportage and Mediation". This generic and historical reevaluation necessitates an explicit construction of the concept of the author or writer

---

18 Lyotard, "Note on the Meaning of Post-," 76.
19 Lyotard, 77.
20 Lyotard, 80.
21 Lyotard, *The Postmodern Explained*.

as witnessing medium, which I present in the third theoretical section titled "The Human Medium Inspecting Itself". This rather prominent authorial self engages with and communicates presentations of heavily mediated realities. An initial, larger theoretical account of socially and medially constructed reality is given later on in this introduction. However, the three more specific aspects of reality that are represented in the writers' actual texts—communing, subjectivity, and violence—are theoretically introduced in the three main chapters, in which they are directly tied to the textual analyses of the texts that have been selected.

The Mediality of Literary Journalism

Most fundamentally, I view the texts analyzed as narratives that make truth claims. As such, they have to be distinguished from fictional narratives. In the same vein, they have to be viewed in light of what Martin Kreiswirth has termed the *narrativist turn* (an erupting critical interest in the ideology, ontology, and epistemology of narrative rather than its function or form). This interest has its roots in the Humanities' linguistic turn and that paradigm's general assumption that language serves as the primary condition for the possibility of both meaning and knowledge. Consequently, "research into social, political, psychological, cognitive, behavioral, philosophic, and cultural questions must be formulated in terms of linguistic issues."[22] Despite growing scientific interest, however, making the distinction between fictional and factual narrative has proven difficult, in part because, as communicative acts, both work similarly in that they communicate "temporal and causal relationships between agents and events".[23] Therefore, whether a narrative can be regarded as true, Kreiswirth has argued, lies mainly in a commitment to truth that devolves from context, contract, and convention.[24]

One of narrative's most defining characteristics as communicative form is its inherent connection to temporality. Paul Ricoeur, for instance, takes "temporality to be that structure of existence that reaches language in narrativity and narrativity to be the language structure that has temporality as its ultimate

---

22 Kreiswirth, "Merely Telling Stories? Narrative and Knowledge in the Human Sciences," 298.
23 Kreiswirth, 313.
24 Kreiswirth, 313.

referent".²⁵ Therefore, rhetorically, narratives that claim to be true are first and foremost structured as allegories. According to the poststructuralist critic Paul de Man, the figure of allegory acknowledges this temporality most explicitly.²⁶ Understood in a broader sense as a narrative "that continuously refers to another pattern of ideas or events",²⁷ allegory signifies an idea of representation that acknowledges (temporal) difference. In contrast to the symbol, de Man has stated, allegory "designates primarily a distance in relation to its own origin, and, renouncing the nostalgia and the desire to coincide, it establishes its language in the void of this temporal difference." ²⁸

De Man's observation has proven particularly useful as an instrument of critique in areas in which positivist or empiricist representation have dominated. In a landmark essay on the rhetorical turn in ethnography, James Clifford has argued that ethnographic writing ought to be understood as fundamentally allegorical.²⁹ Importantly, Clifford offers a way to use some of poststructuralism's main insights for a more elaborate analysis of reality's representation. Based on Clifford's argument, documentary film has also been read in terms of its allegorical structure.³⁰

Similarly, allegory helps to identify literary journalism's fundamental mediality in a twofold structure. Clifford has argued, again with reference to ethnographic writing, that it maintains "a double attention to the descriptive surface and to more abstract, comparative, and explanatory levels of meaning."³¹ Of course, this also holds true for literary journalism's texts. Here, allegory helps us to locate the areas of mediation in the relationships between a particular set of facts, usually stemming from human experience, and that experience's more generalized meanings. Importantly, allegorical mediation between the particular and the general is reciprocal and dynamic in the texts under analysis, since the general simply cannot exist without a corresponding particular and vice-versa.

In literary journalism, as in ethnography, these acts of mediation occur along the basic dimensions of narrative: content and form.³² In texts that claim

---

25   Ricoeur, "Narrative Time," 165.
26   De Man, "The Rhetoric of Temporality."
27   Clifford, "On Ethnographic Allegory," 99.
28   De Man, "The Rhetoric of Temporality," 207.
29   Clifford, "On Ethnographic Allegory."
30   Kahana, *Intelligence Work: The Politics of American Documentary*.
31   Clifford, "On Ethnographic Allegory," 101.
32   Clifford, 98.

to refer to an extratextual reality, they differ mainly in that the allegorical relationships in terms of content have to be situated in events located outside the text and that took place prior to its final publication. Their formal equivalents, however, mainly encompass the actual text's allegorical relations themselves and, therefore, concern the spatial and temporal differences between the text's finalization and its reading. As a consequence, any transcendence of the posited spatial and temporal difference between the particular subjective experiences in reality and their generalized meaning is only temporary. To make matters more complex still, this transcendence's temporality—and this is again in crucial difference to fictional texts—has a material component, in that it is physically embodied by the writer who then materializes it as text. In terms of content, then, writers communicate a certain consciousness, an overall set of values of what it means to live and be a human part of these realities. In terms of form, they communicate a set of formal features that are concretely employed and, hence, are an example of how a human experience can be expressed in arranged letters.

This existential aspect of literary journalism has largely remained unacknowledged in scholarly debates, as I show in the following chapter. That being established, the general theorization of literary journalism is highly contested and contradictory. As I will argue in the following chapter, this is at least in part due to generalized understandings of literature and journalism that are not concerned with the particularities of mediation or communication. One potential reason for this is that, as Christopher Wilson has claimed, there is precious little critical scholarship in the first place.[33] Another scholar, William Dow, has called for "much closer attention to the 'experimental progress' that combinatory and hybrid narrative forms have made and what writers are doing with such forms" and claims that "we also need to see how these forms interact with 'raw material', the actual workings and driving forces of culture and society."[34] My analysis also seeks to contribute to tackling these rather pressing research issues by making a general point about the critical analysis of literary journalism; by identifying and defining a specific strain of experimental drive in contemporary literary journalism that engages with literary journalism's existential mediality.

---

33   Wilson, "The Chronicler: George Packer's The Unwinding (2013)," para. 4.
34   Dow, "Reading Otherwise: Literary Journalism as an Aesthetic Narrative Cosmopolitanism," 119.

When it is considered by scholars, literary journalism often appears as a kind of hybrid between journalism and literature—that is, between fiction and nonfiction. These general binary oppositions risk obfuscating our view of very concrete texts, as I argue in my first chapter, because they themselves are compounds of contested and conflicting ideas. For instance, on the side of literary studies, questions of reference and function have been foregrounded. Literature, depending on the definition of literature one uses, is a term which has been perceived as synonymous with fiction from certain vantage points; therefore, such a thing as literary journalism simply cannot exist. Conversely, on the side of journalism, issues of form, modality, and style in particular have dominated critical discourse, which has been mainly concerned with demarcating this kind of journalism from industrial news journalism; questions of materiality and research methods have largely been taken for granted. Hence, in the very worst case, texts from the tradition of literary journalism can be seen as unworthy bastards: not humble enough to be literature proper, not serious enough to be journalism proper, and impossible either to situate generically or to grasp critically.

Mediatization and Reportage

To make the matter even more complex, the very subjects of recent literary journalism are themselves existentially mediated. Modern western societies and cultures, such as the U.S.A., are themselves constructed via infrastructures and processes of communication that are mediated by technology.[35] Nick Couldry and Andreas Hepp have detailed this material perspective in the following way:

> The fundamentally mediated nature of the social – our necessarily mediated interdependence as human beings – is ... based not in some internal mental reality, but rather on the *material* [emphasis in original] processes (objects, linkages, infrastructures, platforms) through which communication, and the construction of meaning, take place. Those material processes of mediation constitute much of the *stuff* [emphasis in original] of the social.[36]

---

35 Couldry and Hepp, *The Mediated Construction of Reality*, 1; Krotz, "Mediatization: A Concept With Which to Grasp Media and Societal Change," 28–31.
36 Couldry and Hepp, *The Mediated Construction of Reality*, 3.

Thus, as mentioned previously, Western societies take part in a meta-process behind modernity that has been theorized and termed *mediatization*, along with individualization, commercialization, and globalization.[37]

First, according to Friedrich Krotz, mediatization should be understood as a "historical, ongoing, long-term process in which more and more media emerge and are institutionalized."[38] Nick Couldry and Andreas Hepp have argued that this long-term process—the history of mediatization—can be broken down into three successive and overlapping transcultural waves: mechanization, electrification, and digitalization, with a nascent fourth wave, datafication. These waves are characterized by underlying technological changes in the media. According to this history, mechanization began with the invention of the printing press and continued as the industrialization of communication more generally culminated in print mass media. The electrification of communications media began in earnest with the invention of the electronic telegraph, and ended with broadcast media such as the radio and forms of telecommunication like the telephone. Digitalization is tied to the invention of computers, the mobile phone, or the Internet.[39]

Mediatization is by no means a neutral process, even though it may appear as a byproduct of a history of technological evolution. Krotz also pictures mediatization as a "process whereby communication refers to media and uses media so that media in the long run increasingly become relevant for the social construction of everyday life, society, and culture as a whole."[40] Mediatization is primarily driven by the changes in people's communication practices resulting from technological change. For example, an early manifestation of such a shift was observed when orality shifted to literacy. Writing was generally perceived as a technology that stood for increased de-contextualization, distancing, and precision when it first emerged, compared to orality. The change from oral to written culture was a move from sound to visuality, from the dominance of hearing to the dominance of sight and printed texts: in specific, it invited a sense of closure that oral speeches lacked.[41]

One of this study's central claims is that one explicit literary response to mediatization can be found in the genre of reportage. This particular genre

---

37 Krotz, "Mediatization: A Concept With Which to Grasp Media and Societal Change," 25.
38 Krotz, 24.
39 Couldry and Hepp, *The Mediated Construction of Reality*, 34–52.
40 Krotz, "Mediatization: A Concept With Which to Grasp Media and Societal Change," 24.
41 Ong, *Orality and Literacy: The Technologizing of the Word*, 77–114.

emerged in Europe during the second half of the 19th century and had an explicitly artistic drive. Compared to literary journalism, the theorization of reportage in Europe has revolved rather explicitly around the issue of human mediation when faced with a more generally technologically mediated reality. As I demonstrate in the following chapter, Egon Erwin Kisch's short theoretical manifestos help us to trace reportage's genesis as the account of a specifically human medium. Taken together, this historical contextualization of reportage in relation to mediatization supports what Jonathan Fitzgerald's theory claims, that changes in media technology have historically correlated with boosts in innovation within the field of literary journalism.[42]

The Critique of Technical Mediation

As indicated previously, shifts in favor of increased technical mediation have been viewed critically. Many thinkers have pointed out that mediatization generally changes social interaction by causing a kind of separation or even alienation because technical media spatializes, commodifies, and anestheticizes human experience. Shortly after the invention of mass printing, the very reproducibility of symbolic forms made possible by electronic media became an important lens for a harsher critique of the effects of technical mediation on human consciousness. In his highly influential essay "The Work of Art in the Age of Mechanical Reproduction" (1935), Walter Benjamin observed that new mechanical technologies worked in specific ways as media because of their reproductive powers. As a result of the extraction process, rather than production, reproducible art lacked a unique presence in space and time. In film, for instance, the use of the camera essentially subjected the actor to a series of optical tests, according to which the resulting film was compiled. Hence, Benjamin argued that the actor performed for the camera instead of the audience, which led to the audience taking the distanced position of a critic. "Those who are not visible, not present while he executes his performance", Benjamin stated, "are precisely the ones who will control it. This

---

42 Fitzgerald, "Setting the Record Straight: Women Literary Journalists Writing Against the Mainstream," 141.

invisibility heightens the authority of their control."⁴³ Thus, the actor's self-alienation is essentially put to great productive use.

As Benjamin's point only vaguely suggests, the emergence of electronic media technologies, such as cameras and microphones, turned the audience into a new kind of both distanced and involved witness. On the one hand, they affected the audience's experience of reality because their technological representations consisted of a wealth of engaging visual and aural evidence that conveyed a sense of power. This act of witness, as John Ellis has argued,

> enables the viewer to overlook events, to see them from more points of view than are possible for someone physically present: to see from more angles, closer and further away, in slow and fast motion, repeated and refined. Yet at the same time, and by the very act of looking, individuals in the witnessing audience become accomplices in the events they see. Events on a screen make a mute appeal: "You cannot say you did not know."⁴⁴

On the other hand, despite its plural character, this new modality of experience was limited to the audio-visual and had a distancing effect on the audience. Again, according to Ellis,

> the feeling of witness that comes with the audio-visual media is one of separation and powerlessness: the events unfold, like it or not. They unfold elsewhere and – especially in the case of film – another time as well. So for the viewer, powerlessness and safety come hand in hand, provoking a sense of guilt or disinterest.⁴⁵

It is this combination of engagement and distance, which are inherent in newer media technologies such as radio and TV, that has been criticized as having potentially anaesthecizing effects on audiences.⁴⁶

However, the decisive point that Benjamin raised was electronic media's reproducibility more generally. In this vein, the most prominent critique of

---

43   Benjamin, "The Work of Art in the Age of Its Technological Reproducibility: Second Version," 33.
44   Ellis, *Seeing Things: Television in the Age of Uncertainty*, 11.
45   Ellis, 11.
46   Main critical works with regard to U.S. society and culture that pursue this argument in more detail are, for example, Boorstin, *The Image: A Guide to Pseudo-Events in America*; Postman, *Amusing Ourselves to Death: Public Discourse in the Age of Show Business*.

recent mediatization stems, perhaps, from the French philosopher Jean Baudrillard who combined concerns of anaestheticization with concerns about reproduction. Baudrillard sweepingly argued that, in modern mediatized societies, reality disappeared behind a simulated world produced by mass media where "we live, sheltered by signs, in the denial of the real".[47] The main shift, according to Jean Baudrillard, occurs in the moment at which symbolic forms change because "they are no longer mechanically reproduced, but *conceived according to their very reproducibility* [emphasis in original]".[48] According to Baudrillard, it is in this moment that the signs, selected mainly on the basis of their very reproducibility, lose their material referents and give way to processes of simulation that work as perpetual tests according to a binary system of question/answer signals.[49] Baudrillard states with Marshall McLuhan that, in such an environment of mediatized reality, it "is in fact the medium, the very mode of editing, cutting, questioning, enticement, and demand by the medium that rules the process of signification."[50] One main consequence of mediatization, therefore, is the increased empowerment of technical media.

The analysis of the recent mediatization wave of datafication, characterized by computation and information, has to be read as a continuation of these earlier concerns. Today, the test's binary logic, identified by Benjamin, has found its most powerful expression in the computer. Frederic Jameson, for instance, has argued that the computer has changed the ways in which we conceive aesthetic representation and contributes to what he perceives as flatness or depthlessness, as a medium of reproduction rather than production. For Jameson, this is manifest in the expanding culture of the image, a weakening of temporality, and a waning of affect.[51]

The computer's most distinctive feature as medium, however, might be its capacity to mediate itself by way of a kind of reduced reflexivity. Mark B. N. Hansen has argued that "for the first time in history, the technical infrastructure of media is no longer homologous with its surface appearance."[52] This is to say that the computer offers no correlation between its technical storage faculty and sensory human perception. Consequently, Hansen perceives a separa-

---

47 Baudrillard, *The Consumer Society: Myths and Structures*, 34.
48 Baudrillard, *Symbolic Exchange and Death*, 56.
49 Baudrillard, 62.
50 Baudrillard, 65.
51 Jameson, "Postmodernism, or The Cultural Logic of Late Capitalism."
52 Hansen, "New Media," 178.

tion of technics and media that, in turn, illuminates two specific and different functions of media. On the one hand:

> to exteriorize human experience in durable, repeatable, and hence transmissible form; on the other, to mediate for human experience the non- (or proto-) phenomenological, fine-scale temporal computational processes that increasingly make up the infrastructure conditioning all experience in our world today. What is mediated in both cases is, to be sure, human experience, but according to two distinct programs: for whereas media in the first, traditional sense mediates human experience itself (its content is that experience), media in the second sense mediates the technical conditions that make possible such experience – the 'transcendental technicity' underlying real experience in our world today.[53]

In ways similar to Benjamin's camera, today's computers still contain the power to shape reality according to a principle of quantitative selection. As media, they are most effective, as Theodore Porter has argued, "if the world they aim to describe can be remade in their image."[54] People's communication practices change in relation to the patterns of the computer if, as the theory on mediatization suggests, the computer has become relevant for the social construction of everyday life, society, and culture.

Writers as Human Media

Taken together, the demands of allegory, the mediality of literary journalism, and the analysis of mediatization and its historical connection to reportage call for a detailed conception of the writer as a decidedly human medium. The theory that I will present in the following chapter acknowledges the specifically human capacities of perception and sensemaking, as well as the complexities of communication within the framework of professional writing. Such a theory also has to be situated within a larger and cultural, rather than functional, understanding of communication. In *Speaking Into the Air* (1999), John Durham Peters details an idea of communication that emphasizes dissemination rather than dialogue. For Peters, the idea of a perfect union of communicants in mutual understanding is misleading because of the communicants' fundamental

---

53 Hansen, 180.
54 Porter, *Trust in Numbers: The Pursuit of Objectivity in Science and Public Life*, 43.

spatial and temporal differences. Instead, it is the listener or reader who complements the received message as he or she interprets it.[55] It is this imbalance, as Peters shows, which marks the very possibility of social interaction. He argues that "communication should be measured by the successful coordination of behaviors"[56] and understood, thus, as "more fundamentally a political and ethical problem than a semantic one".[57] In sum, Peters's model of communication works well as the basis for a more elaborated theory of the writers or reporters, as the main generative subject in reportage, because it takes their very subjective specificities and ambivalences and their mass-medial function into account.

In line with Peters's larger theory, I conceive of writers of reportage as intentional eyewitnesses who witness by assignment.[58] In my theory, I use the analysis of witnessing provided by German media theorist Sybille Krämer based on the messenger as a figure where acts of inter- and excorporation intersect.[59] I understand these processes to take place with, within, and through the writer or reporter, thereby composing a particular overall mediality of the reporter as communicating human subject. I understand mediation as, according to Andreas Hepp and Friedrich Krotz, referring to "a very fundamental moment of communication as symbolic interaction" or construction of meaning.[60] I pair these with theoretical considerations of reportage by German literary scholar Michael Geisler. He was active during a rather recent wave of reportage theorizing in Germany in the 1970s and 1980s. Crucially, for Geisler, it was the reporter's very self-awareness as medium that defined the genre of reportage, which he distinguished from other journalistic text forms: "The degree to which the reporter is aware of this mediality [*Vermitteltheit*], how he applies it consciously and ultimately also makes the reader aware of it, marks the distance between the report and reportage."[61] In ways similar to Krämer's earlier grammar of witnessing, Geisler identified three areas of mediation, which can be attributed to the writer's sensory experience, the person of the writer, and the written text. He names, first, the selection of the excerpt

---

55 Peters, *Speaking into the Air: A History of the Idea of Communication*, 268.
56 Peters, 268.
57 Peters, 30.
58 Peters, "Like a Thief in the Night," 197.
59 Krämer, *Medium, Messenger, Transmission: An Approach to Media Philosophy*, 83.
60 Hepp and Krotz, "Mediated Worlds – Understanding Everyday Mediatization," 3.
61 Geisler, *Die literarische Reportage in Deutschland: Möglichkeiten und Grenzen eines operativen Genres*, 97.

of reality experienced by the writer; second, the person or character of the reporter; and third, the structuring of the portrayed selection of experienced reality in the text.[62]

Geisler's concept serves as a crucial launchpad for my own concept of the reporter as human medium. I distinguish four mediated domains in which writers of reportage are active, on the basis of both his and Krämer's findings, as well as those of Ashuri and Pinchevski. The first one I will call the area of *work*, namely their very intentional and selective production of experience of reality as mediated by professional journalistic practice and incentives. The second one is the area of *experience*, which concerns the writers' physical experience of the real world as mediated by their senses. The third area I call *interpretation*, since it relates to their explicit self-reflection and to the deliberations that are mediated by thought. The fourth and final area, *transmission*, refers to their communicative interactions with readers mediated by written language, that is to say, text.

The area of *work* is primarily mediated by the power structures and incentives at play in the professional field of freelance journalism. Freelancing is rather typical for works of literary journalism. For instance, Mark Kramer has argued:

> The defining mark of literary journalism is the personality of the writer, the individual and intimate voice of a whole, candid person not representing, defending, or speaking on behalf of any institution, not newspaper, corporation, government, ideology, field of study, chamber of commerce, or travel destination.[63]

Although Kramer somewhat idealizes the literary journalist's independence here, he raises an important point: freelance reporters adopt a professional role that is separate from the journalistic work that occurs within professional power structures.

This aspect includes the fact that writers deal more individually and freely with fundamental issues of knowledge production that are typically negotiated and institutionalized within either newsrooms or publishing houses. The most prominent of these are: Which aspects of reality deserve their specific attention and why? How are these aspects to be processed and turned into a text

---

62 Geisler, 96.
63 Kramer, "Breakable Rules for Literary Journalists."

and why? The first question concerns what is commonly called gatekeeping: an inevitable act of selection that takes place when researching for reportage. The second question concerns the professional principles that they are required to adhere to, such as telling the truth, being disciplined in verification, and maintaining independence.[64] How they select what merits their attention and how they turn the fruit of their attention's labor into a written text is, thus, affected by what Ashuri and Pinchevski call "the conditions of witnessing," the professional relationships with editors and readers in the context of which the texts are produced.[65] Needless to say, these relationships are deeply affected by capitalist incentives. As a contractor working for a publisher, a freelance writer produces and delivers a text that has been commissioned. The text is then printed and turned into a resource in order to attract attention as it performs in the media business's attention economy.[66] In sum, the work is performed both by the reporter, who researches and writes a reportage story, and by the story itself. In both cases, there are strong incentives to create a certain kind of value within a capitalist logic that mediates the work's performance.

In contrast to the area of work, the main mediation taking place in the areas of *experience* and *interpretation* is more explicitly concerned with the making of meaning that occupies the heart of reportage. If this meaning-making is affected in a rather sterile manner by the pervasive qualities of capitalist logic in the area of work, then it is utterly subjective in acts mediating experience and interpretation. Fully embodied by writers, these acts of mediation ascribe meaning to phenomenal experience and make sense through thought. What is central to this integrated approach, which views all human meaning-making as fundamentally body-based, is a broad understanding of aesthetics rooted in the premise that "all meaningful experience is aesthetic experience."[67] Crucially, as Mark Johnson argues, this entails that "[b]ody and mind are not separate realities, but rather aspects or dimensions of a process of organism-environment interaction, in which organism and environment are interrelated, in-

---

64 Kovach and Rosenstiel, *The Elements of Journalism. What Newspeople Should Know and the Public Should Expect*, 5; Chris Wilson lists a range of texts on how these principles can be applied to specifically narrative journalism. Wilson, "Chapter 1: Introduction and First Principles."
65 Ashuri and Pinchevski, "Witnessing as Field," 140.
66 Celis Bueno, *The Attention Economy: Labour, Time and Power in Cognitive Capitalism*; Franck, "The Economy of Attention in the Age of Neoliberalism"; Wu, *The Attention Merchants*.
67 Johnson, *The Aesthetics of Meaning and Thought*, 2.

terdependent and interdefined."⁶⁸ Meaning is produced aesthetically in these processes of interaction, which make up our ideas of ourselves and our world. More specifically, it is past, present, or possible future experience that defines the meaning we assign to people, events, or objects.⁶⁹

Experience and its interpretation have a fundamentally qualitative and temporal character. Following the pragmatist philosopher John Dewey, Mark Johnson argues that the human mediation of experiential situations occurs in particular reactions to particular aspects of a remembered past, a perceived present, or to an imagined future experience.⁷⁰ Although every such experiential situation has a distinctive unifying quality, any attempt to assign meaning thereto or to conceptualize it will necessarily select some of its aspects and will, ultimately, miss the unity of the entire situation.⁷¹ Johnson also shows that any meaning assigned to any experiential situation is felt before it is known. This temporal hierarchy associates feelings and emotions with a sense of immediacy.⁷² This is why they are particularly important in human acts of interpreting past, present, or possible future events. Johnson states:

> Emotional response patterns are, literally, changes in our body state in response to previous changes in our body state caused by our interactions with our environment, and they usually precede any reflective thinking or conceptualization. In that sense, they might be called "noncognitive" (as not conceptual and not propositional); but they are nevertheless at the heart of our cognitive processes, taken in the broadest sense, as concerned with all the ways we experience, make, and transform meaning.⁷³

Johnson has a lot more to say about this distinction, as well as about the importance of emotion and feelings for the human creation of meaning. Most important for the mediation occurring through writers' sensory experience and interpretation, however, is the proximity of emotions and feelings to the sensory perception of particular characteristics of reality and their distinction from later reflective thinking. As primary, physical human acts of meaning-making, emotional responses play an important role in the writer's interpretation

---

68 Johnson, 14.
69 Johnson, 14.
70 Johnson, 15–16.
71 Johnson, 17.
72 Johnson, 19–20.
73 Johnson, 21.

of reality and function as a crucial threshold between sensory experience and interpretation.

Another of the human medium's singular qualities is the fundamental interrelatedness of human organism and environment. This essentially supports Usher's claim to the specific epistemic quality of reporters' 'being there'.[74] The specific processes of this interrelation are detailed in a recent book by the science journalist Annie Murphy Paul. In fact, extra-neural resources are crucial to both human thinking processes and physical activity, surroundings, and human company have all been proven to shape the human interpretation of experience. Murphy Paul distinguishes between *embodied cognition*, *situated cognition*, and *distributed cognition*. Embodied cognition is concerned with the body's role in thinking and, for instance, how hand gestures can enhance the human interpretation of abstract concepts. Situated cognition refers to the effects that place can have on human thinking, such as how environments can instill a sense of human belonging or control and can heighten performance and concentration, for example. Distributed cognition means the ways in which human cooperation affects individual human action and can produce results that exceed the possibilities of a group's members' individual capabilities. Annie Murphy Paul's observations are based on the theoretical considerations outlined in a paper by Andy Clark and David Chalmers. The two philosophers examine how the mind can be extended by technology, such as a notebook, and argued in 1998 that "there is nothing sacred about the skull and the skin"[75] and "once the hegemony of skin and skull is usurped, we may be able to see ourselves more truly as creatures of the world."[76] This view contradicts popular metaphors of the human brain as either a computer or muscle and suggests a discrete entity that is locked in the skull that determines the quality of human thinking, has fixed traits that can be measured, ranked, and compared, and are congruent with the significance of individualism in postmodern Western societies.[77]

The area of *transmission* highlights the mediation that shapes the transmission of physically produced meaning that is stored and distributed in both

---

74 Usher, "News Cartography and Epistemic Authority in the Era of Big Data: Journalists as Map-Makers, Map-Users, and Map-Subjects."
75 Clark and Chalmers, "The Extended Mind," 14.
76 Clark and Chalmers, 18.
77 Murphy Paul, *The Extended Mind: The Power of Thinking Outside the Brain*, 9.

writing and text. It, thus, similarly emphasizes writing's fundamentally social aspect. Most important in this regard is the writers' awareness that acts of reading themselves represent a human experience that entails processes of individual and communal meaning-making. This means, according to the basic premises of reader-response theory, that a text does not really exist until it is read by a reader. This view accords readers a fairly active role as producers of a text's meaning. By reading, then, they enter into collaborative relationships of meaning-making with the text's authors.[78] As Stanley Fish has argued, in so doing readers enter different interpretive communities "made up of those who share interpretive strategies ... for constituting [texts'] properties and assigning [texts'] intentions".[79] Basically, any potential meaning that is communicated in any text is contingent upon its interpretation by its readers, who may interpret it differently at either the same time or at different times. Just like witnesses then, reporters fundamentally depend on the audience's trust.

Still, there are nuances. The reading process at play in nonfiction differs, as Phillip Lopate has argued, from the one involved in reading works of fiction. While fiction may offer the possibility of delving into a created world, potentially to the point of forgetting that reading is taking place at all, nonfiction permanently reminds readers that they are in contact with another, real human being working out a problem. Lopate states: "What makes me want to keep reading a nonfiction text is the encounter with a surprising, well-stocked mind as it takes on the challenge of the next sentence, paragraph, and thematic problem it has set for itself."[80] The experience of these processes of reading and corresponding meaning-making takes place, of course, away from the text. Nevertheless, we can still find traces of the writers' awareness of the readers' agency and their reading for the story of a real human being working to solve a problem within reportage texts. For instance, it can manifest itself rather explicitly in what Chris Wilson, in his study of immersion journalism, has called the second-order narrative: "a coexisting literary story about how the text we're reading ostensibly came to be researched and written."[81] Writers' awareness of readers' agency can also manifest itself more subtly in a text's particular formal or stylistic aspects, such as in its composition or direct reader address.

---

78   Cuddon and Preston, "Reader-Response Theory," 726.
79   Fish, "Interpreting the 'Variorum,'" 483.
80   Lopate, *To Show and To Tell: The Craft of Literary Nonfiction*, 6.
81   Wilson, "Immersion and Second-Order Narrative," 347.

Of course, all four of these domains of mediation should not be seen as equal instantiations of one and the same kind of mediation, but which instead come in different combinations and hierarchies. For instance, as I hinted at previously, a post-structural theorist of literature would point out that the area of transmission rules all of the others, since all acts of mediation are ultimately expressed in text. By contrast, a more strictly Marxist reader would point to the importance of the work's circumstances that pervade all acts of mediation, very much including transmission. However, as will be seen in my concrete analyses of concrete texts, these areas mediate each other as they interact and intersect in occasionally wonderous ways that defy clear-cut distinctions and isolations, but which nonetheless produce impressions of peculiarly mediating subjectivities. My main point with respect to these four areas is not, then, primarily their conceptual analytical separation, but rather their real simultaneous integration into the very real physical presence of a human writer existing in space and time. The main claim of my analysis is that this integrated mediation contrasts the real technological forces at play in mediatization that separate symbolic and material action.

Unlike fictional literature, it is also this integrated character of human mediation in nonfiction that necessitates a narratological approach that does not strictly separate author from narrator. In the following analyses, the texts are understood in the sense of the rhetorical narratologists James S. Phelan and Peter J. Rabinowitz as being designed by their "authors (consciously or not) to affect readers in particular ways."[82] Consequently, this means that the author as a real, existing human being bears responsibility for the narrator as a textual persona. The text thus appears as the rhetorical performance of an author who both narrates and argues for the credibility of his or her narration. To a large degree, the foundations of both of these functions—narration and argumentation—are inevitably intertwined and performed off the page. The writer conducts research for the potential story and this research itself becomes part of the story that he or she ultimately tells in the text. This means that the actions of writers performed off the page can be viewed not just as merely plot-driving scenes, featuring an intra-diegetic narrator in the story being told, but also as instances of the writers' self-characterization in the text as reliable and trustworthy narrators.[83]

---

82 Phelan and Rabinowitz, "Narrative as Rhetoric," 5.
83 In his introduction to reading narrative journalism, Chris Wilson argues this crucial case in much greater detail. He states: "Matters of style and selection really *can't* be

Presence and Production

My theory of the reporter as human medium implies certain consequences for analyses of literary journalism. As mentioned previously, it insists on the very material processes of meaning-making in reportage depending on the very existence and presence of a physical human body as the precondition for communication. This approach is decisive because the human medium's physical presence implies a stronger human agency and carries a specific epistemic quality. Nikki Usher has shown that reporters' 'being there' amounts to a claim to place-based epistemic authority that includes the communication of what this presence means in ways not available to other social actors. "Historically", she argues, "journalists retained this role by exercising power over the platforms people used to access news and by taking advantage of their material resources, professional practices, and routines".[84] Consequently, when seen as *human* media, reporters engage in the very *production* of knowledge, not merely in its neutral transmission.

This perspective amounts to a reconstitution of transmission as generative rather than neutral. As Sybille Krämer has shown, this reconstitution, in turn, only works if the witness's—or the reporter's—audience considers him or her to be credible and when situated within the context of larger intersubjective communication. It is the result of a fundamentally social process, essentially, where knowledge is produced by way of witnessing.[85] This materialist perspective on communication, then, ultimately also serves to draw attention to how, as Raymond Williams has argued, the means of communication are also always means of production.[86]

Taken together, my approach amounts to a rather specific theoretical stance that is concerned with nonfictional narratives that integrate embodied and discursive knowledge in the particular role of the writer as witness or, more generally, as medium. I necessarily depart from some of the main arguments offered in critical debates about narrative in general, which are mostly

---

separated from the interpretive work of a given work of narrative journalism: rather, they tell us *how* a journalist interprets the events he or she reports on." Wilson, "Chapter 1: Introduction and First Principles."

84 Usher, "News Cartography and Epistemic Authority in the Era of Big Data: Journalists as Map-Makers, Map-Users, and Map-Subjects," 248.
85 Krämer, *Medium, Messenger, Transmission: An Approach to Media Philosophy*, 145–146.
86 Williams, "Means of Communication as Means of Production."

based on concepts of narrative fiction or text more generally.[87] For instance, from my point of view, writers of reportage are unable to definitively represent reality because they never work alone. Moreover, they always fundamentally operate in cooperation with their readers and depend upon their attention, understanding, and trust. However, this by no means amounts to them being dead, even metaphorically, as one of the most prominent poststructuralist arguments has posited.[88] These truths or facts are constructed, but not fictional, if reportage texts could still be deemed to communicate true or factual stories. They are subjectively and socially constructed by way of the writers' and readers' mutual acknowledgment of the very possibilities and limits of their own bodies, as well as by the very temporal and spatial separation that is inherent in communication. In the present study, I use this framework of the writer as human medium in two ways; initially, it functions as an existential definition of the authorial subject and the delineation of a specific genre of nonfiction in which the roles of author and narrator are integrated. Subsequently, and more importantly, I use it as a prism through which to identify self-reflection represented in the texts.

Self-Reflection in Recent American Reportage

As my analyses show, each text carries a unique imprint of self-reflection. In each case, the four domains of mediation are manifested, albeit to different degrees, and are shaped in distinct ways. My intention was not to mechanically assign them to different passages, but instead to use them as launchpads for textual analyses that seek to illuminate broader issues—communing, subjectivity, and violence—in modern American society and culture. The texts analyzed here are all products of a human processing of intentional experience and were composed by American writers. The writers all left the comfort of their desks to experience contemporary realities from the perspective of an American subject confronted with the specific task outlined by Foster Wallace. Their self-reflection, thus, showcases the actual display of the self in modern American society. It reflects upon this self's intrinsic construction and agency and

---

87 Kreiswirth, "Merely Telling Stories? Narrative and Knowledge in the Human Sciences," 302.
88 Barthes, "The Death of the Author."

it looks at how this self is part of a larger community that is shaped by human action in both symbolic and material reality.

First and foremost, as I explore in more detail in the third section of the following theory chapter, their self-reflection amounts to the self-affirmation of the reporter as human medium. In nonfictional literature, such as reportage, critique by way of self-reflection often has a defining function. However, many of the most popular analytical concepts used to analyze self-reflection in literary texts, such as metafictionality or autofiction, apply exclusively to fictional literature and hence to a decidedly different kind of mediation. Still, overlaps exist. For instance, as Mary K. Holland has demonstrated, various links between realism and metafiction have been made throughout the course of theorizing the two concepts. One of the main insights into these connections and overlaps is that literature foregrounds the inevitable integration of form and idea.[89] My claim is that reportage writers also foreground a roughly corresponding kind of integration in the texts analyzed, as they integrate the negotiation of concerns pertaining to the material production of both experience and its symbolic meaning.

I have selected the sample of texts according to their date of publication, following David Foster Wallace's iconic essay collection in 1997.[90] As the means of their production indicate, they were all initially produced for publication in an American magazine at short-story-length; only a few were amended and extended in order to be included in book collections. Where this was the case, I have used the newer version for analysis. In order to conform to the generic frame of reportage, I have only selected texts that primarily relied upon the American author's subjective, first-hand experience of reality and combined this with a high degree of self-reflection. The selection also seeks to exemplify the diversity of authorial perspectives that shed light upon specific themes from different subjective angles. Through the selection of three texts by George Saunders and two by John Jeremiah Sullivan, it furthermore examines the diversity of manifestations of self-reflection within the body of a single author's work.

I have organized the nine textual analyses into three thematic chapters in order to illuminate their allegorical rhetorics and cultural and social specificity. These chapters highlight how writers' specific self-reflection as human media

---

89   Holland, *The Moral Worlds of Contemporary Realism*, 53.
90   Foster Wallace, *A Supposedly Fun Thing I'll Never Do Again: Essays and Arguments*.

emphasizes the subjective construction of reality's complex and singular mediality. Against the background of the social and cultural issues at stake, they furthermore ponder the individual and collective human agency in the material and symbolic world- and meaning-making more generally.

The first chapter of textual analyses examines how writers reflect the irreproducibility of human experience as they combine self-reflection with analyses of human communing in tourism. Due to its influential character, I begin with David Foster Wallace's "A Supposedly Fun Thing I'll Never Do Again" (1997).[91] In this text, Foster Wallace combats the despair that he feels aboard a cruise ship with an intense exercise in self-reflection that seeks to unveil the insincerity of the consumerist narratives shaping the experience of the cruise community. Foster Wallace, thus, creates a specific kind of awareness and attentive subjectivity in order to engage with a challenging reality. More optimistic than Wallace, George Saunders describes his experience of Dubai in, rather hopeful, terms as a manifestation of the possibilities of capitalist globalization. In "The New Mecca" (2007),[92] he identifies more basic human similarities and possibilities. He productively engages in social and communicative interactions, subject to the rules of global capitalism of course. Finally, the third text, John Jeremiah Sullivan's "Upon This Rock" (2012),[93] explores the power of religion to create community by means of the shared belief in a narrative. Attending a Christian rock festival, Sullivan contrasts his own inability to believe in God with Jesus's aestheticization of weakness, thereby reflecting on the shared aspects of storytelling in religion and in writing about religion. Although their approaches and interpretations vary, the writers counter the ritual performance of pre-fabricated trust in touristic experience with narratives of more fundamentally uncertain communing in all three texts.

The second analytical chapter looks at texts of reportage that employ authorial self-reflection to profile other human media and thereby illustrate the possibilities of irreproducible, singular human self-creation in contemporary mediatized societies. The first text, George Saunders's "Buddha Boy" (2007),[94] examines the physical possibilities of mind-control, exemplified by a meditating teenage bodhisattva. This is contrasted with Saunders's own acts of mind-control in his interpretation of experience. In this demonstration of his own

---

91 Foster Wallace, "A Supposedly Fun Thing I'll Never Do Again."
92 Saunders, "The New Mecca."
93 Sullivan, "Upon This Rock."
94 Saunders, "Buddha Boy."

mind's agency, he lays the foundation for the case that the capabilities of the human subject to make itself are potentially wider than humanely understandable. In the chapter's second textual analysis, I demonstrate how John Jeremiah Sullivan's "Getting Down to What is Really Real" (2011) playfully juxtaposes the self-awareness of the cast members of a reality TV show with his own self-awareness as the performed character of his writing. As he turns his own self-awareness into an object, he illuminates the reality-TV stars' acting as playful identity construction. In the third text analyzed in the chapter, "Delusion is the Thing With Feathers" (2017),[95] Mac McClelland portrays two ornithologists on a research trip to Cuba. By showing how her own experience differs vastly from those of the two birders, she also points to the constructed character of their subjectivities and to the productive aspects of difference. In all three texts, writers zoom in on their subjects' performance of reflexivity that reveals human subjectivity's existential plasticity and a realm of possibility for change that resists objectification.

With the final group of case studies, I analyze how three texts engage with violence by considering its reflexive mediality and the consequential limits of technological mediation primed for reproducibility. In "Tent City, U.S.A." (2009),[96] for instance, George Saunders recounts the story of his own experience in a homeless camp in Fresno, California. In his self-reflective report on the structural violence of homelessness, he links the precarious social and material conditions in the camp to the fundamentally social aspects of communication. In "Should We Get Used To Mass Shootings?" (2016), Michael Paterniti visits scenes of past mass shootings and reflects upon the effects of the mediation of gun violence. By analyzing how the personal and industrial mediation of past shootings affects potential future acts of violence, he points to deadly violence's fundamentally objectifying character. In the final text under discussion, Rachel Kaadzi Ghansah's "A Most American Terrorist" (2017),[97] the writer's moral production of experience serves as a testament to the racist reality of contemporary U.S. society. Necessary, harrowing, and revealing, her black body's research experience integrates reflections on intention, interpretation, and communication as acts of nonviolent resistance; she reveals racist violence's fundamentally cultural and social roots by detailing the complexities of the making of her own role. As the authors demonstrate in

---

95   McClelland, "Delusion Is the Thing with Feathers."
96   Saunders, *Tent City, U.S.A.*
97   Ghansah, "A Most American Terrorist: The Making of Dylann Roof."

these three texts, the material and symbolic causes and effects of violence are deeply intertwined. As a consequence, the authors' complex acts of mediation turn into urgent acts of witnessing imbued with a moral imperative.

As I detail in the conclusion, the writers' self-affirmation, as decidedly human media, can be read as a reaction to recent developments in media technology. As kinds of supermedia that mimic humans, computers have come to shape modern Western societies and cultures with their capabilities of integrating symbolic and material acts by way of a limited reflexivity under a binary logic. Although this is never directly addressed, writers' increased self-reflection can be interpreted as an answer to such technological mediation, given that it seeks a more humble and humane connection with readers that resists reproducibility and insists on the mediated quality and fundamental ethics of all communication about human experience.

1 Reportage and Mediation

1.1 The Complications of 'Literary Journalism'

Mapping out the theoretical terrain of literary texts most explicitly concerned with the representation of reality—a kind of nonfictional realism—is a complex endeavor. Any theory of such a genre must simultaneously acknowledge the texts' grounding in documentary authorial intention and experiential materiality, as well as the eventual product's very formal, textual character. This multidisciplinary complexity might have been one of the reasons that pushed Barbara Lounsberry to argue that such literature was "the great unexplored territory of contemporary criticism" in 1990.[1] The critical conversation around such texts has shifted noticeably in the thirty years since Lounsberry's book. Literary journalism has become established as a useful point of reference for issues of genre, in addition to assuming the status of an academic discipline in its own right. On the institutional level, this has led to an increase in scholarly work on literary journalism, while the emergence of literary journalism has imposed terminological unity on a rather fractured landscape, on the level of actual critical theory.

However, this unification has occurred in broadly general, predominantly formal, terms. The term "literary journalism" initially surfaced in the U.S. as a way of referring to a kind of journalism more akin to realist novels than to traditional news media.[2] The term can be traced back as far as 1907, to the anonymous "Confessions of 'a Literary Journalist,'" whose author draws a contrast

---

[1] Lounsberry, *The Art of Fact: Contemporary Artists of Nonfiction*, xi.
[2] In 1905, Hutchins Hapgood, an early proponent of the idea of a more literary kind of journalism, suggested turning the journalistic interview into a form of autobiography. He found that a real character could be turned into a type representing a certain social class, which would make for vital literature. Thus, he fused Marxist ideas about literary realism with journalistic methods. However, he did not yet use the term literary journalism. Hapgood, "A New Form of Literature."

between the reporter's two conflicting tendencies towards "objective observation" and "subjective imagination,"[3] while confessing that he is "just telling the story as it appeared to me."[4] As an object of scholarly interest, literary journalism made its first major appearance in 1937 when Edwin Ford published *A Bibliography of American Literary Journalism*,[5] only to disappear once again from critical discourse for almost 50 years.[6] The term resurfaced in 1984, with the publication of *The Literary Journalists: The New Art of Personal Reportage*[7] by Norman Sims.[8] At that time, the term tapped into a multidisciplinary conversation that had been prompted by the proliferation of experimental journalistic texts in the 1960s and 1970s and by Tom Wolfe's bold proclamation of New Journalism.[9]

Following Sims' publication, literary journalism witnessed a surge in interest from researchers who sought to challenge Wolfe's claim to novelty and to trace the genre's history.[10] This development was supported by institutional efforts, such as the foundation of the *International Association of Literary Journalism Studies*, in 2006.[11] As a result, research interest has expanded and become more diverse since then. More recently, scholars have begun to explore literary journalism's diverse global histories and cultural peculiarities.[12]

---

3   Anonymous, "The Confessions of 'a Literary Journalist,'" 376; For a detailed history of American literary journalism, see Hartsock, *A History of American Literary Journalism: The Emergence of a Modern Narrative Form*.
4   Anonymous, "The Confessions of 'a Literary Journalist,'" 371.
5   Ford, *A Bibliography of Literary Journalism in America*.
6   Roiland, "By Any Other Name: The Case for Literary Journalism," 66.
7   Sims, *The Literary Journalists: The New Art of Personal Reportage*.
8   Sims himself credits Sarah R. Shaber with the use of the term in 1980. Sims, *True Stories: A Century of Literary Journalism*, 11.
9   Roiland, "By Any Other Name: The Case for Literary Journalism."
10 Connery, "Discovering a Literary Form"; Kerrane and Yagoda, *The Art of Fact: A Historical Anthology of Literary Journalism*; Hartsock, *A History of American Literary Journalism: The Emergence of a Modern Narrative Form*; Sims, *True Stories: A Century of Literary Journalism*.
11 International Association of Literary Journalism Studies, "About Us."
12 Bak and Reynolds, *Literary Journalism across the Globe: Journalistic Traditions and Transnational Influences*; Keeble and Tulloch, "Introduction: Mind the Gaps, On the Fuzzy Boundaries between the Literary and the Journalistic"; Keeble and Tulloch, *Global Literary Journalism: Exploring the Journalistic Tradition*.

Hierarchical Distinctions and Blurred Boundaries

Despite the (global) notoriety it has attained, the meaning of the term "literary journalism" is still the subject of constant debate and the critical conversation about works that would qualify as literary journalism remains highly fragmented.[13] These disconnections are mainly due to the contradictory premises of literary journalism's twin components. While the qualifier "literary" refers to a rather broadly defined set of textual products, as well as specific formal features, "journalism" can at least signify both certain professional practices of knowledge production and the diverse forms of this knowledge's communication.

On the one hand, then, "literary journalism" gathers a diverse set of conflicting meanings; however, the binary compound "literary journalism" also insinuates a clear boundary between literature and journalism on the other. This is an assumption that has proven problematic in theories of genre. While the term seemed useful for drawing distinctions within the journalistic trade, as well as for studying it, scholars from other disciplines have either ignored or rejected it. During the 1970s and 1980s, shortly before "literary journalism" started to become widely used, a good portion of the critical analyses of New Journalism was based on concepts such as composition, documentary, or the essay. In their readings, scholars used the generic term "literary nonfiction," thereby renouncing any explicit affiliation with journalism.[14] However, other analyses from the same period seem to take issue with the term "literature." Phyllis Frus, for instance, explicitly avoids the term, arguing that honoring exclusively

> selected forms of journalism as literature emphasizes the line that separates the two modes, confirming the late-nineteenth-century notion of literature that arose specifically to exclude journalism and other factual narrative, defining literature as a collection of timeless works of universal value and appeal.[15]

---

13   Keeble, "Literary Journalism," 2018, 2; Wilson, "The Chronicler: George Packer's The Unwinding (2013)," para. 4.
14   See, i.e. Weber, *The Literature of Fact: Literary Nonfiction in American Writing*; Anderson, *Style as Argument: Contemporary American Nonfiction*; Anderson, *Literary Nonfiction: Theory, Criticism, Pedagogy*; Lounsberry, *The Art of Fact: Contemporary Artists of Nonfiction*.
15   Frus, *The Politics and Poetics of Journalistic Narrative: The Timely and the Timeless*, 5.

Other scholarly analyses—particularly those conducted from within the framework of literary studies—approached works of New Journalism as fiction and used terms such as "nonfiction novel,"[16] "documentary fiction,"[17] or "fables of fact."[18]

From a literary studies perspective, this indicates that criticism of "literary journalism", as a term, denotes a genre that is grounded in the problem of shifting definitions of "literature". Historically, these definitions are rife with value judgments and are frequently served to elevate literature above other forms of writing such as philosophy or history. It was Plato who first introduced the idea of different ways of speaking about the world, when he differentiated between reason and mimesis. Significantly, he imbued the distinction with an explicit value judgment. Preferring abstract analysis, Plato viewed the artful imitation of the world as a dangerous and irrational mirror.[19] Plato's student Aristotle, in his influential *Poetics*, inverts his teacher's valuation, using a slightly different taxonomy in which mimesis is elevated over ethics. For Aristotle, mimesis contains an internal logic and unity based on plot. As such, it is mainly concerned with probability and necessity. From this perspective, it stimulates reason because it provides extraordinary insights. Aristotle seems to suggest that mimesis need be neither precise nor true to fact, but is mainly bound to the causal chains expressed in plot. In his view, impossible or fictional events could even be preferable to the truth, on condition that they adhere to a probable or necessary logic.[20]

This elevation of probability or necessity over factual accuracy was also manifested in Aristotle's influential distinction between philosophy and poetry, on the one hand, and history on the other. While poetry is concerned with probability and necessity, according to Aristotle, history is bound to factuality. "Poetry," he argues, "is something more philosophic and of graver import than history, since its statements are of the nature of universals whereas those of history are singular."[21]

---

16 Zavarzadeh, *The Mythopoeic Reality: The Postwar American Nonfiction Novel*; Hollowell, *Fact and Fiction: The New Journalism and the Nonfiction Novel*.
17 Foley, *Telling the Truth: The Theory and Practice of Documentary Fiction*.
18 Hellmann, *Fables of Fact: The New Journalism as New Fiction*.
19 Potolsky, *Mimesis*, 15–22.
20 Potolsky, 39–41.
21 Aristotle, *Poetics*, 17.

Aristotle's distinction strongly influenced debates on literary mimesis in a way that decisively shaped our understanding of literature and complicated its relationship with other modes of discourse, such as history or journalism. For instance, in the 16th century, Sir Philip Sidney elevated the poet over the philosopher and the historian precisely because he avoids explicit mimesis. Sidney viewed the poet as a kind of mediator who "nothing affirms, and therefore, never lieth."[22]

Roughly four hundred years later, in another line of separating reasoning, Austin Warren and René Wellek have argued that literature has its own truth, because it operates in a separate realm. They claimed that "art is substantively beautiful and adjectivally true (i.e., doesn't conflict with truth)."[23] In their view, literature, in contrast to history or philosophy, has a mainly presentational character, rather than a discursive one.[24]

Such distinctions were still dominant when the idea of "literary journalism" arrived upon the scene. In the 1970s, when works of what might be called literary journalism began to force their way into American culture, Northrop Frye still insisted on literature's distinctive quality. He associated literature with autonomy and freedom, while disparaging all other forms of writing as essentially instrumental. Frye argued that in "literature, questions of fact or truth are subordinated to the primary literary aim of producing a structure of words for its own sake."[25] However, by restricting the label of literature to fiction, Frye limited all other forms of text to instrumentality—that is, viewing them as tools—claiming these forms as "words used instrumentally to help human consciousness do or understand something else."[26]

Jürgen Habermas developed Frye's distinction even further shortly thereafter. The German philosopher delineated literature from philosophy, literary criticism, and the "normal (everyday) use of language."[27] Habermas argued that what he called the poetic function was dominant only in literature, whereas in other discourses, "the tools of rhetoric are subordinated to the discipline of a *distinct* form of argumentation."[28] In his argumentation, Habermas

---

22   Sidney, *An Apology for Poetry, or The Defence of Poesy*, 103.
23   Wellek and Warren, *Theory of Literature*, 25.
24   Wellek and Warren, 26.
25   Frye, *Anatomy of Criticism*, 74.
26   Frye, *Anatomy of Criticism*, 74; For a more detailed analysis of this self-defining discourse in literary studies, see Winterowd, *The Rhetoric of the "Other" Literature*, 3–6.
27   Habermas, *The Philosophical Discourse of Modernity: Twelve Lectures*, 199.
28   Habermas, 209–210.

uses the term "fiction" as a synonym for "literature," while "philosophical" is used interchangeably with "discursive," "argumentative," and "scholarly."²⁹ Importantly, this blurring of lines between fiction and literature made a text's fictionality appear characteristic of its function and, hence, made the distinction between fiction and literature appear obsolete.

However, poststructuralist scholars like the French philosopher Jacques Derrida questioned such hierarchical binary distinctions at around the same time. They dramatically replaced such categorizations with a much more general dichotomy between written artefacts and factual experience. From a literary journalism studies perspective, this similarly reduced the difference between factual and fictional texts because poststructuralism was rather uninterested in questions of textual reference.³⁰

Put generally, Derrida challenged Western philosophy's prevailing idea that there existed a truth independent of its representation in language. In Derrida's view, meaning was based on relations of infinite differences and, hence, was always in the process of becoming and was never fully realized until an impasse was encountered.³¹ Indebted to Husserl's phenomenology and likely also Bakhtin's writings on dialogism,³² Derrida's idea of realist representation entailed a wide and encompassing understanding of text and writing as "that which enables the sense and the truth-value of statements or propositions to be communicated from one context to the next."³³ Despite still-popular accusations of extreme relativism, scholars have shown that Derrida did not deny the existence of material reality. More importantly, he emphasized the inevitable differentiation and relationality inherent in our perception thereof.³⁴

Still, like the binary distinctions that it sought to replace, poststructuralism's general line of argument was similarly incompatible with the reality of literary journalism. For in this view, all thought, language, and hence also argumentation could simply be seen as rhetorical. Of course, this does not mean

---

29 Sandler, "Habermas, Derrida, and the Genre Distinction between Fiction and Argument," 106.
30 Cohn, *The Distinction of Fiction*, 7.
31 Cuddon and Preston, "Post-Structuralism."
32 See i.e. Kristeva, "Word, Dialogue and Novel"; Peiró Sempere, *The Influence of Mikhail Bakhtin on the Formation and Development of the Yale School of Deconstruction*.
33 Norris, "Truth in Derrida," 26; Marder, *The Event of the Thing: Derrida's Post-Deconstructive Realism*; Mooney, "Derrida's Empirical Realism."
34 Deutscher, *How to Read Derrida*, 34–36.

1.1 The Complications of 'Literary Journalism' 49

that all language should be regarded as fiction, but instead suggests that a potential distinction between fiction and nonfiction is necessarily only negotiated within a text itself. For example, Roland Barthes, another prominent poststructuralist critic, proclaimed the death of the author.[35]

However, poststructuralism certainly sharpened critical attention. Its ideas had wide ramifications for historical writing, a scientific discourse equally defined by its core referentiality to an existing material world. Most prominently, the American historian Hayden White showed how the distinguishing categorizations between different types of discourse, such as the one employed by Frye, idealized history as real when histories ought, instead, to be regarded as texts with narrative structures.[36] Histories, he argued, "ought never to be read as unambiguous signs of events they report, but rather as symbolic structures, extended metaphors, that 'liken' the events reported in them to some form with which we have already become familiar in our literary culture".[37] Essentially, White pointed out that historical events did not carry meaning in themselves, but that their meaning was constructed by the ways in which historians arranged them to form historical narratives.

So far, these challenges have gone largely unprocessed in scholarship about literary journalism; where they have been taken into consideration, they have contributed to a confusing blurring of boundaries. Informed by poststructuralism, the paradoxical idea of fact *as* fiction proved tempting for a time. In his analysis of New Journalism, for instance, John Hellmann understood artful prose generally as fiction.[38] Later, he used the term "postmodern journalism" to refer to New Journalism, which he argued sought to overcome realism's "inadequacies in the face of the fragmenting, changing world of the postmodern."[39] Leonora Flis observed a blurring of fact and fiction in the documentary novel in her study entitled *Factual Fictions*.[40]

This blurring has had consequences. Dorrit Cohn has argued that "the most pervasive and prominently problematic application of the word *fiction* in re-

---

35 Barthes, "The Death of the Author."
36 White, "Historical Text as Literary Artifact," 89.
37 White, 91.
38 Hellmann, *Fables of Fact: The New Journalism as New Fiction*, 17–18.
39 Hellmann, "Postmodern Journalism," 52–53.
40 Flis, *Factual Fictions: Narrative Truth and the Contemporary American Documentary Novel*, 42.

cent decades has been to narrative discourse in general—historical, journalistic, and autobiographical—as well as to imaginative discourse."[41]

Against the Idealization of Literary Journalism

These theoretical complications have affected the discourse around literary journalism in quite specific ways. Most recent definitions restrict themselves to a combination of particular formal features, associated with literary realism, and a specific professional practice of research advocated by the reporter Tom Wolfe. In 1973, Wolfe boldly asserted that what he called New Journalism "would wipe out the novel as literature's main event" in the context of a debate on American realism.[42] As Tom Connery has shown, most early definitions of literary journalism refer back to Wolfe's definition that blends features of textual form and professional practice.[43] They are centered on a text's similarity to realist fiction on the basis of "intense" and "detailed" reporting.[44] Norman Sims, for example, revisiting Wolfe's list of characteristics from 1984, states that, apart from "immersion reporting, complicated structures in the prose, accuracy, voice, responsibility, and attention to the symbolic realities of a story," he would add "access, attention to ordinary lives, and the special qualities of a writer's connection to the subjects"[45] to the list of literary journalism's defining features.

Such definitions mainly seek to delineate literary journalism from news journalism and are not concerned with critical discourses in literary studies; however, in so doing, they also run the risk of idealizing the genre. This is because they regard journalistic texts that feature formal elements of narrative, such as a personal voice, scene descriptions, or dialogue—always in implicit contrast to news journalism—as exceptionally effective in revealing reality. In another foundational text, for instance, Mark Kramer elevated what Sims called "voice" above the other characteristics that he listed. He argues that the

---

41 Cohn, *The Distinction of Fiction*, 8.
42 Wolfe, *The New Journalism*, 1973, 22.
43 Connery, "Discovering a Literary Form," 3–5.
44 Wolfe, *The New Journalism*, 1973, 15.
45 Sims, *True Stories: A Century of Literary Journalism*, 12.

defining mark of literary journalism is the personality of the writer, the individual and intimate voice of a whole, candid person not representing, defending, or speaking on behalf of any institution, not a newspaper, corporation, government, ideology, field of study, chamber of commerce, or travel destination.[46]

Kramer seems to be ascribing a degree of objectivity superior to that of other kinds of journalism to literary journalism, one that is attained precisely by means of the writer's intensified subjectivity. In a more recent definition of what John Hartsock calls "narrative literary journalism," Hartsock states that this writing tried to "engage in a revelation for the reader about our phenomenal world, one that is conjured imaginatively by means of sensate experience reflected in language, a conjuring that can disrupt taken-for-granted cultural and personal assumptions."[47] He further argues that "narrative literary journalism more actively engages the imagination in the creation of meaning than either the summary lead, inverted pyramid model of journalism or the traditional feature story" and that its goal is "to recover more concretely the illusion of experience."[48] Similar to Aristotle's elevation of art over history and Kramer's promotion of personal voice, Hartsock makes the case that this more subjective kind of journalism is a "more natural way to tell the news."[49]

Other scholars have sought to evade such idealization by emphasizing literary journalism's textual character, albeit rather generally. Richard Lance Keeble, for example, proposes that all journalism be considered as "worthy of critical attention as *literature*."[50] Joshua Roiland suggests that rather than understanding the adjective "literary" as a value judgment or legitimating maneuver, we should take it as referring to "the use of rhetorical elements ranging from scene, character development, plot, dialogue, symbolism, voice, et cetera."[51]

However, I would argue that literary journalism's decisive aspect lies in its material referentiality that includes authorial agency. In one of very few specific critical analyses of these texts as literature, rather than journalism, Phyllis Frus makes an attempt to define the peculiar character of what she calls "journalistic narrative." In reading such texts, she argues, "we are ... unable

---

46 Kramer, "Breakable Rules for Literary Journalists."
47 Hartsock, *Literary Journalism and the Aesthetics of Experience*, 4–5.
48 Hartsock, 15.
49 Hartsock, 20–23.
50 Keeble, "Literary Journalism," 2018, 2.
51 Roiland, "By Any Other Name: The Case for Literary Journalism," 71.

to recover the event outside of textual evidence. All the materials of journalism—documents, personal testimony, or even memories—are communicable only in a form of secondary revision."[52] Literature, Frus explains, is produced by readers when they "read to discover how a text, through its style, 'makes' reality read its content through its form."[53] We cannot determine a journalistic narrative's credibility through a comparison of the narrative to the actual characters and events, due to the fundamental belatedness of any nonfictional narrative—it is always produced after the events narrated have occurred in reality. Instead, per Frus, we can only:

> compare versions to each other, and to other texts, for "truth" cannot be found in the connection between the word and its referent (because this is always deferred); nor can it be arrived at by comparing the plot to the story we already know to have existed. This is because the facts are not there before the narrative about them; ... there are no descriptions of events apart from narratives.[54]

Rather than claim that nonfictional narratives are "true," Frus concludes that "all we ought to say about them is that their referents are material or historical, in contrast to imaginary or hypothetical."[55]

This is very much in line with Dorrit Cohn's categorization. Cohn herself avoids the term literature; instead, she suggests the category of referentiality as the central textual characteristic that distinguishes fiction from other narrative texts. Cohn uses the term "nonreferential narrative" to explain that "a work of fiction itself creates the world to which it refers by referring to it."[56] The category of "referential narrative," by contrast, refers to a world existing outside the text and denotes works of history or journalism. In such texts, she

---

52   Frus, 213; Apart from Frus's study Anderson, *Style as Argument: Contemporary American Nonfiction*; Winterowd, *The Rhetoric of the "Other" Literature*; Mosser, *The Participatory Journalism of Michael Herr, Norman Mailer, Hunter S. Thompson, and Joan Didon: Creating New Reporting Styles.*, all performed rhetorical analyses of works of literary journalism. However, none of them used the actual term "literary journalism."
53   Frus, *The Politics and Poetics of Journalistic Narrative: The Timely and the Timeless*, 5.
54   Frus, 214.
55   Frus, 214.
56   Cohn, *The Distinction of Fiction*, 13.

states, "the synchronous interplay of story and discourse is undergirded ... by the logical and chronological priority of documented or observed events."[57]

Frus's observations also correspond to the concept of literature proposed by James Phelan. Phelan points to the shortcomings of structural narratology in his rhetorical poetics of narrative from 2017. He establishes a narratological paradigm that incorporates both fictional and nonfictional discourse by conceiving of narrative more broadly, as an event produced by a dialogical relationship between a narrator and an audience.[58] Phelan defines a literary nonfiction narrative—a category in which I would include what is meant by the term "literary journalism"—as a work which

> offers the reader a representation of actual people and events that is simultaneously responsible to their existence outside the textual world *and* shaped in the service of some underlying authorial purpose designed to give the people and events a thematic, affective, and ethical significance and force that would not be apparent without such shaping.[59]

As he explains, this understanding certainly entails a different relationship between freedom and constraint, as compared to a novel's narrative fiction. Phelan points out that authors of literary nonfiction are "free to shape the characters and events into his or her vision of their thematic, affective, and ethical significance within the limits imposed by the necessary responsibility to the extratextual existence of those characters and events."[60] The main consequence of this perspective is that the relationship between the textual representation of extratextual realities and the realities themselves are not necessarily that of a clear correspondence, but rather a "constant negotiation between the twin demands of referentiality and the communication of thematic, affective, and ethical significance."[61]

The actual blurring of fact and fiction in nonfictional narratives occurs in this negotiation or shaping. This is a central insight of postmodern literature after all and its challenging of realism's seamlessness can be found in what the Canadian critic Linda Hutcheon has called historiographic metafiction. In her analysis of the parallels between history-writing and literary fiction, Hutcheon

---

57   Cohn, 115.
58   Phelan, *Somebody Telling Somebody Else: A Rhetorical Poetics of Narrative*, 5.
59   Phelan, 72.
60   Phelan, 72.
61   Phelan, 72.

states: "Facts do not speak for themselves in either form of narrative: the tellers speak for them, making these fragments of the past into a discursive whole."[62] Consequently, it is the author's function, not primarily the text's function, that deserves the most scrutiny in the analyses of both historical and journalistic writing.

It is the absence of explicit analyses based on this observation in theoretical discourses about literary journalism, that accounts for a good portion of the fuzziness surrounding literary journalism as the theoretical conceptualization of a genre. In light of the complications stemming from the term "literature," however, it is not my intention to redefine literary journalism as a genre. Instead, I view literary journalism in the same way as John Tulloch and Richard Lance Keeble, who argue—albeit for a slightly different reason—that:

> rather than a stable genre or family of genres, literary journalism defines a *field* where different traditions and practices of writing intersect, a disputed terrain within which various overlapping practices of writing—among them the journalistic column, the memoir, the sketch, the essay, travel narratives, life writing...—camp uneasily, disputing their neighbor's barricades and patching up temporary alliances.[63]

For the sake of textual analyses of literary journalism, then, it generally seems imperative to zoom in on specific practices that integrate material processes of knowledge production and this knowledge's communication with the processes' own geneses and conventional boundaries.

In literary journalism, the relevant practice is embodied by the writer or reporter. Although thinkers, such as Hutcheon, are right to emphasize facts' fictionality and the factuality of fiction, this central contrast cannot be fully resolved. However, the central agency of authors with regard to the negotiation of a text's factuality stakes out the area in which Phelan's negotiation of the demands of referentiality and communication might occur.

---

62 Hutcheon, "Telling Stories: Fiction and History," 239.
63 Keeble and Tulloch, "Introduction: Mind the Gaps, On the Fuzzy Boundaries between the Literary and the Journalistic," 7.

1.2 The Human Qualities of Reportage

One way to enter into a deeper exploration of literary journalism's mediating function is through the genre of reportage; the term has even been used interchangeably with "literary journalism."[1] As I will show, reportage has been conceptualized as "eyewitness account". Therefore, its central workings can be examined via the comparably much more developed analysis of the witness's mediating function. "The division of fact and fiction," John Durham Peters has stated, "so central for historians and sports fans, as well as the structuring principle of media and literary genres, turns on witnessing. An event requires witnesses, a story only needs tellers and listeners."[2] Like journalism performed by humans, witnessing anchors its referentiality to extra-textual reality in an experiencing observer's body.

The main attempts to theorize reportage in Europe in the 19th and early 20th century reflect motives similar to those that drove the shaping of literary journalism in the United States. European writers and thinkers synthesized ideas emerging from literary realism and science, while further emphasizing the problem of communication, during a time of rapid modernization. Like their American counterparts, European writers and thinkers positioned reportage as the human artistic cure, rooted in phenomenological experience, against the capitalist forces of hitherto unconceptionalized mediatization. They observed that these forces were both changing human experience in modern societies and affecting the very communication of that experience. However, the European theorization of reportage was also frequently informed by piercing anti-

---

1   The term reportage was considered at the founding conference of the *International Association of Literary Journalism Studies*. Roiland, "By Any Other Name: The Case for Literary Journalism," 72. Additionally, the IALJS' website refers to its mission as "the improvement of scholarly research and education in Literary Journalism/Reportage."; International Association of Literary Journalism Studies, "About Us."
2   Peters, "Witnessing," 2009, 37.

American criticism of developments in the emerging journalism business and capitalism in general.

In their theoretical debates, Marxist writers and critics, such as Egon Erwin Kisch and Walter Benjamin, went much further than their American colleagues as they elaborated and scrutinized the reportage writer's own mediating function. First, reportage was defined as an eyewitness account with a particular epistemology. Second, and more decisively, it was forged as a real political weapon against the threat of fascism. Strongly influenced by the analysis that fascism was a direct outgrowth of the increasingly technological mediation of reality—and hence false class consciousness—writers were actively looking for a representational form that corresponded with the aesthetics of human sense perception.

Perception Against Profession: The Beginnings of Reportage

The history of reportage as a generic category is complex, dynamic, and intercultural.[3] The word *reportage* has its roots in the French verb "reporter," which in 11th century Anglo-Norman and Middle French meant "to take back." It was not until the 12th century that it acquired the meaning "to bear (witness)."[4] Significantly, in the United States,[5] reportage has to this day been primarily associated with the practice of reporting applied in journalism, or some variation of the news story, "meaning a piece of direct, informative reporting, as opposed to comment."[6] In Europe, however, reportage has acquired the narrower meaning of an "eyewitness account." For instance, in his introduction to *The Faber Book of Reportage* (1987), the English literary scholar John Carey identified the reporter's role of witness and his or her main reliance on human sensory experience as one of the main criteria used in selecting the texts.[7] Similarly, in his introduction to *The Granta Book of Reportage* (2006), English journalist Ian Jack

---

3 Hartsock, *Literary Journalism and the Aesthetics of Experience*, 100.
4 "Report."
5 Hartsock, *Literary Journalism and the Aesthetics of Experience*, 83; Marcus, *Second Read: Writers Look Back at Classic Works of Reportage*; Silvers, *The New York Review Abroad: Fifty Years of International Reportage*.
6 Roy, "Reportage," 696.
7 Carey, "Introduction," xxix.

emphasized that reportage "has this nice sense of the thing seen, the event observed."[8]

Importantly, the theorization of reportage as the explicitly written product of an intentional human eyewitness coincides with the further increase in mechanization and the electrification of the media environment in Western societies. A set of innovations in media technology, such as the invention of the telegraph and the portable photocamera (between 1850 and 1940 for the most part) profoundly changed how human communication worked. In retrospect, the telegraph in particular was associated with a new degree of technological transcendence of time and space and, consequently, the separation of sign and referent that is said to be one of the postmodern's defining characteristics.[9] Until the mid-19th century, what are called reports, dispatches, or travelogues today had been published in a diverse and complex set of print media, such as books, pamphlets, or journals. These various publication formats had been brought about by the steady mechanization of the printing press and contributed to the intensification of translocal communications and, in some ways, also helped establish colonial states.[10] However, the rapid transmission that the telegraph made possible further changed the scale and speed of these communications and contributed to the building of new media-based communities not primarily determined by time and space. The invention of the telegraph, according to Nick Couldry and Andreas Hepp, created "shared rhythms of simultaneous experience and new narratives of commonality", and "new forms of near-instantaneous, reciprocal communication".[11]

The technological development of photography in the early 20th century posed an even more fundamental competition for reporters' texts based on their subjective experience of reality. Key to their rise was the invention of the Leica in Germany, the first hand-held camera to take pictures of unposed action in high quality. Importantly, its mass production in the 1920s coincided with the first transmissions of photographs via telegraph. By the 1940s, at least in the U.S., magazines such as *Life* or *Look* had turned photojournalism into big business.[12] An appreciation of the new media technology accompanied this

---

8   Jack, "Introduction," vi.
9   Carey, "Time, Space, and the Telegraph."
10 Couldry and Hepp, *The Mediated Construction of Reality*, 40–44.
11 Couldry and Hepp, 47.
12 Cmiel and Peters, *Promiscuous Knowledge: Information, Image, and Other Truth Games in History*, 147–150.

rise. Compared to text, the pictures produced by photojournalists appeared superior. On the one hand, cameras were thought to deliver more reliable representations of reality than any description of human perception could muster in text, particularly in the early days of photojournalism.[13] On the other hand, the photograph's supposedly superior representational power resulted in an appreciation of a manufactured effect manifested in a "feel of artlessness".[14] While the interpretation and selection inherent in journalistic writing had become negatively associated with bias, photographers were celebrated if their pictures managed to communicate interpreted essence.[15]

These technological innovations in specific call into question the communication of subjectively experienced reality of a human medium. The telegraph affected both the very production and publication of texts and indirectly contributed to the genesis of the journalistic ideology of objectivity.[16] Photography challenged the very credibility of textual journalistic genres and their phenomenological bases of knowledge.

Reportage has developed alongside such challenges as textual form and professional practice. The genre is an amalgamation of two different generic categories. On the one hand, scholars have traced the form's roots to Herodotus' *Histories*[17] and later to the travelogues of the 17th and 18th centuries.[18] As hinted at previously, however, reportage must also be regarded as a byproduct of the American press's transformation from traditional political-partisan journalism to mass newspapers during the second half of the 19th century.[19] As such, it was accompanied by the emergence of new forms of advocacy journalism that sought to move readers emotionally and positioned

---

13 Hicks, "What Is Photojournalism?," 22–33.
14 Cmiel and Peters, *Promiscuous Knowledge: Information, Image, and Other Truth Games in History*, 151.
15 Cmiel and Peters, 151.
16 Schudson, *Discovering the News: A Social History of American Newspapers.*, 4.
17 Homberg, *Reporter-Streifzüge: Metropolitane Nachrichtenkultur und die Wahrnehmung der Welt 1870–1918*, 42.
18 Homberg, 56; Hartsock, *Literary Journalism and the Aesthetics of Experience*, 95; Geisler, *Die literarische Reportage in Deutschland: Möglichkeiten und Grenzen eines operativen Genres*.
19 Lindner, *The Reportage of Urban Culture*, 7–11; Homberg, *Reporter-Streifzüge: Metropolitane Nachrichtenkultur und die Wahrnehmung der Welt 1870–1918*, 47–49.

the reporter's profession front and center.[20] Early American reporters worked under precarious and highly competitive conditions in the hunt for new and spectacular stories. Along with other factors—such as competition among newspapers and the desire for personal recognition—this encouraged sensationalist exaggeration, embellishment, and even the invention of facts and entire stories.[21]

Some of these developments, and their influence upon local journalism, drew harsh criticism in Europe which was experiencing a similar transformation of its media industries. In the United Kingdom, for example, the poet and critic Matthew Arnold opined in 1887 that this "new journalism... throws out assertions at a venture because it wishes them true; does not correct either them or itself, if they are false; and to get at the state of things as they truly are seems to feel no concern whatever."[22]

The emergence of what was actually called reportage was shaped by developments in the French Third Republic, which witnessed an explosion of publications after 1870. On the one hand, early French reportage was likely influenced by the colonialist writings of travel writers such as Henry Morton Stanley, who worked for the *New York Herald*. His travel account *How I found Livingstone* (1872) was translated into French in 1874.[23] On the other hand, the emergence of reportage was also interwoven with a critique of sensationalist fashions in American journalism, similar to the one advanced by Arnold in the United Kingdom.[24] In a manifesto attached to his novel *Le Sieur de Va Partout, souvenirs d'un reporter* (1880), the French journalist Pierre Giffard launched a debate in which he defended reportage's literary qualities and further emphasized the reporter's role as an eyewitness on the spot.[25] The basis for his

---

20 Homberg, *Reporter-Streifzüge: Metropolitane Nachrichtenkultur und die Wahrnehmung der Welt 1870–1918*, 47–49.
21 Smythe, "The Reporter, 1880–1900. Working Conditions and Their Influence on the News."
22 Arnold, "Up to Easter," 638; Campbell, "W.E. Gladstone, W.T. Stead, Matthew Arnold and a New Journalism: Cultural Politics in the 1880s."
23 Martin, *Les grands reporters: Les débuts du journalisme moderne*, 32–35.
24 Martin, *Les grands reporters: Les débuts du journalisme moderne*; Homberg, *Reporter-Streifzüge: Metropolitane Nachrichtenkultur und die Wahrnehmung der Welt 1870–1918*, 48–52.
25 Homberg, *Reporter-Streifzüge: Metropolitane Nachrichtenkultur und die Wahrnehmung der Welt 1870–1918*, 50–51.

argument was a fierce critique of American sensationalism. In his text, Giffard argued that American reporters exaggerated for capitalist reasons:

> They have no artistic sense. They are note-taking machines. Incidentally, they are neither writers, nor artists, nor critics. We the others have to be all this. The French reader does not support the banal inventory that forms the base of the yankee reporters' baggage.[26]

Significantly, Giffard did not uphold the rough distinction between objective journalism and subjective reportage. Rather, Giffard exposed a conflict within reportage itself with his critique, one that he located in the reporter's self-understanding. By opposing the ideas of the reporter as an industrious producer of sensationalist entertainment and the reporter as an artist, he imbued reportage with an—albeit somewhat vague—artistic and reactionary imperative.

Observation and Experiment

Giffard's critique came at a time of rapid expansion and alongside the press's commercialization, which coincided with the emergence of modern literary realism in the form of naturalism. With his call for precise examination, combined with experimentation within reportage, Giffard's arguments showed similarities to the views of the French novelist Emile Zola, who had published his manifesto *The Experimental Novel* (1880) that same year.[27] In this text, Zola places additional emphasis on the earlier promotion of science in literature by his fellow countrymen Honoré de Balzac and Gustave Flaubert and calls for a fusion of the detailed observation of reality with literary experimentation.[28]

While the French debate only hinted at reportage's potential as an artistic response to the capitalist forces of an emerging entertainment industry, the German discourse resulted in a rather explicit theorization of reportage as a functional genre. Key to the theoretical formation of reportage as a literary genre was the acknowledgment of the reporter's own function as a medium.

---

26   Giffard, *Le Sieur de Va-Partout*, 330–331, my translation.
27   Homberg, *Reporter-Streifzüge: Metropolitane Nachrichtenkultur und die Wahrnehmung der Welt 1870–1918*, 51.
28   Morris, *Realism*, 70–71.

This idea was elaborated a few decades later in Germany, but—crucially—it also took place in an environment of increased technical mediation. Following the end of the First World War, writers faced increased competition from new media, such as film and radio. Along with the end of censorship, these new media contributed to an environment of "information overload" for the German public.[29] In 1916, the German writer Hermann Kesser was among the first to argue that the reporter had to be viewed as an involuntary framer, because nothing could be registered automatically or objectively.[30]

It was the Czech reporter Egon Erwin Kisch, however, who initiated a lively theoretical discussion about reportage in Germany. Kisch was the first to formulate the idea of reportage as an explicitly literary genre. He repeatedly published programmatic manifestos that borrowed from other ideas circulating in cultural debates and reacted to societal and political realities in post-war Germany. Over time, in Kisch's programmatic considerations, the initially apolitical insight that the reporter essentially had the function of a human medium gradually morphed into a political responsibility. A communist writer, Kisch produced a trove of reportage, only parts of which have been translated into English.

Kisch's process of self-definition began with the central insight of the reporter's own role as human medium. In 1918—also under the strong, but compared to Giffard belated, influence of Emile Zola—Kisch sought to elevate the reporter's role. He designated the reporter's work as the "most honest, most factual [sachlichste], most important."[31] In Kisch's view, the reporter's importance was grounded in his or her function as a transmitter of facts in an account that also turned him or her into a kind of mediator. Kisch placed the reporter between the artist and the common citizen as "an intermediary [Zwischenstufe] that both sides are hostile to."[32] Reporters set themselves apart from other journalists through their use of, mainly, phenomenological experience. Unlike columnists, who rarely left their desks, drew their evidence from quotes from other publications, and were by nature "second-hand," Kisch argued that

---

29   Mayer, "Die Epoche der Weimarer Republik," 76.
30   Homberg, *Reporter-Streifzüge: Metropolitane Nachrichtenkultur und die Wahrnehmung der Welt 1870–1918*, 54–55.
31   Kisch, "Wesen des Reporters," 40. Unless explicitly noted, all translations of Kisch's quotes are my own. Emile Zola's *The Experimental Novel* (1880) was not translated into German until 1904, two years after Zola's death.
32   Kisch, 44.

the reporter's research yielded results that were "first-hand, from life."³³ The reporter, according to Kisch, had to process and transmit these facts in a way that strongly resembled Zola's concept of the experimental novelist:

> Of course, the fact is only the compass of his journey, but he also needs a telescope: "logical fantasy". For the autopsy of a crime scene or venue, the overheard utterances of participants or witnesses, and the assumptions presented to him, never provide a *complete* [*lückenlos*; emphasis in the original] image of the circumstances. He has to create the practicalities of the event, the transitions to the results of the inquiries himself and only has to pay attention that the line of his account lead precisely through the facts known to him (the given points of the route). It is now ideal that this curve of probability drawn by the reporter corresponds to the real line connecting all phases of the event.³⁴

While Kisch does not discuss events witnessed first-hand by the reporter here, he does emphasize the distinction that the reporter must make between facts and presentation, account and image. Kisch also emphasizes the reporter's self-awareness as a medium who actively shapes the facts.

Zola's clear influence on Kisch indicates the existence of a link between the theorization of realist fiction and reportage. For instance, Kisch celebrated the French writer as the "greatest reporter of all times" in his collection of works of what he called "classic journalism" from 1923.³⁵ Kisch credited Zola with introducing the "infinite realms of truth into the novel" and argued that, in his journalism, Zola was "as ravishing as in his novels" because he "started out from the fact and the autopsy."³⁶ The most explicit parallel, however, can be found in the specific idea of the reporter as a medium, which corresponds to Zola's merging of observer and experimenter in the novelist. In *The Experimental Novel*, which was translated into German in 1904, Zola had argued that the observer "ought to be the photographer of phenomena; his observation ought to represent nature exactly."³⁷ The experimenter, on the other hand:

---

33 Kisch, 41.
34 Kisch, 41.
35 Kisch, *Klassischer Journalismus: Die Meisterwerke der Zeitung*, 405.
36 Kisch, 405.
37 Zola, "The Experimental Novel," 165.

is he who, by virtue of a more or less probable but anticipatory interpretation of observed phenomena, institutes an experiment in such manner that in the logical framework of prevision, it furnishes a result which serves as a control for the hypothesis or preconceived idea.[38]

Despite the aforementioned correspondences, Kisch appeared more cautious than Zola in his assessment of the reporter's ability to represent reality. In his text, Zola introduced the idea of a certain "determinism of the phenomena under study"[39] that not only affects the particular series of events recounted by the novelist, but also turns the experimental account itself into an observation.[40] Kisch avoided this determinism, however, by upholding the separation of fact and fantasy when talking about the reporter. As shown above, he asserted that there could never exist a complete image of the circumstances. The curve of probability in the account corresponded to the real line of events only on an ideal level.

Reportage's Political Turn

In retrospect, Kisch's insistence on the separation between observation and account, between fact and fantasy, already anticipated the conception of reportage as more narrowly the account of an eyewitness, and consequently the genre's politicization. In the famous preface to his collection of reportage *Der rasende Reporter* (1925), Kisch clearly embraced a more modest and scientific conception of reportage. By now, Kisch had abandoned his previous concept of logical fantasy. Instead of Zola, Kisch took the philosopher Arthur Schopenhauer as his main point of departure.[41] The facts, or objects, were now seen to be speaking entirely for themselves, while Kisch located the good reporter's main drive in his desire to experience first-hand in an environment of untruths:

---

38 Zola, 165.
39 Zola, 166.
40 Zola, 166.
41 In "On Writing and Style," from which Kisch quotes, Schopenhauer had distinguished between writers who write for the things they write about and writers who write for the sake of writing itself. In Schopenhauer's view, the former write because they had a certain thought or experience, the latter write for money. Schopenhauer, "On Writing and Style."

The reporter has no tendency, he has nothing to justify and no stance [*Standpunkt*]. He has to be an unbiased witness and to testify unbiasedly, as reliably as it is possible to give testimony... The good [reporter] needs the ability to experience for his business, which he loves. He would experience if he did not have to report on it. But he would not write without experiencing. He is neither artist nor politician or scholar.[42]

What is important, then, is Kisch's early insistence on the reporter's distinct quality as witness and that it include a kind of distanced objectivity. However, it is just as important to remember that Kisch conceived of this idea of the unbiased reporter against the backdrop of the Weimar Republic's social segmentation which, in the years following the end of the First World War, alternated between stabilization and inflation-related chaos.[43] Kisch took the sense of the reporter's work to lie in "the dedication to his object" as they found themselves "[i]n a world, immeasurably flooded by the lie... a world that wants to forget itself and thus only strives toward falsehoods."[44] Furthermore, he characterized the ideal reporter's "independence from the effect of the moment [*Unabhängigkeit von der Augenblickswirkung*]" as "perhaps un-American."[45] While Kisch's formulated stance can be characterized as non-partisan, the material basis in first-hand phenomenological experience indicated a certain political concern that he had yet to articulate.

Kisch's bold positioning, against bias and cheap sensationalism, had significant repercussions. A year later, in a Weimar Republic that the critic Leo Lania viewed as "virtually living second-hand,"[46] Lania praised Kisch for having the courage to feel the present's contours, "to view it ever anew, to auscultate it—to experience it."[47] He further credited Kisch with attaching a name to the "modern direction," in respect of the departure from artistry and romanticism. In his view, Kisch was raising interest in the activity of objective description, in what he saw as a time of a fragmenting division of labor and a general need for public attention.[48] However, this did not mean that Kisch's reportage was apo-

---

42 Kisch, *Der rasende Reporter*, VI–VII.
43 Peukert, *The Weimar Republic: The Crisis of Classical Modernity*; Feldman, *The Great Disorder: Politics, Economics, and Society in the German Inflation, 1914–1924.*).
44 Kisch, *Der Rasende Reporter*, VIII.
45 Kisch, VIII.
46 Lania, "Reportage als soziale Funktion," 5.
47 Lania, 5.
48 Lania, 5.

litical. In fact, his actual reportage differed rather significantly from what was announced in the programmatic preface. As Keith Williams has shown, Kisch's reportage pieces in *Der rasende Reporter* (1925) sought to "subvert concepts propagated by the capitalist media and unmask the economic and political interests lying behind them."[49]

It did not take long for Kisch to theorize this political turn more explicitly. Following the end of both the First World War and the Russian Revolution, Kisch not only traveled extensively throughout Europe and the Soviet Union,[50] but he also worked for the bourgeois press and determined that "the disclosure of many things has to be rejected as politically or economically damaging by newspapers."[51] Kisch definitively abandoned Emile Zola as his writer of reference, replacing him with the American John Reed. Kisch praised Reed's account of the Soviet Revolution, *Ten Days That Shook the World* (1919), as "the most important book for the understanding of the present."[52] In a preface to the second translation of Reed's book from 1927, Kisch claimed that

> Emile Zola defined art as a piece of truth seen through a temperament. To us, contemporaries of the World War, of revolutions successful and unsuccessful, this definition does not suffice anymore. To us, art is a piece of truth seen through a *revolutionary* [Kisch's emphasis] temperament.[53]

Zola's fall in Kisch's estimation was connected to what Kisch felt was an absence of commitment in Zola's writing that he associated with a detachment from reality. One year later, in 1927, Kisch called Zola a "bourgeois socialist... tired of reportage"[54] who, "from the landscape of reality deserts into a quite naïvely imagined land of fantasy."[55]

Kisch amended his conception of the reporter at around the same time, whom he nonetheless still characterized as an eyewitness who is reliant on sensory perception: "Every reporter," he wrote in 1928, is a "writer and journalist who is intent on factually describing circumstances or events for their own

---

49   Williams, "The Will to Objectivity: Egon Erwin Kisch's 'Der rasende Reporter,'" 94.
50   Williams, 93.
51   Kisch, "Was Reporter verschweigen müssen," 116.
52   Kisch, "Soziale Aufgaben der Reportage," 11.
53   Kisch, "John Reed, Ein Reporter auf der Barrikade," 104.
54   Kisch, "Die sozialistischen Typen des Reporters Emile Zola," 62.
55   Kisch, "Soziale Aufgaben der Reportage," 10.

sake through his own visual inspection [*um ihrer selbst willen aus eigenem Augenschein*]."[56] Importantly, this explicit witnessing of the reporter also had clear political consequences. Kisch called it the social "awareness that by far the majority of all seemingly so heterogeneous events and the interest they cause rests on the same basis."[57]

Kisch did not explicitly distinguish between reportage's form and function in his writings. However, he acknowledged that they did not always go hand in hand in his last theoretical texts. "It's difficult to posit the truth precisely without losing drive or form", Kisch wrote in one of his last manifestos in 1935. "[R]eportage means making work and way of life visible—these are often unwieldy, grey models in today's times."[58] He openly admitted that he had not yet found a solution to the problem that he had identified. "With all our power," Kisch urged, "we have to seek a form for an expression of our awareness that satisfies all the ideal principles of an absolute aesthetics."[59]

In the U.S., concern with reportage's more explicitly political function was more pronounced. The American writer Joseph North, strongly influenced by Kisch, tried to infuse Kisch's ideas into theoretical American literary debates in socialist circles. However, North defined the genre mainly in terms of its superior potential to affect readers, similar to the conceptualization of photojournalism. He argued that it could transcend the gaps inherent in communication and make readers "feel the facts".[60] For instance, North repeatedly stressed what he perceived as the transcending power of reportage in a preface to the reportage section of a 1935 anthology of proletarian literature. The reporter's writing, North argued, "must result in an experience, which in turn induces a mode of action" and claimed that reportage "helps the reader *experience* the event recorded."[61] He called reportage "one of the best weapons in the literary arsenal" and insisted that it "is the presentation of a particular fact, a specific event, in a setting that aids the reader to experience the fact, the event."[62] No

---

56   Kisch, 9.
57   Kisch, 9.
58   Egon Erwin Kisch, "Reportage als Kunstform und als Kampfform," in *Reporter und Reportagen: Texte zur Theorie und Praxis der Reportage der Zwanziger Jahre*, ed. Erhard Schütz, (Giessen: Achenbach, 1974), 47.
59   Kisch, "Reportage als Kunstform und als Kampfform," 45.
60   North, "Reportage"; Dingledine, "'Feel the Fact': The 1930s Reportage of Joseph North, John L. Spivak and Meridel Le Sueur."
61   North, "Preface to 'Reportage,'" 211.
62   North, 212.

real challenge to North's conceptualization of reportage arose in the US that could develop into a debate.

Fascism and the Writer as Producer

In Europe, however, Kisch's ideas had only started to set in motion a more urgent search for the right form for expressing an awareness that could counter fascism. It was the German-Jewish critic Walter Benjamin who forcefully articulated what Kisch had grasped only superficially. Walter Benjamin had fled Germany for Paris only weeks after the burning of the Reichstag and Hitler's taking of power in mid-March 1933. He had already criticized fascism and he would theorize it as a socially unjust manipulation of the proletariat, by way of a specific kind of mediation made possible by new media technologies, in the years that followed. In his famous essay "The Work of Art in the Age of Technological Reproduction" (1935), he argued that fascism:

> attempts to organize the newly proletarianized masses while leaving intact the property relations which they strive to abolish. It sees its salvation in granting expression to the masses—but on no account granting them rights. The masses have a *right* to changed property relations; fascism seeks to give them expression in keeping these relations unchanged. *The logical outcome of fascism is an aestheticizing of political life.*[63]

This aestheticizing of political life, Benjamin argued, was made possible by reproductive media technologies such as photography or film, which—simply put—address their audience as passive consumers experiencing readily available reality, rather than involved co-producers who are aware of a decisive temporal distance between themselves and the work of art.

This argument is crucial because it is connected to a more nuanced critique of reportage. Walter Benjamin and Siegfried Kracauer, among others, claimed that reportage did not, by nature, fulfill its social function in favor of the proletariat, as some of their younger comrades had claimed.[64] According to this argument, reportage carried the potential to aestheticize and thereby glorify

---

63 Benjamin, "The Work of Art in the Age of Its Technological Reproducibility: Second Version," 41.
64 Schütz, *Kritik der literarischen Reportage*, 13–14.

misery. If reportage, with its focus on particulars, only managed to portray the surface of life, then it would not lead to just change but would instead act like a kind of propaganda of the existing.[65] This line of critique was based on critical analyses of photography or film. Siegfried Kracauer argued in one of the most prominent passages of reportage critique from his ethnographic study of white-collar workers, *The Salaried Masses* (1930):

> A hundred reports from a factory do not add up to the reality of the factory. Reality is a construction. Certainly, life must be observed for it to appear. Yet it is by no means contained in the more or less random observational results of reportage; rather, it is to be found solely in the mosaic that is assembled from single observations on the basis of comprehension of their meaning. Reportage photographs life; such a mosaic would be its image.[66]

Krakauer's problematization of reportage was connected to a problematization of class—and to the fact that witnessing always implies speaking for somebody else. In a 1930 review of Kracauer's book, Benjamin asserted that: "in a class society social existence is inhuman to the degree to which the consciousness of the different classes, far from being adequate, is highly mediated, inauthentic, and displaced."[67] Writers contributed to such false consciousness because their bourgeois privilege of education and literary instruments made for individual modes of production that nevertheless resulted in standardized literary products. Benjamin argued that even "the proletarianization of the intellectual hardly ever turns him into a proletarian",[68] because the intellectual's bourgeois education created a sense of solidarity with the bourgeoisie that differed markedly from a true proletarian's constant being on alert.[69] In 1930, Benjamin praised Kracauer's approach for its difference from the radical left-wing reportage he found to be demagogic. However, he had not yet formulated a definition of an authorial stance that he himself had deemed adequate.

Benjamin found the solution to this fundamental problem of authorial subjectivity in a class society in the Soviet Union, in which a group of writers was working to expose the alienation of automized everyday life by defamiliarizing

---

65 Schütz, 13–15.
66 Kracauer, *The Salaried Masses: Duty and Distraction in Weimar Germany*, 32.
67 Benjamin, "An Outsider Makes His Mark," 306.
68 Benjamin, 309.
69 Benjamin, 309.

automized representation.⁷⁰ Crucially, these Soviet Futurist factographers like Sergei Tretiakov understood facts themselves as results of processes of production. In the 1920s, the young Soviet Union, like the Weimar Republic, had experienced an explosion of new media technologies. Devin Fore has argued, "the factographers understood acts of signification not as veridical reflections or reduplications of an ontologically more primary reality, but as actual and objective components of everyday, lived experience."⁷¹ In such a "society on the cusp of the modern media age the distinction between the object and its image grew increasingly tenuous."⁷² The *ocherks*, the factographers' literary texts, have been characterized as experiments between literature and science, comparable to sketches, essays, and reportage.⁷³

Referring to Sergei Tretiakov's concept of the operative writer, Walter Benjamin situated the writer of reportage, more explicitly than Kisch had, within the capitalist forces of the apparatus of cultural production and introduced self-reflection as potential relief. In "The Author as Producer," written in 1934, but which remained unpublished during his lifetime, Benjamin rejected what he perceived as the dogmatic connection between the political line of a writer's work and its literary quality. Instead, he fused the two and introduced the category of literary tendency. "The correct political tendency of a work," he argued, "includes its literary quality *because* it includes its literary *tendency*."⁷⁴ According to Benjamin, this literary tendency was embodied by the author whose "work will never be merely work on products but always, at the same time, work on the means of production."⁷⁵ Benjamin consequently demanded of the author "*to think*, [emphasis in the original] to reflect on his position in the process of production. We may depend on it: this reflection leads, sooner or later, for the writers who *matter*... to observations that provide the most factual foundation for solidarity with the proletariat."⁷⁶ This solidarity, then, was based on the writer's transformation "from a supplier of the productive apparatus into an engineer who sees it as his task to adapt this apparatus to the purposes of the proletarian revolution."⁷⁷

---

70 Williams, "'History as I Saw It': Inter-War New Reportage," 40–41.
71 Fore, "Introduction," 6.
72 Fore, 6.
73 Fore, 9; Hartsock, *Literary Journalism and the Aesthetics of Experience*, 106–116.
74 Benjamin, "The Author as Producer," 80.
75 Benjamin, 89.
76 Benjamin, 91.
77 Benjamin, 93.

Of course, Kisch's theorization of the reporter or writer, and later Benjamin's conception of same, can be read as the reporter's increased politicization as one who becomes transformed from a neutral observer into an actor in class struggle. However, this politicization was always tied to the transformation of the political landscape and the simultaneous industrialization and technologization of the media. And most importantly, it went hand in hand with the increasing self-awareness of the writer's own role as a human medium.

1.3 The Human Medium Inspecting Itself

The theoretical background of the existential character of such human media, albeit not explicitly tied to reportage, has recently been scrutinized further; John Durham Peters, for instance, has emphasized the fundamental connection between witness and medium when he called the former a "paradigm case of a medium: the means by which experience is supplied to others who lack the original."[1] Such a general assertion, however, necessarily functions against the backdrop of more detailed and contested ideas of media and communication. In her incisive study, German media philosopher Sybille Krämer has built upon—among others—Durham Peters's observations in order to account for a kind of material shift in media theory. Her fundament is the distinction between the concepts of sign carrier and medium. Signs are generally thought of as being material and, hence, as perceptible and sensible. Yet this materiality of the sign itself is considered secondary to the sign's comparatively invisible meaning. Media, however, are conventionally imagined as primarily showing the perceptible message while making themselves disappear behind it. Roughly put:

> the procedural logic of signs fulfils the metaphysical expectation to search for meaning over and beyond the sensible, but the functional logic of media reverses this metaphysical expectation by going over and beyond the meaning and confronting the sensibility, materiality, and corporeality of media concealed behind it.[2]

This reversion is key to my study's theoretical stance because it corresponds to the ways in which the focus is extended from the textual product to the reporter's materiality.

---

1 Peters, "Witnessing," 2009, 26.
2 Krämer, *Medium, Messenger, Transmission: An Approach to Media Philosophy*, 35.

In her analysis of media's materiality, Krämer distinguishes between two larger theoretical frames: the technical transmission model and the personal understanding model of communication.[3] While both concepts presume a distance and difference between sender and receiver, which communication attempts to overcome, their specific understandings of this bridging of difference diverge strongly. Communication works asymmetrically and unidirectionally in the model of technical transmission, which goes back to the work of Claude E. Shannon and Warren Weaver; its main goal is to produce connections between entities that remain different.[4] According to Krämer, "it is precisely through and in the successful transmission that the sense of being distant from one another is stabilized and reinforced."[5]

In contrast, the personal understanding model, which stems from Jürgen Habermas's work, views communication as a symmetrical, reciprocal interaction that functions like a dialogue. Its communicative performance, Krämer states, "consists not only in establishing a connection across distance, but also in fostering agreement and creating a unified society whose goal is precisely to overcome distance and difference."[6] In the former model, media—with all their imperfections—are indispensable because they establish connections "despite and in the distance"[7] which separates sender and receiver. In the latter model, however, media function imperceptibly as they "provide undistorted and unmediated access to something that they themselves are not".[8] In both communication models, media process communication as they function as thirds between sender and receiver that are not absolutely neutral.

Krämer's theory essentially amounts to a rehabilitation of the technical transmission model. In her theory, the processing of communication is called transmission and Krämer's transmission has four key attributes:

(1) Transmissions presuppose a difference that is not reducible to spatial or temporal distance. (2) The role of the mediator is not always to bridge and level this difference, but also to maintain it. Media... thus make it possible to *deal* with this difference. (3) The function of the messenger... is to *make something perceptible*. ... (4) This is possible through a transformation that mani-

---

3 Krämer, 21.
4 Krämer, 21–22.
5 Krämer, 23.
6 Krämer, 22.
7 Krämer, 23.
8 Krämer, 23.

fests a difference by neutralizing what is 'singular' in each case. Medial mediation thus creates the impression of *immediacy*.[9]

Krämer conceives of the medium as messenger in her model, which corresponds to these attributes. Although this model might already suggest a human figure, Krämer really sketches the messenger more generally, thereby also encompassing non-human entities that function like media in the sense of a transmitter.

The Mediality of Witness and Reporter

Still, her theory fits the early conceptions of the reporter, due to its rather general functional approach. Consequently, I use Krämer's theoretical considerations in order to illuminate the reporter's specific mediality. The aim is to understand his or her very being as an "elementary dimension of human life and culture", rather than to distinguish him or her from other media.[10] As I hope to show, it is precisely the general character-encompassing technical media of Krämer's theory that help me to identify the very human nature of the reporter's ontology as medium. Krämer's own analysis of witnessing as specific transmission is particularly illuminating in this respect because it connects the theoretical considerations on media with the specific definition of the reporter as eyewitness.

A witness is a particularly complex medium because it both creates and transmits knowledge to a receiver; it essentially *produces* knowledge. This mechanism is profoundly social because it only works under the premise of the receiver's trust in and credibility of the witness.[11] Looking at legal witnessing, Krämer has conceived a grammar of witnessing containing five different aspects: (1) the witness's fundamental creation of evidence; (2) that this evidence was created by way of physical presence and sensory perception; (3) this private experience, in turn, is translated into a public statement; (4) this statement is part of a dialogue or interaction with its audience; and (5) the witness's credibility is decisive.[12] Importantly, witnesses are always human

---

9   Krämer, 165.
10 Krämer, 75.
11 Krämer, 144–146.
12 Krämer, 146–149.

beings, in particular when examined through the lens of media. This creates an insoluble tension between the witness's depersonalization in its function as transmitting medium and his or her existential quality as an experiencing human being.[13] On the one hand, this tension manifests itself in the relationship between the witness and the experienced event, which cannot be neutrally perceived.[14] On the other, it is present in the discursification of the witness' experience and in his or her speech acts in dialogue with the unknowing audience.[15]

The theorization of the witness—what Sybille Krämer and Sigrid Weigel have called testimony studies—has largely occurred in two different camps that lean towards emphasizing either the witness's depersonalization or his or her humanity. The study of discursive testimony usually encompasses epistemological questions concerning the possibilities of objectivity, which are concerned with witnessing as a knowledge practice.[16] Studies of embodied testimony, conversely, usually revolve around existential questions of memory, suffering, or trauma and concern the immediate embodiment of the experience of violence.[17] While the conversations concerning the former strand of testimony studies have largely taken place in philosophy, media, or law theory, debating the latter—intensified in particular by the literary processing of the Holocaust—has occurred in critical theory predominantly. From this field, it has brought forth various analyses at the intersection of violence and culture, via the concepts of the survivor and the martyr for instance.[18]

Reporters do not neatly fit into this binary categorization. The two strands of discursive and embodied testimony refer to the two distinct meanings of witness as neutral third (testis) or as survivor (superstes) first described by Émile Benveniste, as Krämer and Weigel show.[19] While journalism has been associated with informing the public by speaking the truth, it is important to note that, as Krämer and Weigel argue, "the truth at stake in the customary disclosure of information remains a feature of linguistic utterances that lay claim

---

13 Krämer, 151.
14 Krämer, 152.
15 Krämer, 153.
16 Krämer and Weigel, "Introduction," xi.
17 Krämer and Weigel, xii.
18 Krämer and Weigel, xiii–xxv; Kilby and Rowland, *The Future of Testimony: Interdisciplinary Perspectives on Witnessing*.
19 Krämer and Weigel, "Introduction," xi.

to validity irrespective of the person making the utterance."²⁰ Consequently, if reporters themselves are to be understood as human media, as in the genre of reportage, then they must engage in both discursive and embodied witnessing and must be subject to the larger tensions inherent to both types.

More importantly, then, reporters as media should primarily be distinguished as *professional* witnesses in public service. As such, Tamat Ashuri and Amit Pinchevski have pointed out that reporters essentially function "as actors in an institutionalized practice of witnessing with its specific combination of competence and circumstance."²¹ This also applies to organized humanitarian witnesses such as NGO workers or human rights watchers.²² However, whereas such humanitarian witnesses also usually occupy the position of the survivor witness,²³ reporters generally hold a more decidedly unaffiliated position. War correspondents, for instance, have been ruled under international law not to be compelled to testify in war crimes proceedings.²⁴ Moreover, what sets reporters apart from other quite specifically interested professional witnesses is their acting in the public's, rather general, interest. "Journalism's first loyalty", as Bill Kovach and Tom Rosenstiel have argued, "is to citizens."²⁵ This primary obligation to readers or viewers holds, at least in theory; in practice, however, it identifies one central conflict within reporters between what Krämer has referred to as their production of evidence and their physical experience, their discursification of private experience, and the expectations of their audience or readership.²⁶ As argued previously, such conflicts are negotiated, rather than resolved. Hence, as Tamar Ashuri and Amit Pinchevski have argued, the very conditions of a reporter's witnessing "are never divorced from ideology."²⁷ The specific theorization of the reporter as witness sharpens the awareness of such inherent conflicts and aporiae.

---

20 Krämer and Weigel, xi.
21 Ashuri and Pinchevski, "Witnessing as Field," 139.
22 Hartog, "The Presence of the Witness," 14–15; Norridge, "Professional Witnessing in Rwanda: Human Rights and Creative Responses to Genocide."
23 Hartog, "The Presence of the Witness," 15.
24 Spellman, "Journalist or Witness? Reporters and War Crimes Tribunals."
25 Kovach and Rosenstiel, *The Elements of Journalism. What Newspeople Should Know and the Public Should Expect*, 52.
26 Krämer, *Medium, Messenger, Transmission: An Approach to Media Philosophy*, 147–148.
27 Ashuri and Pinchevski, "Witnessing as Field," 140.

Self-Reflection: Embodied Interplay of Confirmation and Critique

One tool at the hand of writers to address such contradictions is the expression of self-awareness regarding their inherent existence in acts of mediation. In written text the intricate interconnection of acts of argued and narrated mediation effectively expresses a writer's self-awareness as a human medium who actively shapes and produces meaning, rather than uncovering a meaning that exists independently. Significantly, as I aim to show in my analyses, this subjective self-awareness does not necessarily result in solipsistic introspection, but has the potential to build a sense of community. Exhibiting considerable confidence, writers who are self-aware in this way exemplify the possibilities of collaborative human experience and action. This "exemplary character of production," as Benjamin has pointed out, carries the potential to "turn readers ... into collaborators."[28] Crucially, the mere acknowledgment of the core role of the mediating function in literary journalism also entails a collaborative idea of human communication that counteracts classical realism's anesthetic qualities, which David Foster Wallace has criticized previously. Benjamin's and Wallace's positions suggest a quality of self-awareness that serves to enhance intersubjective communication and collaboration because it is particularly relatable to other humans.

This assertion is backed up by philosophical investigations of self-knowledge more generally. According to this line of work, self-reflection is a basic trait of human beings. Crucially, it is precisely this ability that signifies the social basis of both individual human consciousness and subjectivity. At its core lies a complex dialogical interaction that George Herbert Mead has described as follows:

> It is by means of reflexiveness—the turning back of the experience of the individual upon himself—that the whole social process is ... brought into the experience of the individuals involved in it; it is by such means, which enable the individual to take the attitude of the other toward himself, that the individual is able consciously to adjust himself to that process, and to modify the resultant of that process in any given social act in terms of his adjustment to it. Reflexiveness, then, is the essential condition, within the social process, for the development of mind.[29]

---

28 Benjamin, "The Author as Producer," 89.
29 Mead, *Mind, Self, and Society*, 134.

When seen from this perspective, human self-reflection is a rather general basis for human social existence. Humans perform it in countless and different complex ways, depending on the context. Unlike the kind of test that Walter Benjamin observed taking place in the actor performing for the camera, self-reflection is a kind of internal evaluation vis-à-vis the other with a theoretically indeterminable outcome. It is unlike any kind of test performed by any technical medium, such as the camera or the computer, and it has no clear criteria but is simply one characteristic of the modern subject's (self-)creation.

Still, more specific tendencies or risks have been identified against this larger backdrop. Claudia Jünke, for instance, has argued that, throughout the 20th century, the modern subject has reconstructed itself from within a dialectics of self-weakening and self-affirmation.[30] Florian Lippert and Marcel Schmid have also pointed out that this process of (individual and collective) self-making is the expression of a collective psychology that is necessary for modern democracies, given that it can be influenced by fears of self-weakening through potential change that is prompted either by self-reflection, or by an inability to self-distance and reflect.[31]

Consequently, any display of self-reflection in reportage carries three main aspects. It is—at the same time—a kind of skill that is employed intentionally; an act of self-affirmation; and an act of self-weakening. This insight carries two main epistemological and existential consequences. If we view reporters as decidedly human media, it is—apart from the physical mediation described previously—their ability to reflect upon themselves that marks them as such. If we view reporters as particularly trustworthy or sincere communicators, again, then their self-reflection might also decisively contribute to this effect. As Ursula Renz has argued with regard to self-knowledge, on the one hand, "our being a person or mental subject depends in a constitutive way on some form of epistemic self-intimacy."[32] On the other hand, she further states that "we are also used to thinking that what qualifies someone as wise person is, among other things, the unusual extent or depth of his or her self-knowledge."[33] Importantly, then, self-reflection can work as a kind of reflexive meta-critique

---

30   Jünke, "Selbstschwächung Und Selbstbehauptung – Zur Dialektik Moderner Subjektivität," 9.
31   Lippert et al., "Read Thyself: Cultural Self-Reflection and the Relevance of Literary 'self'-Labels," 3–4.
32   Renz, "Introduction," 2.
33   Renz, 2.

that encompasses both existential and epistemological concerns. As indicated previously, David Foster Wallace and Walter Benjamin seem to view critical self-weakening as a necessary precondition for successful self-affirmation in their claims that a sense of heightened scrutiny or more encompassing awareness has to be introduced into the ways in which writers cover reality.

However, there are important nuances to self-reflection. Self-aware perspectives in human social conduct are part of what the French sociologist Luc Boltanski calls the *metapragmatic register*; it consists of diverging acts of critique and confirmation and is composed of moments, which are "marked by an *increase in the level of reflexivity* during which the attention of participants shifts from the task to be performed to the question of how it is appropriate to *characterize* what is happening."[34] In these moments, priority is given to the self-referential question "of knowing exactly what one is doing and how it would be necessary to act so that what one is doing is done *in very truth*."[35] On this spectrum, the metapragmatic register of confirmation re-confirms an already existing state of reality as *the* reality—often by way of institutional action. Critique, however, points out this state's temporality, thereby emphasizing the possibility for change.[36] Humans in the roles of critics or spokespersons perform acts of critique and confirmation respectively. In the case of critique, the critic takes personal responsibility for his or her assertions. Spokespeople performing acts of confirmation, however, do not typically engage on a personal level. Still, critique cannot exist independently of confirmation, as Boltanski argues:

> The instances of confirmation, vigilant about the risk critique makes them run, shut their eyes to the evanescent character of what holds the place of foundation for them, to which critique counter-poses its lucidity. But critique ignores – and this is the form of unconsciousness peculiar to it – what it owes to the labour of confirmation that supplies it with the axis without which it would be condemned to drift aimlessly.[37]

Consequently, self-reflection in reportage has to be regarded as embodied interplay between acts of confirmation, related to certain standardized modes and methods of knowledge, and their critical questioning. Essentially, then,

---

34   Boltanski, *On Critique: A Sociology of Emancipation*, 67.
35   Boltanski, 68.
36   Boltanski, 99.
37   Boltanski, 103.

self-reflective reporters as human media engage in acts of self-affirmation precisely by way of potential self-weakening.

In general, however, this introduction of critique or self-weakening is neither a necessary nor a typical function of media. Scholars have repeatedly observed that the success of a medium's performance strongly depends upon the medium's own disappearance; that "mediation is designed to make what is mediated appear unmediated."[38] W.J.T Mitchell has referred to this as media's creation of "zones of immediacy" for themselves.[39] Sybille Krämer has also called this tendency "aesthetic self-neutralization"[40] and has identified its roots in Aristotle's, and later Thomas Aquinas's, conceptions of the transparent medium.[41]

Still, media are not autonomous entities, existentially speaking. They can only occupy middle positions between two sides. Therefore, Krämer also calls media "bodies that can be disembodied" and attributes them a "transitory corporeality".[42] As a critical function, medial self-reflection works in ways similar to what Luc Boltanski has called *existential test*.[43] Based on subjective experience, its critical operation (Boltanski calls it radical, rather than reformist) is not institutionalized and is marginal, at least initially. In Boltanski's view, it carries the potential to reveal reality's contingency by way of exemplary experience. The human medium's self-reflection, then, is a conscious and intentional affirmation of its own corporeality first and foremost. With reference to the concrete cases of reporters, it is precisely self-reflection that foregrounds the human medium's fundamental function—namely mediation—as typically veiled, but existing as their self-reflection. As I argue in the conclusion, however, it does not work in the sense of "noise, dysfunction and disturbance [that] make the medium itself noticeable"[44] but as a productive autocritique, the function of which is to establish a connection between humans that is based on a more transparent authorial self-depiction.

---

38 Krämer, 31; This aspect of media is absolutely central to the work of other German media theorists, such as Lorenz Engell, Joseph Vogl, or Dieter Mersch, whom Krämer builds upon. See, for instance, Engell and Vogl, "Vorwort"; Mersch, "Wort, Bild, Ton, Zahl: Eine Einleitung in die Medienphilosophie."
39 Mitchell, "Addressing Media," 12.
40 Krämer, *Medium, Messenger, Transmission: An Approach to Media Philosophy*, 31.
41 Krämer, 32–33.
42 Krämer, 34.
43 Boltanski, *On Critique: A Sociology of Emancipation*, 113.
44 Krämer, *Medium, Messenger, Transmission: An Approach to Media Philosophy*, 31.

2 On Real Communing: Mediating Coordinated Experience

2.1 Authenticity and Uncertainty in Touristic Experience

If it is to function properly, the human medium always works within a social context governed by intersubjective trust. Texts that feature an operative kind of self-reflection are therefore frequently concerned with how and under what circumstances humans cooperate and interact. In many texts then, the human medium's exemplary integration of material and symbolic sensemaking of human experience is typically juxtaposed with analyses of said collective human experience and coordinated human behavior. The more or less explicit parallel, depending on the text, is found in the ongoing, dynamic, and often implicit negotiations of trust and consent that occur both between writer and reader as well as social actors involved in the coordination of human action on a cultural and societal level more generally.

In such instances, writers of reportage contrast their own acts of material and symbolic meaning-making with the ways in which collective human behavior is organized and mediated. Most notably, they explore the potential differences in human interaction that such contrasting illuminates. They thereby emphasize their own humanity as media and analyze the complexities of human social behavior.

In a modern Western society such as the U.S., instances of human social action are often affected by the spatializing, commodifying, or dismantling effects of capitalism. Just like the writers themselves, capitalism functions both as a set of ideas in symbolic sensemaking as well as a concrete material force that changes physical reality. Therefore, particularly sharp considerations of such material and symbolic shaping of human experience can be found in textual representations of touristic experiences, for instance. In this typical setting, human experience itself is the product to be manufactured and managed. This active, intentional production of human experience of course is akin to the ways in which the writers themselves produce experience to be processed and sold to readers. However, as writers identify and ponder fundamental differences, they also raise important ethical questions rooted in their own, inevitably social humanity.

The texts analyzed include the reportage written by David Foster Wallace, about his experience on a cruise and its communal sense of leisure; George Saunders's visit to Dubai and the descriptions of the communal function of globalized luxury tourism; and John Jeremiah Sullivan's attendance at a Christian rock festival, where he observed the communal celebration of religion.

In their texts, they all position themselves as self-aware singularly producing human media, in contrast to the re-producing of reality that shapes these instances of manufactured and managed human communing in tourism. More specifically, all three writers identify fundamental uncertainties that occupy the core of communal acts of the material and symbolic construction of everyday realities. They often illustrate these uncertainties by way of intersubjective conflicts between themselves as professionals in service of the rather general human curiosity of their readers and the interests and actions of others taking part in or producing such touristic experience. Importantly, they thus also all critically highlight tourism's reflexivity. That is, how the very mediation of communing in tourism informs the communing itself with often ideological means, through the shared embodying of belief in both preexisting consumerist and religious narratives.

Concerns with uncertainty in touristic experience are reflected more specifically in concerns with alienation and authenticity and their constructed nature. Recent critical analyses of tourism have therefore raised questions about who authenticates, how and why.[1] Similarly to texts of reportage then, acts of construction of authenticity illuminate issues of power and responsibility. From a producer's standpoint, authenticity can be manufactured industrially. On the end of the consumer however, akin to the relationship between writer and reader, authenticity is always experienced subjectively as a produced, temporal human feeling.

This connection is central to the arguments made in all three texts. Still, from within this framework there exists a range of different perspectives onto authenticity in tourism. Early critical attention to authenticity in tourism focused on the authenticity of the tourist's object, the destination, or experience. This perspective goes back to Daniel Boorstin's provocative book *The Image: A Guide to Pseudo-Events in America* (1961). Boorstin argued that traveling

---

1 Rickly and Vidon, "Introduction: From Pseudo-Events to Authentic Experiences."

had stopped being about spontaneous experience. As tourism, it had become commodified as a series of pre-fabricated, inauthentic pseudo-events seeking to transcend time and space.[2] In one of the first systematic analyses of tourism, *The Tourist: A Theory of the Leisure Class* (1976), Dean MacCannell rejected Boorstin's nostalgia but maintained that tourism was marked by a kind of staged authenticity that worked, because it enabled the off-duty worker to experience an idealized enactment of him- or herself. He argued that it was:

> only by making a fetish of the work of others, by transforming it into an 'amusement' ('do it yourself'), a spectacle (Grand Coulee), or an attraction (the guided tours of Ford Motor Company) that modern workers, on vacation, can apprehend work as a part of a meaningful totality.[3]

This experience had a unifying effect on societies, MacCannell argued, because the experience of the work of others alleviated the alienating effects of people's own experience as workers: "The alienation of the worker stops where the alienation of the sightseer begins."[4]

Alongside a recent shift in scholarly attention the very experiential aspects of authenticity have come into focus. Daniel Knudsen has argued that all consciously experienced authenticity could be classified as fantasy because a sense of alienation, stemming from the transformation from a biological to a societal human being, remains in every human's unconscious.[5] Importantly then, in tourism, the very fundamental uncertainties in human communing are manifested in the ways in which authenticity is produced and felt individually.

Existential authenticity, as this concept has been termed, is concerned with what is commonly known as "being true to oneself" and the very modern quest to attain this state of being. Rather than concerning the authenticity of either objects or experiences, this approach is concerned with the ways in which authenticity is itself a (temporal) experience that is produced within and between tourists and with the people with whom they interact.[6]

Intrapersonal authenticity refers to the dimension of existential authenticity that concerns the sensual and symbolic aspects of the body as the source

---

2 Boorstin, *The Image: A Guide to Pseudo-Events in America*.
3 MacCannell, *The Tourist: A New Theory of the Leisure Class*, 6.
4 MacCannell, 6.
5 Knudsen, "Afterword: Authenticity and Life."
6 Rickly and Vidon, "Introduction: From Pseudo-Events to Authentic Experiences," 5–7.

of the authentic self. Here, the body is both a signifying display of personal human identity and a subject that produces feeling by way of its sensory organs. As such, the body and its drives are controlled, for instance in contexts of labor, which may result in a sense of existential inauthenticity or alienation.[7] Ning Wang argues that tourism makes the experience of personal authenticity possible because "sensual pleasures, feelings, and other bodily impulses are to a relatively large extent released and consumed and the bodily desires (for natural amenities, sexual freedom, and spontaneity) are gratified intensively."[8] Intrapersonal authenticity also refers to acts of self-making or self-identity that are realized in touristic contexts because the routinization of everyday lives hardly leaves space for experimentation with identity.[9]

Interpersonal authenticity, on the other hand, refers to the ways in which communal experience matters in touristic contexts. Wang mentions family tourism as a way to "achieve or reinforce a sense of authentic togetherness".[10] She also references Victor Turner's concept of *communitas*, which means an ideal "inter-personal relationship among pilgrims who confront one another as social equals based on their common humanity."[11] Tourism, she argues, can have similar effects, given that "the pleasure of tourism exists not only in seeing exotic things, but also in sharing and communicating this pleasure with other tourists who are seeing the same sights together."[12]

In their specifics then, these different aspects of authenticity help to again identify a fundamental kind of uncertainty as the more general characteristic of communing that unites the three texts. Uncertainty is an existential fact of all social actions, and the waves of mediatization have further affected the complexity of Western societies because they have illuminated their constructed character. In theory, everyday realities are the specific instantiations of the complex material and symbolic constructs that social theorists call social worlds. They are highly mediated products of material infrastructure and communication made and performed by humans.[13] Nick Couldry and Andreas Hepp define the social world as:

---

7   Wang, "Rethinking Authenticity in Tourism Experience," 361–362.
8   Wang, 362.
9   Wang, 363.
10 Wang, 364.
11 Wang, 364.
12 Wang, 365.
13 Couldry and Hepp, *The Mediated Construction of Reality*, 6–7.

the intersubjective sphere of the social relations that we as human beings experience. Those relations are rooted in everyday reality, a reality nowadays always interwoven with media to some degree. The social world is, in turn, differentiated into many domains of meaning, even though it is also bound together by multiple relations of interdependence and constraint.[14]

Put rather generally, then, everyday reality is the outcome of communal human actions that occur in certain differentiated and intersecting domains based on the shared practical orientations of the humans acting therein.[15]

Such communal human action is highly temporal. It is typically based on a shared "meaningful belonging that provides a basis for action–and orientation–in common."[16] The highly contested term that comes to mind is 'community'. Couldry and Hepp use the term 'collectivities'[17] because they are also concerned with digital realities. I prefer Studdert and Walkerdine's 'communing' or 'communal being-ness' because these terms emphasize the temporary quality of such material and symbolic human togetherness in space and time and indicate that they involve "actions and movement, being and becoming".[18] Luc Boltanski has argued that the social world, as a construct, and its specific manifestations in everyday reality undergird a radical uncertainty, because any real construct of reality is inevitably positioned against the backdrop of all of everyday reality's possible and different constructions. Boltanski identifies dispute and fragility as core characters of social bonds; this is because humans possess bodies and, hence, are capable of only taking one particular point of view on the world at a time.[19]

As analyzed in the following case studies, this radical uncertainty at the heart of the social world is particularly apparent in the relationship between writer and reader. Critical endeavors in reader response theory have shown that this relationship is similarly marked by a fundamental uncertainty with regard to the reader's interpretation of texts. As shown earlier, awareness of the fragility of this connection has increased alongside mediatization and conceptions of the postmodern.

---

14   Couldry and Hepp, 20.
15   Couldry and Hepp, 20.
16   Couldry and Hepp, 168.
17   Couldry and Hepp, 168.
18   Studdert and Walkerdine, *Rethinking Community Research: Inter-Relationality, Communal Being and Commonality*, 29.
19   Boltanski, *On Critique: A Sociology of Emancipation*, 57–61.

As the case studies also show, however, writers engage differently with these uncertainties that mark both the communing in the social world they experience as well as the relationship they aim to establish with readers.

First, very much in the vein of Daniel Boorstin's critique, David Foster Wallace details the alienation that results from inauthentic bodily and communal experience on a cruise that exploits trust for economic gains, and drafts a critical response in text. George Saunders pitches an optimistic belief in a basic kind of human sameness that is situated in the human potential to be kind as a countermeasure to individualized consumerism. And as he experiences interpersonal authenticity with fellow festivalgoers, John Jeremiah Sullivan affirms a basic human weakness that consequentially results in a tolerant ethic that acknowledges the human need to believe. All three texts identify a general ideological force that aims to brush over uncertainties. Yet they also locate possibilities of change and difference in the specific human interactions perceived as authentic, due to their very embracing of uncertainties.

2.2 The Desperate Medium in David Foster Wallace's "A Supposedly Fun Thing I'll Never Do Again" (1997)

As mentioned, David Foster Wallace made no secret of his motivation to create a form of literature that could confront the mass mediation of American society in either interviews or essays. However, Foster Wallace, who committed suicide in 2008, also left an exemplary body of work. While he is primarily known for his short fiction and his magnum opus *Infinite Jest* (1996),[1] written between 1992 and 2008, Foster Wallace also produced a substantial trove of innovative yet controversial reportage, essays, and commentary, which influenced and inspired other writers of literary journalism.[2] For John Jeremiah Sullivan, Foster Wallace "got his finger into a certain wound and was moving it around,"[3] and Leslie Jamison stated that the "multiplicity of [his] perspectives feels almost like an ethical stance; the refusal of the single view."[4] An experimental fiction writer, Foster Wallace had no journalistic training and he never claimed to be a reporter. Nevertheless, he was very interested in non-fiction literature. As a reader, he preferred the writings of George Orwell or Joan Didion to those of Tom Wolfe or Hunter S. Thompson, whose texts—except for *Hell's Angels* (1967)[5]—he found to be "naïve and narcissistic."[6] Foster Wallace seemed

---

1   Foster Wallace, *Infinite Jest*.
2   On Wallace's influence, see most recently and explicitly Roiland, "Derivative Sport: The Journalistic Legacy of David Foster Wallace"; See also Lorentzen, "The Rewriting of David Foster Wallace"; Kraus, "Viewer Discretion: The Trajectory of Writer-Worrier David Foster Wallace"; Sullivan, "Too Much Information."
3   Roiland, "Derivative Sport: The Journalistic Legacy of David Foster Wallace."
4   Roiland.
5   Thompson, *Hells Angels: A Strange and Terrible Saga*.
6   Jacob, "Interview with David Foster Wallace," 153–54.

uncertain about where and how he wanted to draw the line between fact and fiction, significantly and particularly in his early career.[7]

In general, Foster Wallace has been established as one of the most formative writers of his generation, due to his experimental approach to form and interest in affect. Robert Seguin has observed a:

> disparity one often senses between the scintillating intensity of Wallace's texts ... and the weirdly earnest, unfashionable ... ideas that they are often thought to espouse: how we must seek new ways to sincerely communicate our authentic selves, and be mindful and attentive to the world outside us, amidst the tornadic roar of an addictive culture of image and mass spectacle that seeks only to fortify our essential narcissism.[8]

In one of the most daring critical readings of Foster Wallace's work, Adam Kelly affiliated him with other writers such as George Saunders or Jennifer Egan and identified a new kind of sincerity in their texts. Kelly sees these texts as "defined by their undecidability and the affective response they invite and provoke in their readers"[9]. He observes in their writers' positions a "sturdy affirmation of non-ironic values, as a renewed taking of responsibility for the meaning of one's words".[10] This rather forward-looking sincerity acknowledges that it can never achieve purity, that it always has to be understood "in inextricable conjunction with ostensibly opposing terms, including irony and manipulation".[11] This awareness necessitates what Kelly calls the "aesthetically generative undecidability";[12] this is the insight that a text's affective power "cannot fully be separated from, and is in fact in large part constituted by, the appropriation of affect for manipulative ends".[13] There is no guarantee of the writer's sincerity in the written text either for the writer or for the reader, because either acceptance or rejection of the writer's authenticity happens "off the page, outside repre-

---

7   Roiland, "The Fine Print: Uncovering the True Story of David Foster Wallace and the 'Reality Boundary.'"
8   Seguin, "Form, Voice, and Utopia in David Foster Wallace," 220.
9   Kelly, "The New Sincerity," 206.
10 Kelly, 198.
11 Kelly, 201.
12 Kelly, 204.
13 Kelly, 204.

2.2 The Desperate Medium in Wallace's "A Supposedly Fun Thing I'll Never Do Again"   91

sentation"[14] and depends "upon the invocation and response of another".[15] In certain ways, then, Kelly even reads Foster Wallace's fiction as a kind of nonfiction, or at least as a fiction with nonfictional purposes.

Arguably, David Foster Wallace's most popular piece of actual nonfiction is his reportage titled "A Supposedly Fun Thing I'll Never Do Again."[16] Marshall Boswell called it "one of Wallace's most beloved and widely read works" that contains "all the hallmarks of Wallace's inimitable style."[17] In the text, Foster Wallace tells the story of his becoming the alienated, and hence desperate, object of a produced, pre-fabricated experience of escape from everyday life while on a week-long cruise. Josh Roiland has noted that this trope of escape into fantasy is prominent in Wallace's nonfiction, which generally seeks to communicate an "imperative to be present."[18] According to Lukas Hoffmann, this imperative to be attentive and conscious is presented as a remedy for the despair and anxieties that mortality causes in humans in "A Supposedly Fun Thing."[19] Hoffmann classifies the text as post-ironic, partly because it emphasizes the ubiquitous mediation of experience in contemporary American society and culture.[20]

Importantly, however, Foster Wallace's (self-)reflections upon mediation are deeply intertwined with the text's primary theme; touristic experience and his emphasis of mediation clearly serve a larger critical cause. The anxiety and despair that Foster Wallace feels onboard the cruise is rooted in the particular experience of alienation brought about by capitalist drives in tourism, which essentially manufactures, manages and sells human experience. Foster Wallace juxtaposes the inauthenticity he perceives in both the produced experience of being pampered and this production's very interpretation (provided by the cruise company in PR brochures aboard) with an extensive display of self-reflection that encompasses the mediating aspects of his role as a human

---

14   Kelly, 205.
15   Kelly, 205.
16   Foster Wallace, "A Supposedly Fun Thing I'll Never Do Again." A shorter version of the story was first published in *Harper's* magazine in January 1996, entitled "Shipping Out."
17   Boswell, *Understanding David Foster Wallace*, 180.
18   Roiland, "Getting Away From It All: The Literary Journalism of David Foster Wallace and Nietzsche's Concept of Oblivion," 31.
19   Hoffmann, *Postirony: The Nonfictional Literature of David Foster Wallace and Dave Eggers*, 165.
20   Hoffmann, 151.

medium. He emphasizes the very aesthetic and material qualities of his mediation that are absent, repressed, or disguised in the limiting objectification of human experience on the cruise ship, even as he details the ambiguities and pluralities of how he works, experiences, thinks, and tells. He embodies both symbolic and material meaning-making—human communing and communication—as deeply uncertain and mediated or shaped by forces that can both connect and alienate humans.

A Pseudojournalist

The most basic and decisive mediator of Foster Wallace's experience on the cruise, its subjective interpretation, and its transmission to readers is his professional role. In the text's very first paragraph, Foster Wallace writes that he had been on a "journalistic assignment."[21] The professional relationship between Foster Wallace and *Harper's* magazine shapes both his experience and the resulting text. Foster Wallace reflects, somewhat ambiguously, on the effects of this relationship in terms of the pressure it makes him feel about, and the ways in which his purported role as a journalist affects, his interactions onboard with the personnel and other passengers, not to mention the ways in which it influences his own behavior.

The assignment pressures Foster Wallace in two different ways. On the one hand, this pressure is due to the assignment's comparatively high financial stakes. Foster Wallace indicates that what he calls a "tropical plum assignment" by "a certain swanky East-Coast magazine" might be too much for him compared to a previous article about a state fair: "[T]his time there's this new feeling of pressure: total expenses for the State Fair were $27.00 excluding games of chance. This time *Harper's* has shelled out over $3000 U.S. before seeing pithy sensuous description one."[22] On the other hand, Foster Wallace also claims that the pressure he feels stems from a lack of specificity regarding the expected outcome of the assignment. "They say all they want is a sort of really big experiential postcard—go, plow the Caribbean in style, come back, say what you've seen."[23] By detailing these fundamentals of the text's genesis, Foster Wallace illustrates that his experience is intentionally

---

21   Foster Wallace, "A Supposedly Fun Thing I'll Never Do Again," 256.
22   Foster Wallace, 256.
23   Foster Wallace, 257.

produced within a capitalist framework that he associates with journalism. Furthermore, he indicates that this very framework has the potential to shape his very experience by affecting his mental well-being.

In addition, Foster Wallace repeatedly refers to rather concrete ways in which the capitalist framework manifests itself in the text. Several examples take us back to the financial dependency and uncertain expectations outlined at the beginning. For instance, after relaying an almost page-long litany of experiences, Foster Wallace asks the reader and himself: "Is this enough? At the time it didn't seem like enough."[24] Elsewhere, Foster Wallace admits to not being sure how many examples he needs to include to provide a sense of the pampering services onboard[25] or that he was actively looking for "some really representative experiences."[26] The assignment is more explicitly alluded to when he anticipates the process of editing and potential deletion of passages[27] or mentions discussions about the forwarding of a skeet-shooting bill to *Harper's*.[28] Taken together, these little asides signify that, in economic terms, Foster Wallace sees himself as being in the situation of a contract journalist and wants the reader to be aware that this has affected the resulting text.

According to Foster Wallace, the journalistic assignment also impacted the very nature of his experiences on board. In the text, both his own and other people's purported understanding of his role simultaneously creates and hampers direct experience. For example, Foster Wallace names two instances in which he was denied a demand as a result of his journalistic role. In the first episode, Foster Wallace describes how he asked the restaurant staff for kitchen leftovers to attract sharks, which:

> turned out to be a serious journalistic faux pas, because I'm almost positive the maître d' passed this disturbing tidbit on to Mr. Dermatitis [Foster Wallace's nickname for the ship's hotel manager, Ed.] and that it was a big reason why I was denied access to stuff like the ship's galley, thereby impoverishing the sensuous scope of this article.[29]

---

24   Foster Wallace, 257.
25   Foster Wallace, 290.
26   Foster Wallace, 320.
27   Foster Wallace, 293.
28   Foster Wallace, 344.
29   Foster Wallace, 262.

As Foster Wallace states, this incident is connected to a later interaction with the hotel manager in question, in which Wallace asks for permission to inspect the ship's sewage system. At the time, Wallace is unaware of a scandal involving another cruise ship that was found to have dumped garbage into the sea. The interaction is described in such a way as to create a sense of surprise about how his request is received:

> Even behind his mirrored sunglasses I can tell that Mr. Dermatitis is severely upset about my interest in sewage, and he denies my request to eyeball the V.S.S [acronym for what Foster Wallace calls the VACCUUM SEWAGE SYSTEM, Ed.] with a complex defensiveness that I couldn't even begin to chart out here.[30]

Later, having been made aware of the scandal at the dinner table, Foster Wallace assumes that the hotel manager really thinks that he might be "some kind of investigative journalist with a hard-on for shark dangers and sewage scandals."[31] Although potentially exaggerated and slightly ironic, all of these cases illustrate that, in Foster Wallace's view, the context of the journalistic assignment not only had the potential to affect the final product, but also the experiences he has already had on board in virtue of other people's—in this case the hotel manager's—perception of him.

Furthermore, Foster Wallace's purported self-understanding as a voluntary, albeit naïve journalist also affects his own dealings and perceptions. For instance, when waiting to board the ship before the cruise, Foster Wallace reflects on his own attention:

> A major advantage to writing some sort of article about an experience is that at grim junctures like this pre-embarkation blimp hangar you can distract yourself from what the experience feels like by focusing on what looks like items of possible interest for the article.[32]

Similarly, Foster Wallace notes that he repeatedly felt compelled to leave his cabin to actively create experience, as a result of his assignment on another occasion:

---

30   Foster Wallace, 305.
31   Foster Wallace, 305.
32   Foster Wallace, 274.

> I'd have to sort of psych myself up to leave the cabin and go accumulate experiences, and then pretty quickly out there in the general population my will would break and I'd find some sort of excuse to scuttle back to 1009. This happened quite a few times a day.³³

By characterizing his "journalistic" attention as a distraction, Foster Wallace describes a conflict between the way in which he would behave under normal circumstances and the way in which he behaves as a journalist, who is intentionally looking for potential content for his article. The same principle might apply to the reflection on his general lack of willingness to leave the cabin, which was affected by the pressure of his assignment.

Elsewhere, Foster Wallace relates that his own interpretation of his role affected his interaction with crew members. When meeting and chatting with a Polish waiter named Tibor, for instance, Foster Wallace admits that he would rather not act as a journalist in these interactions:

> He doesn't know I'm on the *Nadir* [Foster Wallace's nickname for the cruise ship, Ed.] as a pseudojournalist. I'm not sure why I haven't told him – somehow I think it might make things hard for him... I never ask him anything about Celebrity Cruises... because I feel like I'd just about die if Tibor got into trouble on my account.³⁴

Similarly, Foster Wallace states that he refrained from treating Winston, his table tennis opponent and the ship's DJ, in a journalistic way:

> As with good old Tibor, I don't probe Winston in any serious journalistic way, although in this case it's not so much because I fear getting the 3P [another one of Foster Wallace's nicknames, Ed.] in trouble as because (nothing against good old Winston personally) he's not exactly the brightest bulb in the ship's intellectual chandelier, if you get my drift.³⁵

For both Tibor and Winston, Foster Wallace anticipates the potential consequences of his journalistic work, which is why he treats these two differently and admits to meeting them on a mere human level that allows for more gen-

---

33 Foster Wallace, 297.
34 Foster Wallace, 322.
35 Foster Wallace, 329.

erosity. In this way, they serve as another indication of Foster Wallace's awareness of the effect of his assignment on his experiences onboard.

All in all, Foster Wallace reflects deeply on the ways in which the professional parameters of his participation in the cruise potentially affect the outcome of his work. If one accepts his own declarations, Foster Wallace acts simultaneously as a journalist and as a non-journalist. Economically speaking, Foster Wallace presents himself as a journalist, although he is certainly not a professional. He openly admits to not being able to conduct research or to treat all of the objects of his research with the same distance. These episodes can appear ironic precisely because they show legitimate issues deriving from the intentionality that the economic framework of journalism creates, but that are not usually mentioned in works of journalism. The only possible irony then is that, rather than being concerned with the question of whether or not what he is telling his readers is true, Foster Wallace instead focuses on the issues of what, in the context of an assignment, might affect any textual representation of reality as it is experienced.

The Recording Human

The main demand of Foster Wallace's assignment, as mentioned previously, is to deliver "a sort of really big experiential postcard."[36] In the text, Foster Wallace interprets this task literally. Yet, he also sees it as his duty to reflect upon what it means to write literally about human experience. Foster Wallace obsessively details not only the basic physical and sensory qualities of his experiences, but also their occasional physical effects and interconnectedness. He also misses almost no opportunity to point out how human experience is mediated by other human beings or by Foster Wallace himself. Most importantly, however, Foster Wallace characterizes his own ways of experiencing reality as plural and decidedly human, thereby criticizing the reductive aspects of the visual media dominating touristic experience.

Although Foster Wallace laments the vagueness of the instructions he has been given, in fact, his task is rather specific. In his words, it is his job to "go, plow the Caribbean in style, come back, say what you've seen."[37] This of course

---

36 Foster Wallace, 257.
37 Foster Wallace, 257.

2.2 The Desperate Medium in Wallace's "A Supposedly Fun Thing I'll Never Do Again"

limits experience to its visual manifestation and Foster Wallace does not hesitate to ignore his job description, by almost mockingly reporting on more than what his eyes have perceived. For example, in the paragraph immediately following the description of his task, Foster Wallace presents a collage of things he has seen, only to suddenly break with sight itself altogether:

> I have seen a lot of really big white ships. I have seen schools of little fish fins that glow. I have seen a toupee on a thirteen-year-old boy. (The glowing fish liked to swarm between our hull and the cement of the pier whenever we docked.) I have seen the north coast of Jamaica. I have seen and smelled all 145 cats inside the Ernest Hemingway Residence in Key West FL. I now know the difference between straight Bingo and Prize-O, and what it is when a Bingo jackpot "snowballs." I have seen camcorders that practically required a dolly.[38]

Notably, Foster Wallace starts each of the first five sentences of this paragraph by dutifully stating what he has seen, as if to argue that seeing alone is not enough for him to do his job properly; however, he adds that he has also smelled the cats in the fifth sentence. In the sixth sentence (not counting the bracketed one), Foster Wallace then moves on to include knowing into the scope of human experience, which suggests a connection to consciousness. The paragraph is remarkable not for its imagery, but for both its initial foregrounding and subsequent abandonment of, and ultimate return to, what is *seen*. Visuality, Foster Wallace seems to suggest, forms a vital part of human experience, but by no means can the latter be reduced thereto.

This stance is manifested in Foster Wallace's critique of cameras and camcorders, whose enormous size he alludes to in the final sentence of the passage cited above. In particular, Foster Wallace makes a point of his dislike of the ubiquity of cameras both on and off the boat. When he describes the bus transfer from the airport to the pier, for example, he observes "a tremendous mass clicking sound in here from all the cameras around everybody's neck. I haven't brought any sort of camera and feel a perverse pride about this."[39] After arriving at the pier, the mass of cameras again catches his attention. "I count over a dozen makes of camera just in the little block of orange chairs within camera-discernment range. That's not counting camcorders."[40] On the follow-

---

38   Foster Wallace, 257.
39   Foster Wallace, 271.
40   Foster Wallace, 275.

ing page, Foster Wallace proudly states: "I have now empirically verified that I am the only ticketed adult here without some kind of camera equipment."[41]

At first glance, the cameras may help Foster Wallace differentiate himself from the other image-recording passengers as media and help him position himself as a writer who relies on the use of pen, paper, and memory. However, Foster Wallace undermines this initially clear distinction in his character study of a passenger he calls Captain Video. In Foster Wallace's telling, Captain Video is a "sad and cadaverous guy" who "camcords absolutely *everything*."[42] However, Foster Wallace also admits to having observed similarities between himself and Captain Video that "tend to make me uncomfortable, and I try to avoid him as much as possible."[43] This observation further cements Foster Wallace's self-characterization as being primarily human. Despite his aversion to the constant use of cameras, he can relate to an actual human being behind one of them. Once again, the issue is general ubiquity, not singular use.

In place of visual impressions and the use of a camera, then, Foster Wallace explores and emphasizes the interconnected and complex interdependencies of sensuous impressions. For instance, Foster Wallace describes the feeling of physically being on a moving ship in detail:

> Even in heavy seas, 7NC Megaships don't yaw or throw you around or send bowls of soup sliding across tables. Only a certain subtle unreality to your footing lets you know you're not on land. At sea, a room's floor feels somehow 3-D, and your footing demands a slight attention good old planar static land never needs. You don't ever quite hear the ship's engines, but when your feet are planted you can feel them, a kind of spinal throb—it's oddly soothing.[44]

In this passage, touch, balance, and hearing are all interwoven to form a kind of sensory collage located and centered in Foster Wallace's body, where the impressions coalesce. Consequently, the workings of body and brain are impossible to separate, as Foster Wallace more explicitly describes in the following paragraph about walking:

> When heavy waves come straight at a Megaship's snout, the ship goes up and down along its long axis – this is called *pitching*. It produces a disorient-

---

41   Foster Wallace, 276.
42   Foster Wallace, "A Supposedly Fun Thing I'll Never Do Again."
43   Foster Wallace, 308.
44   Foster Wallace, 283.

ing deal where you feel like you're walking on a very slight downhill grade and then level and then on a very slight uphill grade. Some evolutionary retrograde reptile-brain part of the CNS is apparently reawakened, though, and manages all this so automatically that it requires a good deal of attention to notice anything more than that walking feels a little dreamy.[45]

In both passages, Foster Wallace notes how different perceptions contribute to the sense of being on a cruise ship. In the first description, he observes the interconnectedness of touch and hearing that is related to balance, and he observes the unfamiliarity of the fact that walking demands attention. In the second description, Foster Wallace emphasizes how the brain apparently synchronizes sensory impressions to such a degree that walking no longer demands attention. Rather, it is the unfamiliarity itself that can only be perceived with extra attention. As this juxtaposition seems to suggest, Foster Wallace emphasizes the mere existence of inter-sensual connections and their potentially different and contradictory effects as something notable in itself.

As much as Foster Wallace highlights and almost celebrates these connections, he also observes the weirdness of their absence. Following his observation that his cabin's bathroom smells like artificial lemon, for instance, he notes that:

[the] cabin itself, on the other hand, after it's been cleaned, has no odor. None. Not in the carpets, the bedding, the insides of the desk's drawers, the wood of the Wondercloset's doors: nothing. One of the very few totally odorless places I've ever been in. This, too, eventually starts giving me the creeps.[46]

The very absence of smell, as disconnected, has an emotional resonance as it elicits a kind of anxiety in Foster Wallace. He seems to argue that there is no way for a human being to shut off their senses. Thus, apart from the complexity and plurality of the senses, he also emphasizes their ubiquity.

In addition to these rather general considerations about human perception, Foster Wallace points to its specific physical mediation almost tirelessly. The sensory perceptions in the text are mediated either by other human beings, or by Foster Wallace himself. After hearing about various cruise incidents from

---

45   Foster Wallace, 283.
46   Foster Wallace, 303.

a couple at the airport prior to departure, for example, Foster Wallace notes that "the lady (kind of a spokesman for the couple) isn't sure; it turns out she sort of likes to toss off a horrific detail and then get all vague and blasé when a horrified listener tries to pump her for details."[47] Here, Foster Wallace adds a qualifying observation that puts what he had heard earlier into a new context. He leaves the actual content uninvestigated, however—namely, whether or not what the woman said was correct. The focus is less on the impression itself than on its mediation, which is a recurring theme in the text.

Foster Wallace makes this concern with mediation particularly apparent in his examination of the sincerity of other passengers or staff members. For instance, he develops a particular affection for Tibor, the Polish waiter, who simply means what he says.[48] He is, however, repulsed by Mona, a teenaged passenger who lies to the staff and shows a lack of gratitude towards her grandparents.[49] By carefully characterizing and examining other characters as media in this way, Foster Wallace once again emphasizes the mediated nature of human interaction in general. In order to make his point, he even focuses his attention on a particular facial expression, the professional smile:

> You know this smile – the strenuous contraction of circumoral fascia w/ incomplete zygomatic involvement – the smile that doesn't quite reach the smiler's eyes and that signifies nothing more than a calculated attempt to advance the smiler's own interests by pretending to like the smilee.[50]

Similar to what occurs in his analyses of sincerity, Foster Wallace here analyzes a particular way of smiling or, rather, of seeing a particular smile. The problem with this type of smile is not that it is just a basic expression of human joy; it is mediated by a particular intention which objectifies its addressee. Foster Wallace's respect for Tibor, however, indicates that the professional smile also affects the smilers themselves. In her famous study *The Managed Heart: Commercialization of Human Feeling* (1983),[51] Arlie Russell Hochschild argued with regard to the professional smiles of flight attendants that they, too, lose the authenticity of their selves. Beyond this specific critique of the commercialization of human emotion and interpersonal connection, Foster Wallace's analysis also

---

47 Foster Wallace, 269.
48 Foster Wallace, 321–322.
49 Foster Wallace, 282–283.
50 Foster Wallace, 289.
51 Hochschild, *The Managed Heart: Commercialization of Human Feeling*.

2.2 The Desperate Medium in Wallace's "A Supposedly Fun Thing I'll Never Do Again"

points to the very general potential of the mediation of human communication and its experience.

Significantly, Foster Wallace's sensory perceptions are mediated by previous experience. More specifically, Foster Wallace describes instances in which earlier experiences on the ship influence the ways in which he perceives. For example, when another cruise ship lines up alongside Foster Wallace's ship in a Mexican port, Foster Wallace starts:

> to feel a covetous and almost prurient envy of the *Dreamward*. I imagine its interior to be cleaner than ours, larger, more lavishly appointed. I imagine the *Dreamward*'s food being even more varied and punctiliously prepared, the ship's Gift Shop less expensive and its casino less depressing and its stage entertainment less cheesy and its pillow mints bigger.[52]

Of course, the envy that Foster Wallace describes feeling here is based on his experience on his ship. Whether or not this envy is merited does not seem important to Foster Wallace, only that it is the effect of the experience of looking at the other ship, after having spent a few days on a similar cruise. It is he himself who has mediated the impression of this other ship through the memories that he has accumulated over the course of the previous days. Another episode in which Foster Wallace mediates his own experience occurs when he drinks more coffee than usual:

> I normally have a very firm and neurologically imperative one-cup limit on coffee, but the Windsurf's coffee is so good... and the job of deciphering the big yellow Rorschachian blobs of my Navigation Lecture notes so taxing, that on this day I exceed my limit, by rather a lot, which may help explain why the next few hours of this log get kind of kaleidoscopic and unfocused.[53]

In this passage, Foster Wallace speculates about how his consumption of coffee might have affected his perception and, ultimately, the text he writes. He also provides two reasons for having drunk more coffee than usual, thereby indicating that even the coffee-drinking was mediated by an earlier bout of coffee-drinking and the attendance of a lecture.

Foster Wallace's attempts at depicting both the complexities and ways in which human experience is mediated can be read as intense and occasionally

---

52 Foster Wallace, "A Supposedly Fun Thing I'll Never Do Again," 315.
53 Foster Wallace, 335–336.

theatrical exhibitions of the self-reflection of a human medium. If they potentially appear theatrical, this is because Foster Wallace's concern with self-awareness presses into almost every niche of his perception. His ambition to gather material for an experiential postcard occasionally almost blows up the postcard itself. However, this is not to say that Foster Wallace is being ironic. Rather, in these instances, he seems to be adamant about simply telling a story that is different from the one his readers might expect to read.

The Objectified Human Subject

As a human medium, who ultimately also delivers a text to be read, Foster Wallace exhibits a clear awareness of how he, as a writer, reflects upon the material that he has gathered and how he shapes it into a comprehensive argument. This is manifested on at least two different levels in the text. On the one hand, Foster Wallace makes the subjective assessments and intentions (or lack thereof) that he brings to the experience as a human being comparatively transparent. On the other hand, he presents an explicit meta-argument as a result of his reflections and deliberations. The arguments on both levels are connected in the text's main narrative conflict, as the display of Foster Wallace's very human subjectivity is juxtaposed with the objectivity he laments on the meta-textual level.

On the level of his concrete experience onboard, Foster Wallace makes a point of emphasizing his own humanity, since he exhibits the subjectivity that he brings to the experience by referring to his memory, taste, and values. His subjective memory, in particular, as he repeatedly shows, mediates his experience. As Foster Wallace waits to board a bus at the airport, for instance, he observes that a

> crowd-control lady has a megaphone and repeats over and over not to worry about our luggage, that it will follow us later, which I am apparently alone in finding chilling in its unwitting echo of the Auschwitz-embarkation scene in *Schindler's List*.[54]

Of course, the comparison of the two scenes, one the prelude to a cruise, the other a part of a filmed representation of the Holocaust, are utterly subjective.

---

54   Foster Wallace, 270.

2.2 The Desperate Medium in Wallace's "A Supposedly Fun Thing I'll Never Do Again"

Foster Wallace here, early on in the narrative, asserts that he holds a particular, singular view, which is different from that of the mass of other passengers, and which is manifested in his particular memory of having watched a particular movie. However, Foster Wallace also reflects on the particular workings and potential pitfalls of memory as a mediator of experience when, after having observed that a lot of people look Jewish to him, he adds that he is "ashamed to catch myself thinking that I can determine Jewishness from people's appearance."[55]

What might be called "subjective taste" serves as another mediator of Foster Wallace's experience. While pre-boarding, Foster Wallace looks at the other passengers, bluntly judging the appearance of older men in shorts:

> Men after a certain age simply should not wear shorts, I've decided; their legs are hairless in a way that's creepy; the skin seems denuded and practically crying out for hair, particularly on the calves. It's just about the *only* body-area where you actually want *more* hair on older men.[56]

In contrast to other similar passages in which Foster Wallace frequently comments on his reasons for particular judgments, here he simply comments that he has "just decided" to view the hairlessness of older men's legs as problematic and worthy of commentary. Additionally, this passage is a commentary on the meaning of human experience itself. The hairless-legs observation has no connection to Foster Wallace's argument about the cruise as such. As a spontaneous question of taste, however, it appears worthy of inclusion simply because it is part of his overall human experience.

Much to the contrary, Foster Wallace's absolute prioritization of sincerity over other values characterizes the personal value system that he brings to the experience as a key interpretative frame. Furthermore, it also decisively shapes his argument about the cruise experience. One of the clearest expressions of this is Foster Wallace's critique of the writer Frank Conroy's own experiential essay about a cruise. After reading it twice, Wallace contends that it is "sinister and despair-producing and bad"[57] because both its content and its contextualization are insincere. With regard to content, Foster Wallace argues that the essay's:

---

55   Foster Wallace, "A Supposedly Fun Thing I'll Never Do Again," 272–273.
56   Foster Wallace, 272–273.
57   Foster Wallace, 286.

real badness can be found in the way it reveals once again the Megaline's sale-to-sail agenda of micromanaging not only one's perceptions of a 7NC Luxury Cruise but even one's own interpretation and articulation of those perceptions.[58]

In Foster Wallace's view, the essay is insincere because its intention is not to speak the truth, but rather to influence the clients' perception of a product that has already been sold to them. What irks Foster Wallace even more, however, is that this agenda of control extends into the essay itself, and that even the very perception of the essay is influenced:

[the] really major badness is that the project and placement of 'My Celebrity Cruise...' are sneaky and duplicitous and far beyond whatever eroded pales still exist in terms of literary ethics. Conroy's 'essay' appears as an insert, on skinnier pages and with different margins than the rest of the brochure, creating the impression that it has been excerpted from some large and objective thing Conroy wrote.[59]

Both content and context, in Foster Wallace's view, create the impression that the text's main function is artistically argumentative when, in actual fact, it is a commercial. In effect, it not only betrays the reader, but also, in Foster Wallace's view, "messes with our heads and eventually starts upping our defenses even in cases of genuine smiles and real art and true goodwill."[60] Foster Wallace deems such textual insincerity particularly dangerous, precisely because it has the potential to affect not merely a single experience, but rather the entire perception of a human being taken cumulatively. In these passages on the "essaymercial,"[61] Foster Wallace describes how his ethical sense, as a human reader, influences the experience, since it directly affects his interpretation of the experience and leads him to judge it quite decisively. Moreover, his ethical deliberations also inevitably connect to other levels of the text and consider how awareness itself might be shaped and influenced, much in the same way as Foster Wallace's overall argument about the experience of being on the cruise.

On the text's third page, Foster Wallace concedes that his own value system might be off when he judges other passengers who are enjoying themselves.

---

58   Foster Wallace, 287.
59   Foster Wallace, 287.
60   Foster Wallace, 289.
61   Foster Wallace, 288.

2.2 The Desperate Medium in Wallace's "A Supposedly Fun Thing I'll Never Do Again"   105

Looking back on his experience, Foster Wallace states that he has "filled almost three Mead notebooks trying to figure out whether it was Them or Just Me."[62] The result of this process of figuring out is a central argument that Foster Wallace makes about his experience in general. In this meta-narrative argument, Foster Wallace expresses his conclusions about his experience onboard and, thus, transmits the awareness that his experience is mediated and how it is processed in his mind. In the argument itself, in ways similar to Boorstin, Foster Wallace claims that a cruise makes for an insincere experience, because it objectifies the passenger while it aims to produce an impossibly pleasurable feeling of being human that represses the existence of time and human desire.

Foster Wallace develops this argument in various bursts of retrospective general comments about the cruise that are interspersed throughout the text, while nonetheless remaining connected. In a first comment, Foster Wallace claims that the cruise company offers a specific product, a feeling, "a blend of relaxation and stimulation, stressless indulgence and frantic tourism, that special mix of servility and condescension that's marketed under configurations of the verb 'to pamper.'"[63] This pampering, as Foster Wallace explains, includes not only the production of pleasantness, but also the repression of unpleasantness. On the cruise, this is manifested in "the construction of various fantasies of triumph over just this death and decay."[64] Here, Foster Wallace goes into more detail, identifying three different ways of triumphing: self-improvement, play, and the active construction and evocation of fantasy through the ads and brochures on the ship.[65]

Invoking personal experience, Foster Wallace denounces these fantasies as flawed. Time, for instance, cannot be overcome, he argues, reflecting on the general choices and narrowing of options time demands from him. "It's dreadful. But since it's my own choices that'll lock me in, it seems unavoidable."[66] Foster Wallace counters the promise of micromanaged pleasures that enable the passengers to do "Absolutely Nothing" with a reference to the embryonic state:

---

62   Foster Wallace, 258.
63   Foster Wallace, 260.
64   Foster Wallace, 263–264.
65   Foster Wallace, 264–268.
66   Foster Wallace, 268.

> I know how long it's been since I had every need met choicelessly from someplace outside me, without my having to ask or even acknowledge that I needed. And that time I was floating, too, and the fluid was salty, and warm but not too-, and if I was conscious at all I'm sure I felt dreadful, and was having a really good time, and would have sent postcards to everyone wishing they were here.[67]

Almost forty pages later, Foster Wallace connects the embryo's lack of self-awareness to what he calls the "Dissatisfied Infant part of me, the part that always and indiscriminately WANTS."[68] While the unborn embryo, by nature, has every need met, the infant, also by nature, is constantly dissatisfied. Foster Wallace, thus, argues that the cruise promises to make its passengers feel like embryos, even though they have already been born and are insatiable. "The thing to notice is that the real fantasy here isn't that this promise will be kept, but that such a promise is keepable at all. This is a big one, this lie."[69] Potentially accepting this lie, then, could turn Foster Wallace into a merely consuming object, one totally devoid of agency. However, Foster Wallace clings to his subjectivity as a force of resistance by invoking his own memory and taking ownership of his desires as weapons against objectification. Consequently, the argument laid out by means of these instances of aestheticized self-reflection details the concrete conflict within a human subject embedded in a system driven by objectifying forces, such as the tourism industry.

The Desperately Dialoguing Narrator

In opposition to the ads, commercials, and brochures onboard, Foster Wallace seeks to communicate his experience sincerely by exhibiting an awareness of at least three different aspects of his own transmitting function as a medium. He indicates that he is aware of his taking part in a larger conversation with readers. In different asides, he cautiously comments on experiencing and narrating, distancing himself from both actions in the process. However, Foster Wallace also productively engages with the potentially distancing aspects of his

---

67   Foster Wallace, 268.
68   Foster Wallace, 316.
69   Foster Wallace, 316.

2.2 The Desperate Medium in Wallace's "A Supposedly Fun Thing I'll Never Do Again"

narrating and experiencing functions as a reporter by creating immediacy effects and acting as an experiential stand-in for readers. Furthermore, he plays with various formal elements of text itself, thereby emphasizing its mediated character.

Foster Wallace's display of his own awareness of his communicative relationship with readers includes reflections on the difference between himself and his readers. His comments about narration and experience, in particular, can create a distancing effect. When waiting in line to board the cruise ship, for instance, Foster Wallace observes certain fellow passengers and elaborates about his uncertainty regarding one particular group in a footnote, namely the men identified as working for the Engler Corporation:

> I was never in countless tries able to determine just what the Engler Corporation did or made or was about, but they'd apparently sent a quorum of their execs on this 7NC junket together as a weird kind of working vacation or intracompany convention or something.[70]

Foster Wallace almost celebrates his own uncertainty here. He emphasizes his inability to determine anything about the Engler Corporation, as well as how this inability leads him to speculate cautiously. Elsewhere, having supposedly had too much coffee, Foster Wallace is blunter about his inability to make sense of an experience:

> I seem now to be at the daily Arts 6 Crafts seminar in some sort of back room of the Windsurf Café, and aside from noting that I seem to be the only male here under 70 and that the project under construction on the table before me involves Popsicle sticks and crepe and a type of glue too runny and instant-adhesive to get my trembling overcaffeinated hands anywhere near, I have absolutely no fucking idea what's going on.[71]

Here, Foster Wallace admits to not trusting his own perception to the degree that he denies that he understands anything. In both passages, Foster Wallace suggests that he sees it as his job to tell the reader not only about what he has experienced, but more importantly about what he has been unable to either experience or make sense of.

---

70   Foster Wallace, 270.
71   Foster Wallace, 337.

Along the same lines, Foster Wallace comments on instances in which he was unable or unwilling to narrate. While observing another cruiser in a Mexican port, Foster Wallace states that he "cannot convey to you the sheer and surreal scale of everything,"[72] hereby emphasizing the difficulty of separating signal from noise in his transmission. Later, when anticipating a formal dinner, Foster Wallace also reflects on the possible effects of his telling: "Look, I'm not going to spend a lot of your time or emotional energy on this," he tells a potentially male reader before advising him to *"bring Formalwear."*[73] These two instances display Foster Wallace's awareness of the potential limits of his own basic narrating function as medium; namely, its potential to convey inaccuracies or simply to bore the reader. Overall, the display of such limits makes Foster Wallace appear aware of the differences between him and his surroundings and that of his readers, thereby producing potentially distancing effects.

However, Foster Wallace also attempts to close the distances that he exposes in these passages, by repeatedly invoking the possibility of immediacy. On a narrative level, this happens in those passages in which he aims to create spatial and temporal immediacy, by merging his experiencing and telling. One example is the text's very opening line:

> Right now it's Saturday 18 March, and I'm sitting in the extremely full coffee shop of the Fort Lauderdale Airport, killing the four hours between when I had to be off the cruise ship and when my flight to Chicago leaves.[74]

By placing a claim to temporal immediacy at the very beginning of the text, Foster Wallace implies that he wrote the entire piece at the Fort Lauderdale airport and that readers are reading it at the same time that he is writing it. This integration becomes unsustainable, however, when he later starts another paragraph about an experience on the ship that necessarily happened earlier: "Right now it's Thursday 16 March 0710h., and I'm alone at the 5C.R.'s Early Seating Breakfast, Table 64's waiter and towering busboy hovering nearby."[75] Foster Wallace allows the two timelines to collide, by applying another "right now" to a different time, thereby creating an impasse that ironically highlights his undertaking's inherent temporality. These attempts at creating immediacy

---

72 Foster Wallace, 310.
73 Foster Wallace, 347.
74 Foster Wallace, 256.
75 Foster Wallace, 320.

can be read as contradictory images. They are also critical comments by Foster Wallace about the bare possibility of his task of delivering an experiential postcard, since they emphasize the experiential gap between writer and reader.

Foster Wallace also engages with a potential solution to the experiential gap between himself and his readers by addressing them directly, invoking the potentially similar experience they would have in his place. When describing the sea off the Mexican coast, for instance, Foster Wallace suggests what the reader sees: "You can see why people say of calm seas that they're 'glassy.'"[76] Here, through a simple reference to the reader's vision and the common experience of seeing, the inversion of writer and reader appears to work. However, it gets more complicated when Foster Wallace describes his interaction with Winston, suggesting that the reader feels what he feels:

> Interfacing with Winston could be kind of depressing in that the urge to make cruel sport of him was always irresistible, and he never acted offended or even indicated he knew he was being made sport of, and you went away afterward feeling like you'd just stolen coins from a blind man's cup or something.[77]

Here, Foster Wallace describes a more complex feeling. By emphasizing this irresistible urge—which is understood to be universal—and Winston's reaction to that urge, Foster Wallace evokes a very specific feeling in the reader. Compared to the more objective phenomenon of sight in the passage above, this invocation of the reader's feelings appears to be more difficult. The very complexity of feeling highlights its intrinsically subjective character, one that could not be attributed to the objective seeing examined in the earlier passage. Here, the implication of the subjective nature of experience is more powerful than the potential closure of the experiential gap between writer and reader.

Foster Wallace's engagement with his transmitting function in his relationship with readers extends to the text's formal dimension, as Foster Wallace plays with the mediating specifics of text itself; he refers to or even analyzes other texts in order to highlight his text's intertextuality. With his footnotes, he points to his main text's supposed context. Furthermore, his idiosyncratic capitalization and italicization reflect any text's potential to emphasize and communicate prioritization.

---

76   Foster Wallace, 307.
77   Foster Wallace, 330.

At least some parts of Foster Wallace's text are not directly informed by his experience onboard, but by other texts. Foster Wallace mentions, for instance, that he has written papers on Herman Melville's novel *Moby Dick* and that he teaches Stephen Crane's short story "The Open Boat."[78] He lists both works because they appeared to have informed his association of the ocean with death and fear, thereby referring to a text's potential power to influence experience.[79] In the same vein, acknowledging the possible effects of texts on their readers, Foster Wallace addresses the aforementioned essaymercial by the writer Frank Conroy in a PR brochure.[80] The essaymercial's genesis is, in turn, rooted in another text. Conroy was commissioned to write the PR text for the cruise company, after having published a different article in a travel magazine.[81] Intertextuality is also alluded to by means of the generic forms of other texts that Foster Wallace imitates or quotes, such as the experiential log that he writes,[82] the label on the porthole's glass in his cabin that he provides,[83] or in the invitation to the hypnotist's presentation that he quotes.[84] He provides further context for this text by foregrounding different aspects of his own text's intertextuality. However, and more importantly, he also demonstrates the interplay between text and context, showing how they can be difficult to separate when text itself is the object of the experience conveyed through text.

This concern with the interplay of supposed text and context is also reflected in Foster Wallace's extensive use of footnotes. Applied to various ends, the use of footnotes suggests a commentary on the possibility of a kind of intertextual context. For instance, Foster Wallace uses them to communicate factual background,[85] his capability to memorize information about shark attacks,[86] the explanation of a word's meaning in brackets,[87] a simple rhetorical question directed at the reader,[88] a comment on his own propensity towards prejudice,[89]

---

78   Foster Wallace, 262.
79   Foster Wallace, 261.
80   Foster Wallace, 285–290.
81   Foster Wallace, 288.
82   Foster Wallace, 320–353.
83   Foster Wallace, 301.
84   Foster Wallace, 349.
85   Foster Wallace, 259–260.
86   Foster Wallace, 262.
87   Foster Wallace, 263.
88   Foster Wallace, 264.
89   Foster Wallace, 272.

the characterization of his fellow passengers through the narration of scenes at the dinner table,[90] or even a footnote within a footnote.[91] That these examples cannot be reduced to mere meta-narrative commentary, such as a reference, but instead include all kinds of narrative modes on different diegetic levels suggests that Foster Wallace at least partly uses footnotes in order to comment on their potentially arbitrary relationship to the main text. In fact, they mostly fulfill the particular meta-textual function that their formal difference suggests that they should. However, the occasional break with their reduction to this particular function suggests their openness to all sorts of potentially different textual functions. Once again, text and context—or meta-text—are difficult, if not impossible, to keep apart.

Foster Wallace not only highlights the potential sameness of text; he also points to its inherent difference and potential for subjective emphasis and judgment. His use of capitalization and italics are two particular areas in which this phenomenon is manifested. Italics, for instance, appear to be used to specify one particular aspect of a word's meaning. Early on, Foster Wallace writes that he has "learned that there are actually intensities of blue beyond *very, very bright* blue."[92] The emphasis achieved through the use of italics here evokes the color's intensity. The emphasis occurs in relation to other kinds of blue. Similarly, he foregrounds the effects of the reassurances on the part of the cruise staff that everybody is having a good time. "It's more like a feeling. But it's also still a bona fide product – it's supposed to be *produced* in you, this feeling."[93] Here, Foster Wallace emphasizes the conscious choice of the verb "produce" over and against other possible verbs and, thus, the impact of his argument.

By contrast, the unusual capitalization of a word's first letter signifies a generalization. When, as noted above, Foster Wallace writes that he was "trying to figure out whether it was Them or Just Me"[94] he alludes not to a specific conflict between him and other cruise passengers, but rather to the more fundamental dilemma of subjective judgment. This also applies to indirect capitalization, when Foster Wallace quotes and acknowledges something. For instance, he quotes from the room service menu "Thinly Sliced Ham and Swiss

---

90 Foster Wallace, 280–283.
91 Foster Wallace, 296, 306.
92 Foster Wallace, 257.
93 Foster Wallace, 260.
94 Foster Wallace, 258.

Cheese on White Bread with Dijon Mustard" and comments that "the stuff deserves to be capitalized, believe me,"[95] thus pointing to the general idea of a tasty sandwich. By highlighting such different formal features of text, Foster Wallace communicates an awareness of text's plural and ambiguous character as a technical medium, one that nevertheless remains permanently open to dialogue with itself. Foster Wallace further displays the capability of text to communicate the very subjective richness and complexity of human consciousness that he sees as being repressed in the objectifying PR brochures on board.

This case can also be made in relation to the overall communicative interaction that Foster Wallace envisions as taking place between himself and his readers. His excessive invocation of a dialogue, which is open to differences of meaning and its potential absence, can be read as a desperate urging on the part of an isolated subject to make and uphold human connection through dissemination.

Self-Reflection Against Alienation

The intense, occasionally even hyperbolic, ways in which Foster Wallace seeks to display an awareness of the different aspects of his role as a medium transmit an urgent concern with authenticity in which self-reflection has a relieving function. Importantly, he positions this display of self-reflection as human medium in contradistinction to the absence of the authentic experience on the ship. His detailing of his construction of an authorial self-identity engaging in a communal act of meaning-making with readers introduces a multifaceted critical perspective on the cruise experience that, in effect, appears both symbolically and materially inauthentic. The self-reflection of his mediate subjectivity functions as a potential means by which to cure the despair—the bodily manifestation of existential inauthenticity—that Foster Wallace describes feeling while onboard. This despair, in turn, stems from a feeling of alienation caused by the capitalist forces of the cruise industry. Having read Frank Conroy's essaymercial as "an ad that pretends to be art," Foster Wallace draws the following conclusion:

> This is dishonest, but what's sinister is the cumulative effect that such dishonesty has on us: since it offers a perfect facsimile or simulacrum of good-

---

95   Foster Wallace, 296.

will without goodwill's real spirit, it messes with our heads and eventually starts upping our defenses even in cases of genuine smiles and real art and true goodwill. It makes us feel confused and lonely and impotent and angry and scared. It causes despair.[96]

As hinted at previously, the despair that Foster Wallace feels is a result of the experience of being turned into an object by being lied to. Foster Wallace argues with the entire cruise experience, which promises an unachievable "respite from unpleasantness,"[97] and claims that this objectification is a characteristic of the cruise economy and tourism more generally. For him, it is also a deep-seated aspect of American culture. In a port in Cozumel, Mexico, Foster Wallace describes how he feels ashamed of being associated with the mass of other passengers and how this has led him to try to distance himself in various ways. However, as he admits, this does not quite work:

> But of course all this ostensibly unimplicating behavior on my part is itself motivated by a self-conscious and somewhat condescending concern about how I appear to others that is (this concern) 100% upscale American. Part of the overall despair of this Luxury Cruise is that no matter what I do I cannot escape my own essential and newly unpleasant Americanness.[98]

Here, Foster Wallace indicates that the objectification he experiences onboard can also lead to a loss of self-esteem. This loss of self-esteem, the loss of interpersonal trust, and the loss of self-confidence, along with the suspicion that all of these losses cause, are the main problems with objectification in Foster Wallace's view. This loss, at least in Foster Wallace's case, leads to a feeling of alienation. The experience of existential inauthenticity has both inter- and intrapersonal roots and is reinforced by the ways in which the two interact.

The secondary display of self-reflection in the text, then, must be read as a reaction against Foster Wallace's primary experience of alienation. Thus, the form operatively *unveils* the content in Foster Wallace's text, right as his exposure to the aesthetics and contradictions inherent in every aspect of his role as medium make the cruise economy's narrowed and limited aesthetic and contradictory character apparent. As Foster Wallace suggests, the contradictions and weaknesses that he desperately experiences, exposes, and names, are not

---

96   Foster Wallace, 289.
97   Foster Wallace, 263.
98   Foster Wallace, 311.

to be lamented as objective disconnections, but, if acknowledged, instead contain the potential to produce connections between subjects, be it in the form of self-confidence or interpersonal trust.

2.3 The Believing Medium in George Saunders's "The New Mecca" (2005)

George Saunders's reportage has received little attention, despite its peculiar and timely morals and aesthetics. Saunders, predominantly a writer of fiction, is best known for his short story collections and for his experimental novel *Lincoln in the Bardo* (2017). However, Saunders has also written numerous essays and accepted reporting assignments from American magazines such as GQ or *The New Yorker* in which he actively explores different social and cultural phenomena associated with contemporary reality. A collection of his essays, entitled *The Braindead Megaphone*, was published in 2007.

In one of these texts, "The New Mecca,"[1] Saunders travels to Dubai after the terrorist attacks of September 11th and experiences the emerging megacity as an ambivalent utopia of consumer culture. As such, Mike Featherstone has argued: "it offers a world beyond scarcity and hardship, the dream of abundance, yet its modus operandi is through the commodity form, the calculus of monetary value."[2] Saunders mirrors this ambivalence in the self-reflection of his identity as human medium. Unlike Foster Wallace, he is not very interested in inauthenticity. Rather, his reportage focuses on the ways in which authenticity is subjectively produced and imagined by way of the collective fantasies that touristic experience begets. Saunders emphasizes the very will to believe in the possibilities of global consumerism as a countermeasure to its fracturing aspects. Dubai's fantastic material reality as a transnational social space featuring iconic architecture[3] is, thus, reflected in the symbolic reality of fantastic possibility. If it matters at all then, authenticity in Saunders's touristic experience matters as fantasy that illustrates a very general human desire.

---

1   Saunders, "The New Mecca."
2   Featherstone, *Consumer Culture and Postmodernism*, xxiii.
3   Sklair, "Iconic Architecture and the Culture-Ideology of Consumerism."

Most importantly, Saunders interprets the uncertainties that are thus exposed in human interaction as potential material for coordination and cooperation.

The few critical comments that have been made about Saunders's reportage have mainly appeared in reviews. In a short discussion of Saunders's nonfiction, Joshuah Bearman ascribes to Saunders a: "chameleon-like ability to tell [his character's] stories in their voices while also inserting his own, which manages to humanize his subjects, and himself, together."[4] Bearman further argues that Saunders seems to trust his own power to grasp the world around him and that he "seems to do very little reporting, eschewing most external detail for his own internal conflicts and empathetically observational experience."[5] In a review of *The Braindead Megaphone*, Josh Rosenblatt argues that Saunders exhibits an: "optimistic belief in the value of human understanding and generosity. As far as he's concerned, the only answer to our current geopolitical predicament is sympathy, understanding, and an open-armed acceptance of our undeniable sameness."[6] Like Foster Wallace, then, Saunders's reportage can be described as a humanist endeavor that emphasizes the similarities between humans and that argues for the particular urgency of human communication; this is no coincidence. George Saunders and David Foster Wallace were contemporaries who were aware of one another, while Foster Wallace was still alive. They even met occasionally to discuss their writing. For Saunders, they were: "like two teams of miners, digging at the same spot but from different directions."[7] For instance, Adam Kelly's conceptualization of "new sincerity" discussed in the previous chapter on Foster Wallace brackets certain similarities between the two writers in greater detail.[8]

More traditional scholarly attention to George Saunders's work, like Kelly's, has almost exclusively been directed at Saunders's fiction. What is most relevant for my analysis of Saunders's reportage is how his short stories have been read against the backdrop of neoliberalism and the all-encompassing individualization and social atomization that it gives rise to. In his

---

4   Bearman, *Journeys with George (Saunders), or Why Magazines Should Hire More Fiction Writers, Part 2*, para. 9.
5   Bearman, para. 3.
6   Rosenblatt, *Elements of Style*, para. 12.
7   Lovell, "George Saunders Has Written The Best Book You'll Read This Year," 24.
8   Kelly, "The New Sincerity"; Kelly, "Language Between Lyricism and Corporatism: George Saunders's New Sincerity."

narrative explorations of neoliberalism, Saunders's focus lay on the representation of the American working class and of how its experience of precarity and immobility overwhelms its subjects.[9] In these representations, scholars have argued, Saunders has sought to evade the trap of neoliberalism's all-encompassing power by reconfiguring the possibilities of being human and affectively making contact with readers.[10]

In the analyzed text then, Saunders allegorically mirrors the rather general human potential for peaceful coexistence he identifies in Dubai in the ways in which he carries himself as a medium engaging in human interaction. Featuring the integrating aspects of his role as a medium, Saunders in particular reflects upon the general power of human cognition to make connections and to interpret specific experiences. First, Saunders's self-reflection is manifested in his self-characterization as an ordinary human being subjected to the laws of global capitalism. Second, it is apparent in his accepting acknowledgment of the mediated character of his experience, and in an emphasis on the consequences of the experience, rather than its quality. Third, Saunders reflects deeply on his own acts of interpretation on various occasions. Fourth, he is keen to keep a close connection to his readers via the playful use of textual devices, direct addresses to the reader, and personal voice. Hence, his self-awareness of his status as a merely human medium does not beget a sense of desperation. Rather, in Saunders's case, it reinforces a basic belief in human sameness and the possibility of bridging the temporal and spatial gaps that are inherent in mediated human experience.

Paid—or Not—to Have Fun—or Not

In 2005, Saunders went on assignment to Dubai for the men's magazine *GQ*, which covered all of his expenses. When Saunders checks into his luxury hotel, the Burj Al Arab, Saunders notes that the fact that *GQ* is covering his expenses is key to the production of the experience he has in Dubai:

---

9   Rando, "George Saunders and the Postmodern Working Class"; Schoene, "Contemporary American Literature as World Literature: Cruel Cosmopolitanism, Cosmopoetics, and the Search for a Worldlier American Novel"; Boddy, "'A Job to Do': George Saunders on, and at, Work."
10 Schoene, "Contemporary American Literature as World Literature: Cruel Cosmopolitanism, Cosmopoetics, and the Search for a Worldlier American Novel"; Millen, "Affective Fictions: George Saunders and the Wonderful-Sounding Words of Neoliberalism."

> I am so thrilled to be checking in! What a life! Where a kid from Chicago gets to fly halfway around the world and stay at the world's only seven-star hotel, and GQ pays for it![11]

Here, Saunders not only declares it to be a privilege to be paid to visit Dubai and the Burj Al Arab, but also characterizes himself as an ordinary and inexperienced American from Chicago. Saunders gets to be an ordinary consumer of an exclusive experience only because a magazine is footing the bill. This context of global consumerism frames Saunders's reportage and marks the experience that he writes about as having been produced.

More specifically, the framework of the experience's production is more broadly human than it is professional. For instance, the way Saunders refers to his assignment might suggest that he is primarily being paid to consume, not to ultimately deliver a product. The consequence of this more universal framework is economic dependency. Upon arrival at the Burj Al Arab, for instance, Saunders finds out that GQ is unable to pay the hotel bill directly and that he himself cannot cover it:

> Because, for complicated reasons, GQ couldn't pay from afar, and because my wife and I share a common hobby of maxing out all credit cards in sight, I had rather naively embarked on a trip halfway around the world without an operative credit card: the contemporary version of setting sail with no water in the casks.[12]

Due to his bank's withdrawal limit, Saunders is only able to pay part of the amount for one night's stay, at the hotel, and is repeatedly asked to pay the rest. His inability to pay changes the character of the experience that Saunders had so enthusiastically anticipated. Instead of joy, he begins to feel envy and anxiety. Saunders writes that he "couldn't enjoy any of it, because I was too cowed to leave my room. I resisted the urge to crawl under the bed."[13] Hence, the assignment itself is presented as decisively shaping Saunders's experience. It is the very fact that he is on assignment that puts him in the position of experiencing the feeling of being unable to pay the bill in a luxury hotel. Thus, GQ puts Saunders in a situation that he would not even have been able to afford to

---

11 Rosenblatt, *Elements of Style*, para. 12.
12 Saunders, 38.
13 Saunders, 40.

be in under normal circumstances. In a way then, the magazine places him *out of place*.

At the same time, Saunders behaves as if he is—if not necessarily out of place—certainly out of his comfort zone with regard to his disregard for professional standards. On at least one occasion, Saunders explicitly refers to the fact that he is not a professional journalist. When he explores the more political questions of Dubai's wealth and safety against the backdrop of 9/11 and potential terrorist threats, Saunders talks to different anonymous sources. However, in noting that their explanations contradict each other, Saunders comments that he is grateful to not have a professional journalist's obligations: "Good point, I say, thanking God in my heart that I am not a real Investigative Journalist."[14] The assignment consequently also involves Saunders being placed in professional situations that, under normal circumstances, he would never find himself in.

For Saunders, however, this sense of feeling *out of place* does not result in alienation. Rather, it continually presents possibilities for human connections. While trying to pay for the first night's stay, Saunders meets visitors to the Burj Al Arab who had paid fifty dollars just to see the place. Angered by the behavior of hotel staff, he decides to invite them up to his room:

> I snuck them up to my room, past the Personal Butler, and gave them my complimentary box of dates and the three-hundred-dollar bottle of wine. Fight the power! Then we all stood around, feeling that odd sense of shame/solidarity that people of limited means feel when their limitedness has somehow been underscored.[15]

As Saunders details here, the framework of global consumerism serves to emphasize the sameness of the conditions people from all backgrounds face under global capitalism—namely, the fact that capital rules. Here, being denied a joyful experience because of a lack of funds has the psychological consequence of producing solidarity, rather than separation or alienation.

Saunders notes this kind of connection between people living under the same general, systemic conditions with regard to his role as a writer. When he enters another luxury hotel, Saunders observes an Indian man who is cleaning a marble staircase by hand and explores the feeling this sight produces in him:

---

14 Saunders, 47.
15 Saunders, 41–42.

> Part of me wants to offer help. But that would be ridiculous, melodramatic. He washes these stairs every day. It's not my job to hand-wash stairs. It's his job to hand-wash stairs. My job is to observe him hand-washing the stairs, then go inside the air-conditioned lobby and order a cold beer and take notes about his stair-washing so I can go home and write about it, making more for writing about it than he'll make in many, many years of doing it.[16]

Saunders then tries to imagine whether or not this stair-washer would surrender his job to another Indian with no job at all:

> Does this stair-washer have any inclination to return to India, surrender his job to this other guy, give up his hard-won lifestyle to help this fellow human being? Who knows? If he's like me, he probably does. But in the end, his answer, like mine, is: That would be ridiculous, melodramatic. It's not my job to give up my job which I worked so hard these many years to get. Am I not me? Is he not him?[17]

In Saunders's view, the capitalist conditions resulting in the basic human need for a job contain the potential to create a sense of global human sameness. Saunders also hints at this possibility when he imagines that the other Indian might, like himself, feel inclined to give up his job in an act of solidarity. Although they are subjected to the same rules, the basis for this potential sameness is, as Saunders seems to suggest in his concluding rhetorical questions, fundamental human difference.

Even though Saunders's experience in Dubai is determined by the assignment and by the economic dependency it entails, he also describes it as fundamentally human because it is—particularly in Dubai—so permeated by the workings of global capitalism. Saunders appears highly aware of the fact that he is both consumer and worker (or producer) at the same time. For him, this is not a cause for depression, but rather an occasion to explore unique possibilities for human understanding. There, opportunities arise for human solidarity which potentially relieve anger and anxiety, even at times of alienation caused by economic distress.

---

16 Saunders, 54.
17 Saunders, 54.

The Subjective Effect of Objective Experience

This trusting aspect of Saunders's character is on display in how he deals with his primary physical experience. In fact, Saunders never questions his own sensory perceptions. In describing his visit to Dubai, the question of whether or not what he perceives might be real or not is simply of no concern to him. For example, the first luxury hotel Saunders stays at, the Madinat, resembles a theme park version of an Arabian village. Saunders is excited by his surroundings despite their apparent fakeness:

> Wandering around one night, a little lost, I came to the realization that authenticity and pleasure are not causally related. How is this "fake"? This is real flowing water, the date and palm trees are real, the smell of incense and rose water is real. The staggering effect of the immense scale of one particular crosswalk – which joins two hotels together and is, if you can imagine this, a four-story ornate crosswalk that looks like it should have ten thousand cheering Imperial Troops clustered under it and an enigmatic young Princess waving from one of its arabesque windows – that effect is *real*. You feel it in your gut and your legs. It makes you feel happy and heroic and a little breathless, in love anew with the world and its possibilities.[18]

Here, Saunders anchors the potential realness of the experience not in reality—in this case in the authenticity of the ancient Arabian village that has been built—but within himself and in the effect that the experienced reality has on his body. The fact that he feels a positive effect in his gut and in his legs makes reality real enough for him. It is these physical effects that, in turn, also prompt acts of interpreting reality in general, that are not only found in the passage above, but are practically inseparable from the experience.

Saunders similarly foregrounds the importance of his subjective, physical reaction to the experience when he visits an Arabian Ice City, a festival where kids get to experience artificial snow:

> On their faces: looks of bliss, the kind of look a person gets when he realizes he is in the midst of doing something rare, that might never be repeated, and is therefore of great value. They are seeing something from a world far away, where they will probably never go.

---

18   Saunders, 24–25.

> Women in abbayas video. Families pose shyly, rearranging themselves to get more Snow in the frame. Mothers and fathers stand beaming at their kids, who are beaming at the Snow.
> *This is sweet*, I scribble in my notebook.
> And it is. My eyes well up with tears.[19]

Saunders describes himself here as being emotionally touched by an experience he does not even mark as subjective. Experience and interpretation are intertwined in his assertion that what he sees is simply "sweet." Thus, he infers that only his own reaction to the experience might be subjective. The sweetness of the sight, however, he deems universal. Only a few lines later, this perspective is reinforced when he states that if "everybody in America could see this, our foreign policy would change."[20] In these instances, Saunders's dynamics as a human subject who functions as medium are placed front and center, since they track the complexities of his interpretation of reality, rather than reality itself. It is not primarily the experience, but rather Saunders's reaction to the experience, that is the story.

The potential universality that Saunders ascribes to his personal experience is also manifested in his narration of passages mainly about sensory experience. On these occasions, he repeatedly switches both between the authorial "I" and the communal "we", and the reader as subject. When he writes about his experience at the Al Maha Resort, this occurs particularly abruptly:

> For lunch, we have a killer buffet, with a chef's special of veal medallions.
> I go back to my villa for a swim. Birds come down to drink from my private pool. As you lower yourself into the pool, water laps forward and out, into a holding rim, then down into the Lawrencian desert. You see a plane of blue water, then a plane of tan desert. Yellow bees – completely yellow, as if you spray-painted – flit around on the surface of the water.[21]

Although Saunders initially makes it clear that it is he himself who intends to swim, he narrates the scene in the second-person singular. In suggesting that the reader swim, Saunders switches between himself and the reader as the subjects of the scene. Drawn rather hyperbolically, the change in subject in

---

19 Saunders, 49–50.
20 Saunders, 50.
21 Saunders, 44.

this scene must not be read as an intentional mapping out of a zone of immediacy for Saunders as the medium or a bridging of the medial gap between writer and reader. Rather, it is a comment on Saunders's stance versus the status of experience itself. The subject that experiences can simply be interchanged, but the experience stays the same and is bestowed with a steadfast stability, if not the status of an object.

This interpretation can be further supported by a closer look at the quality of his experience. In fact, a lot of the experiences he reacts to could be categorized as secondhand. Still, Saunders rarely treats the information that he is given with suspicion. Instead, he ponders its potential ethical consequences or the effects it has on him more carefully. When exploring the exploitation of foreign workers in Dubai, for instance, Saunders simply pitches different subjective, singular opinions, as well as a newspaper report against each other. He hears from an American with fifteen years of experience in the local oil business[22] that: "the workers tell you again and again how happy they are to be here,"[23] he reads about an exemplary case in a local newspaper,[24] he recounts that: "a waiter shows me exactly how he likes to hold his two-year-old, or did like to hold her, last time he was home, eight months ago,"[25] and he quotes a Kenyan security guard, who says: "I expect, in your writing, you will try to find the dark side of Dubai? Some positive, some negative? Isn't that the Western way? But I must say: I have found Dubai to be nearly perfect."[26] These secondhand experiences simply lead him to conclude that any evaluation of Dubai is complicated, which indicates that he treats all of these secondhand experiences equally and does not evaluate them based on their merits. As interpretations of experience deriving from other human beings, they appear to have value in themselves.

Due to the fact that experience is bought, manufactured, and thus objectified and potentially reproduced, at least in the case of his trip to Dubai, it loses its economic value on the information market. For Saunders, however, this makes experience interesting in a more general sense, as it serves to connect humans from different backgrounds. If experience is objectified, its effects are nevertheless still subjective. This is precisely what Saunders empha-

---

22   Saunders, 31.
23   Saunders, 32.
24   Saunders, 32.
25   Saunders, 33.
26   Saunders, 33.

sizes with his examinations of his physical reactions to the experience he has. As a consequence, his ways of interpreting the experience and its effects come to occupy center-stage.

Confusion and Possibility

Saunders employs various modes of thinking to make sense of his experience and of its effects. Occasionally, he bases his judgments on rather general, personal premises that view human nature through an optimistic lens. Elsewhere, he imagines hypothetical alternatives to experienced reality in order to classify his experience. Ultimately, in a circular kind of thinking, the experiences themselves become objects for his reflections. All of these modes of interpretation have, as their premise, a conscious ethical openness and the possibility for human understanding and connection that this openness enables.

As suggested above, Saunders bases the interpretation of his specific experience on general assertions about human nature. Argumentatively speaking, these general claims are either prompted by specific examples Saunders experiences or they serve to make sense of the reality he encounters. Furthermore, Saunders's use of generalities to interpret experience demonstrates how Saunders uses logic to attribute meaning to reality. In general, they all communicate an idea of basic global human sameness. Saunders explicitly establishes this view early on, while floating in a tube through a water park. Based on his experience floating next to American soldiers, German women, and Arab teenagers, Saunders claims to have an epiphany:

> Given enough time, I realize, statistically, despite what it may look like at any given moment, we *will* all be brothers. All differences will be bred out. There will be no pure Arab, no pure Jew, no pure American. The old dividers – nation, race, religion – will be overpowered by crossbreeding and by our mass media, our world Culture o' Enjoyment.[27]

Saunders's general projection of humanity here takes the form of a biological and teleological narrative of human development. Saunders locates the source of this generally optimistic idea of human nature's development in a general human trait: "We, the New People," he states, "desire Fun and the Good Things

---

27   Saunders, 29.

of Life, and through Fun, we will be saved."[28] This idea of human sameness based on the prioritization of the desire to have fun then serves Saunders as the basis for other general assertions. For instance, he justifies the hostility of a member of the Taliban towards the United States with a rather general explanation: "What one might be tempted to call simplicity" he argues, "could be more accurately called a limited sphere of experience" which essentially causes a difference in meanings that are ascribed to reality.[29]

He underscores this explanation using a different mode of thinking—specifically, imagination—by means of which he entertains a hypothetical example to help make sense of his experience. In the case of the Taliban, he seeks to make sense of the tears that he shed observing the Arab kids having fun in the snow, by imagining a deportation of a member of the Taliban to the military prison in Guantánamo "where he's treated as if he personally planned 9/11... How must this look to him? How must we look to him?"[30] Here the imagined case of a Taliban member ultimately serves Saunders as a means to ask readers to imagine themselves viewing American behavior through the eyes of a foreigner—just like he viewed the Arab kids. By imagining this case, Saunders seeks to make sense of the actions of others and to foster understanding among seemingly different groups of people. Elsewhere, Saunders describes how imagination also has the power to divide, since it can anticipate hostile action by others. After undergoing an experience of anxiety at the Burj Al Arab, Saunders characterizes the emotional reaction in the same terms as his imagined interpretation of reality:

> I experienced a sudden fear that a group of Disapproving Guest Services People would appear at my remote-controlled door and physically escort me down to the lobby ATM (an ATM about which I expect I'll be having anxiety nightmares the rest of my life), which would once again prominently display the words PROVIDER DECLINES TRANSACTION.[31]

Saunders here marks out anxiety as subjective imagination and, thus, situates imagination as a powerful cognitive tool for influencing his own behavior.

---

28   Saunders, 29.
29   Saunders, 51.
30   Saunders, 52.
31   Saunders, 40.

Imagination shapes the ways in which he interprets and experiences reality and can be activated and used productively.

However, in Saunders's case, imagination cannot just be read as a mere instrument for producing argumentative support for generalizations that make sense of experience. Saunders also reflects on his own ways of sensemaking. This sensemaking is manifested in a kind of aside that seeks to provide additional context to a general assertion. Before relaying his mini-epiphany about the future sameness of all human beings for instance, Saunders addresses the reader on a meta-level, framing what is about to come:

> A disclaimer: it may be that, when you're forty-six and pearl white and wearing a new bathing suit at a theme park on your first full day in Arabia, you're especially prone to Big Naïve Philosophical Realizations.[32]

There might be, Saunders suggests here, at least one more level of reflection above the bare interpretation of an experience of reality. Furthermore, by addressing the reader directly, he suggests once again that this might be true for the reader as well, were the reader in Saunders's position.

Ultimately, however, these reflections on Saunders's own ways of interpreting result in a kind of meta-moral writer's code. This becomes apparent when Saunders is faced with contradictory inputs and complexity. In the passage quoted above, in which he is faced with contradictory statements by credible yet anonymous "People Who Know,"[33] Saunders not only indicates that he is happy not to be an investigative journalist, but he also admits to feeling a sort of relief. The header of the passage reads: "THE TRUTH IS, I CAN'T DECIDE WHAT'S TRUE, HONESTLY."[34] Truth, for Saunders, becomes not a search, or the result of a search, but a decision under these circumstances of contradiction and complexity. Not having to make this decision, which he associates with professional journalism, is a relief. This relief then turns into a general ethical guideline. In the text's final lines, after having concluded that: "what one finds in oneself will most certainly be found in The Other,"[35] Saunders describes how he counsels himself on the flight back home: "Fuck concepts. Don't

---

32 Saunders, 28.
33 Saunders, 46–47.
34 Saunders, 46.
35 Saunders, 55.

be afraid to be confused. Try to remain permanently confused. Anything is possible. Stay open, forever, so open it hurts, and then open up some more, until the day you die, world without end, amen."[36] In this passage, Saunders paints conscious confusion as a virtue, as a necessary way of being in the world, precisely because it contains the potential for human understanding.

Potentially Bonding Text

Saunders assumes this very potential on the level of the communicative relationship he has with his readers. Here, he communicates an awareness of how the text, as a vehicle of transmission, shapes his message. Furthermore, throughout the text, as hinted at repeatedly above, he seeks to bridge the experiential gap between himself and the reader, employing an informal, conversational tone that communicates intimacy.

Saunders's use of various formal elements, which, in turn, shape the content, heralds Saunders's self-awareness as a medium transmitting text. For instance, Saunders uses a total of nineteen sub-headers spread over the 34 pages of his piece to frame the subsequent prose text. Although printed in identical typographical layout, these sub-headers consist of different modes of speech. In the case of the first sub-header, for example: "PUT THAT STATELY PLEASURE PALACE THERE BETWEEN THOSE OTHER TWO,"[37] Saunders employs the imagined voice of a unified body of high-handed hotel-builders in Dubai addressed to workers to foreshadow his exposé of the then-recent building boom in the city. The header of the text's penultimate section, in which South-Indian workers try to visit the Emirates Towers on their day off, reads similarly: "LOOK, DREAM, BUT STAY OUT THERE." One sub-header consists of a question directed at readers,[38] another of a quote.[39] There are foreshadowing summaries of the narrative content that is to follow,[40] or the conversational admission directed at readers mentioned earlier: "THE TRUTH IS, I CAN'T DECIDE WHAT'S TRUE, HONESTLY."[41] The diversity of these sub-headers sug-

---

36 Saunders, 55.
37 Saunders, 21.
38 Saunders, 50.
39 Saunders, 45.
40 Saunders, 23, 43, 47.
41 Saunders, 46.

gests their self-referential function, since they playfully point to the inevitable interplay of form and content in text, which points to the medium's flexibility and general openness.

The same can be argued about other formal elements that communicate a certain type of distinct meaning and work exclusively with text. For instance, Saunders forms a: "partial list of wise things cabdrivers said to me in Dubai"[42] that is distinctly formatted and consists of five numbered quotes. Taken together in this way, they illustrate both the plurality of cabdrivers and Saunders's intent to acknowledge and literally incorporate other perspectives into his text. Furthermore, Saunders repeatedly uses italics in order to emphasize particular words, and thus clarify the meaning of his text,[43] or to mark a passage as quoted internal monologue.[44] Similarly, the extensive capitalization he employs serves—just like in David Foster Wallace's reportage—to emphasize concepts with distinct meaning informed by the specific context of the written piece. The "Haves" and the "Have-Nots,"[45] for instance, signify the wealthy and the poor. Text, winkingly exhibited in its own formal plurality, always appears both as mere text and as a context directed simultaneously at both another text and the reader, thereby revealing its own dialogical potential.

However, Saunders's awareness of the plasticity of text is displayed by hints at the potential for the text's formal elements to connect with readers. More directly, the personal, casual voice and direct reader addresses that Saunders employs can be viewed as a concrete manifestation of textual intimacy. At least partly, this implies personal intimacy is grounded in the use of informal or even vulgar language. For instance, Saunders characterizes a few of Dubai's architectural ambitions as "the supercool parts – the parts that, when someone tells you about them, your attention drifts because these morons have to be lying,"[46] lets the readers know that he had been "blissfully farting around"[47] inside a luxury hotel, or tells them that an artificial skiing hall contains "basically a shitload of crushed ice."[48] He also blurs the line between written and oral language in

---

42   Saunders, 34.
43   Saunders, i.e., 28 and 29.
44   Saunders, 30.
45   Saunders, 31.
46   Saunders, 22.
47   Saunders, 29.
48   Saunders, 49.

his use of fillers. When unable to pay for his room at the Burj Al Arab, for example, he writes that he was: "trying to explain, like some yokel hustler at a Motel 6 in Topeka, that I'd be happy to pay half in cash now, half on checkout if that would be, ah, acceptable, would that be, you know, cool?" With his use of these expressions, Saunders presupposes an intimacy with the reader that not only permits, but encourages the casualness of orality and the specificity of context it implies.

This reduction of distance is also demonstrated in Saunders's direct reader addresses that work both as the self-characterization of a stand-in for readers and as attempts at bridging the gap between writer and readers. In fact, Saunders opens his piece by stating the presupposition that he and the reader might be in the same position regarding Dubai: "If you are like I was before I went to Dubai, you may not know exactly where Dubai is."[49] He then moves on to speculate openly about the readers' knowledge about Dubai: "You may also not know, as I did not know, what Dubai is all about or why someone would want to send you there. You might wonder: Is it dangerous?"[50] As hinted at above, such instances of directly addressing the reader can, on the one hand, be read as reflecting Saunders's internal, circular, self-interrogating process of interpretation. On the other hand, however, they are also attempts at forming a bond with the reader through text. This is particularly apparent in a passage in which Saunders imagines the reader as being American, as he ponders the possible deportation of a simple man from rural Afghanistan accused of terrorism:

> My experience has been that the poor, simple people of the world admire us, are enamored by our boldness, are hopeful that the insanely positive values we espouse can be actualized in the world. They are, in other words, rooting for us. This means that when we disappoint them... we have the potential to disappoint them bitterly and drive them away.[51]

In this way, Saunders marks himself out as being part of an American community with his readers, while simultaneously also imagining a community of people not belonging to this American community. Here, he explicitly presupposes a connection between writer and reader that is not based on their fundamental humanity, but on the assumption that Americans are reading his ar-

---

49 Saunders, 21.
50 Saunders, 21.
51 Saunders, 52.

ticle in an American magazine. Thus, Saunders shows that text not only works to communicate the possibilities of human connection through text, but that it also communicates the representation of real physical, material presence.

Basic Belief

To conclude, in "The New Mecca," Saunders casts himself as an actively producing human medium, one who reflects both the contingency of material experience and its symbolic interpretation, as he turns both into objects of subjective cognition. He molds global consumerism as a master mediator that both creates and hinders experience. Saunders's self-reflection, as fundamentally human medium, reveals a belief in the unifying power of intra- and interpersonal authenticity as productive fantasies. Despite the fact that he ultimately claims to resist conceptualization, Saunders explicitly resorts to a general, emotional concept of basic human sameness in order to make sense of his experience as well as of his role as a writer. For in this role, his self-characterization as an ordinary guy from Chicago enables him to actively claim similarity or even intimacy with readers as well as the people who inform his first-hand experience on the ground in Dubai: "I've been to Dubai and I believe,"[52] Saunders establishes on the text's third page. It would have been more apt for Saunders to claim that he has been to Dubai and *still* believes, because his experience in Dubai simply reinforces an already-existing belief in basic human sameness.

However, this similarity is always marked as made up by Saunders in the circularity of his interpretations. As he gradually elaborates on his reasons for believing in humanity, he also shows an awareness of temporality. Saunders is familiar with the human capability to be kind and good because he has experienced human kindness and goodness in the past. As long as this capability exists, the possibilities for it to be employed are everywhere. They potentially also alleviate the divisive forces of global consumerism, which Saunders situates in the fragmentation of human experience. Fiercely hopeful as he is, however, Saunders insists on the idea of human sameness against the backdrop of this difference. For him, it is precisely this difference that carries the openness to human understanding and peace—but only if the contingencies and aesthetic character of experience and language are acknowledged.

---

52   Saunders, 23.

Saunders's self-reflection as human medium ultimately marks out the individualization of human experience combined with the loss of religion or spirituality as the basic problems of mediatized, globalized, and fantastic postmodern reality. The generalizing of Saunders's touristic experience in Dubai only works convincingly in tandem with his embodied belief in basic human sameness. Thus, ontologically, his self-reflection appears exemplarily as a basic human necessity that serves to introduce a critical perspective onto the globalized consumerism that both he himself as well as his readers and subjects live under.

2.4 The Incapable Medium in John Jeremiah Sullivan's "Upon This Rock" (2012)

Despite the critical praise that it has garnered, John Jeremiah Sullivan's writing has evaded the attention of critical scholarly analysis to date. However, his essays and reportage have been reviewed in different media outlets and Sullivan has given interviews about his writing. Upon its initial publication in 2011, Sullivan's essay collection *Pulphead* (2011) received rave reviews. The book was hailed as: "the best, and most important, collection of magazine writing since [David Foster] Wallace's *A Supposedly Fun Thing I'll Never Do Again*."[1] Sullivan himself was praised as: "a writer interested in human stories, watching, remembering, and sticking around long enough to be generally hospitable to otherness."[2] Sullivan himself admits to being inspired by Wallace.[3] However, his perspective on life is more conciliatory and relaxed than Wallace's. In an interview with the British magazine *New Statesman*, he stated:

> My view of life tends to be that everybody is stuck in a more or less absurd and tragic situation, just by virtue of the reality of death, if nothing else. So I don't think of it as a great moral deed to extend empathy and compassion to people who wouldn't otherwise seem to deserve it. I'm not surprised people end up weird and hobbled.[4]

Sullivan's ethical stance connects to a similarly relaxed epistemological position. As he stated in an interview with the *Sewanee Review* in 2018, truth, for him, is not attainable but can only be worked towards in a performative

---

1   Kraus, "Examining Pop Culture's Heroes, and Himself."
2   Wood, "Reality Effects: John Jeremiah Sullivan's Essays."
3   Roiland, "Derivative Sport: The Journalistic Legacy of David Foster Wallace."
4   Derbyshire, "John Jeremiah Sullivan."

process, which one can fail at, because of the limitedness of our very human brains.⁵ Viewing truth as virtually unattainable for Sullivan, is:

> only problematic if you believe that truth's remoteness from our reality gives you permission to fuck around. And that's not what I believe at all. I see the top of the mountain from a distance. Some kind of absolute is probably there. I believe it's there. And I'm pretty positive we can't reach it, or even get close enough to wield it without hurting ourselves, without fooling ourselves. Writers keep trying to climb the mountain, if they're serious. For one thing, it's less boring. And also, why wouldn't you want to be less of an idiot?⁶

Importantly, then, for Sullivan, the limits of human physicality have specific consequences in which the categories of ethics and epistemology cannot be kept apart.

Sullivan expresses this stance of virtual incapability prominently in *Pulphead*'s first essay, "Upon This Rock," which was previously published in a slightly different version in GQ in 2004. For the piece, Sullivan travels to a Christian rock festival in rural Pennsylvania. As scholars have maintained, at Christian rock festivals—essentially managed leisure events—the attendants' communing can produce interpersonal authenticity through a shared experience of liminality, youthful impressionability, and embodied performativity.⁷ In the highly self-reflective text, however, Sullivan paints a more ambivalent picture of the communing taking place at the festival. On the one hand, the text can be read as a somewhat remorseful acknowledgement of Sullivan's personal inability to believe in God and, hence, to experience the sense of *communitas* that is being forged at the festival. On the other hand, Sullivan describes the production of his experience—different from the planned and managed production of the festival itself—as collective and uncertain, but no less full of possibility. On a symbolic level, Sullivan's personal inability to believe mirrors his personal inability to make clear sense of his overall experience as a medium between the believing festivalgoers and his readers. On a material level, Sullivan's personal inability to produce his experience corresponds intentionally and singlehandedly to his inability to share the unified and predetermined experience of his fellow festivalgoers. Ultimately, then, his self-reflection

---

5   Hill, "A Conversation with John Jeremiah Sullivan," 53–54.
6   Hill, 54.
7   Pastoor et al., "Rock of Our Salvation: Ideological Production at the Christian Youth Music Festival."

exemplarily maps out the limits of individual human agency in the symbolic and material making of reality precisely by way of depicting (religious) belief as the main interpersonal mediator. In his telling, the symbolic and material are inevitably interlocked in his very physical existence.

This physical integration comes with a thematic inversion. Sullivan reflects so intensively upon his own role in the process of constructing an argument about experiencing Christian rock that this metanarrative about the production of meaning turns into the main story. This self-reflection of Sullivan as a human medium is manifested in three key points. First, Sullivan characterizes his experience at the Creation festival as having been accidentally produced. Second, as the main vehicle for making sense of the experience at the Creation festival, Sullivan resorts to the memory of his own stint as an evangelical. Third, Sullivan characterizes the contingent communicative relationship with his readers as more susceptible to inaccuracy than his physical perceptions.

The Willing Recruit Themselves: Experience as (Near) Accident

In contrast to the predetermination associated with journalistic or touristic experience, Sullivan depicts the actual experience at the festival as almost unintentional. He details how the initial planning of his trip failed in different ways. Rather than being the product of personal initiative and careful planning, his experience turns out to be the result of a curious sequence of human interactions, at the end of which a near accident prompts the very interactions with young Christian believers that he had initially been seeking. By prominently laying out the conditions governing his research at the very beginning of the text, Sullivan emphasizes their importance for the resulting experience. In his ironic telling, Sullivan was simply unable to follow through on his pre-established plans, due to his own weakness vis-à-vis challenges by capitalism and media technology. As a medium, then, Sullivan does not characterize himself as a shrewdly calculating journalist, but rather as the fortunate benefactor of other humans' willingness to interact.

Sullivan discards two plans before attending the Christian rock festival. The first plan is only ever imaginary, and Sullivan does not even try to realize it. In the outline of this plan, Sullivan would have played the role of a distanced observer who places himself: "at the edge of the crowd and take notes on the scene."⁸ He imagines his experience at the festival as an almost industrial act, involving a pre-planned gathering of pieces brought together purely for the sake of money. He even sees the writing process following his time at the festival as ironically rational: "Fly home, stir in statistics. Paycheck."⁹ Interestingly, however, Sullivan characterizes this imagined industrial rationality as unprofessional. While it might pay him, it would not play to his professional pride, since the industry does not: "give out awards for that toe-tap foolishness."¹⁰ For a professional like Sullivan, it is clearly not enough to make money as a writer, that is, to have his writing mediated by monetary compensation. Acknowledging his human vanity, Sullivan strives for a kind of reward beyond monetary compensation: a materialized form of respect that only other humans could give him via their recognition.

Sullivan's second plan is based on intentionally produced human interaction resulting from his personal initiative. This plan goes awry because its execution is mediated by technology. In an online search in chat forums, which he appears unable to perform, Sullivan fails to find willing festivalgoers to go with him. Sullivan posts advertisements for his rideshare online that are met with suspicion. One of them says: "I'm looking for a few serious fans of Christian rock to ride to the festival with me… Male/female doesn't matter, though you shouldn't be older than, say, 28, since I'm looking at this primarily as a youth phenomenon."¹¹ Eventually, Sullivan states, the potential festivalgoers:

> stopped chatting with me and started chatting among themselves, warning one another about me. Finally one poster on the official Relient K site hissed at the others to stay away from my scheme, as I was in all likelihood 'a 40 year old kidnapper.' Soon I logged on and found that the moderators of the site had removed my post and its lengthening thread of accusations altogether, offering no explanation… I called my lawyer, in Boston, who told me to 'stop using computers' (his plural).¹²

Again, Sullivan presents himself as almost too human to follow through with his plan, as this would entail an ability to create trust in a communicative situation mediated by computers. If pride prevents him from following through

---

8   Sullivan, "Upon This Rock," 3.
9   Sullivan, 3.
10 Sullivan, 3.
11 Sullivan, 4.
12 Sullivan, 5–6.

on his first idea, it is the very absence of his physical humanity in these online postings that appears to raise the suspicion of him to the other potential festival attendees. Reflecting upon these issues, Sullivan quickly establishes a tension between himself, as a decidedly human medium, and the very calculating, economic aspects of his research, such as planning, compensation, and casting.

In the absence of his own personal capabilities, Sullivan relies upon interpersonal cooperation. When he ultimately arrives at the festival, he does so only with the help of others. First, following the abandonment of his second plan, Sullivan wins support from GQ magazine's assistant editor, whom he describes as being better at using the internet than he is (the editor discovers, for example, that Sullivan was actually planning to attend the wrong festival). It is the editor who gets Sullivan a vehicle to drive to the festival and a place to stay while there.[13] The big RV does not meet all of Sullivan's requirements, but in their exchanges the editor manages to overcome Sullivan's reservations: "Once I reached the place, we agreed (for he led me to think he agreed), I would certainly be able to downgrade to something more manageable."[14] Unable to make arrangements and decisions by himself, Sullivan commits to actually going to this new festival called Creation only because of the assistant editor's efforts and dedication to the idea of Sullivan attending the festival.

Second, Sullivan also describes Debbie and Jack, the couple who lend him the RV, as gently pushing him towards attending the festival. Sullivan characterizes them as genuinely human, Debbie with a: "face as sweet as a birthday cake beneath spray-hardened bangs"[15] and Jack as: "tattooed, squat, gray-mulleted, spouting open contempt for MapQuest."[16] Like Sullivan who has had a bad experience with computers, Jack trusts humans more than technology: "He'd be giving me real directions."[17] Ultimately, following a tour with instructions around the vehicle, it is Jack who exemplarily shows Sullivan the way: "Jack pulled down the step and climbed aboard. It was really happening."[18] Of course, Sullivan's emphasis on both his editor's and the RV lenders' agency marks himself out as being overly and unrealistically passive in all his

---

13   Sullivan, 6–7.
14   Sullivan, 6–7.
15   Sullivan, 7.
16   Sullivan, 7.
17   Sullivan, 7.
18   Sullivan, 8.

preparations for the trip. This passiveness, however, has to be read as a form of irony. This irony creates a sense of distance between Sullivan and reality, since reality appears to produce Sullivan's experience by itself and Sullivan is only very passively present in it. Furthermore, since this irony emphasizes Sullivan's own lack of will and intention, it points to the crucial role of intention in the creation of a narrative about reality. This irony very much foregrounds the question of Sullivan's personal individual agency because it makes the absence of intention appear strange.

Third, he describes his discovery of the Christian youth, he had originally envisioned himself travelling to the festival with, as something fundamentally unintended. In attempting to prevent Sullivan from causing an accident with his huge vehicle, they practically recruit themselves. What is key to their encounter is precisely the oversized RV. While Sullivan is uncomfortable with the vehicle because it deprives him of individual agency, he also identifies it as the very reason why the interaction he is seeking with the other festivalgoers ends up taking place. As he tries to find his camping spot, Sullivan is helped by teenage volunteers, whose guidance he more than appreciates:

> They pulled out their walkie-talkies. Some time went by. It got darker. Then an even younger boy rode up on a bike and winked a flashlight at me, motioning I should follow. It was such a comfort to yield up my will to this kid. All I had to do was not lose him. His vest radiated a warm, reassuring officialdom in my headlights. Which may be why I failed to comprehend in time that he was leading me up an almost vertical incline. [19]

The need for help that makes necessary the yielding of his will that Sullivan describes here is entirely the result of the enormous size of his vehicle. At the same time, his dependence on the guide, as well as the near-accident that follows are intimately connected and lead to another encounter. As the RV briefly skids down toward the tents of other festivalgoers and Sullivan anticipates a horrible accident, he suddenly receives instructions from a stranger and his vehicle is being pushed up the hill from behind by a group of young West Virginians. These youths end up becoming the group that he will spend the following days at Creation with:

---

19   Sullivan, 11.

> I'd assumed that my days at Creation would be fairly lonely and end with my ritual murder. But these West Virginia guys had such warmth. It flowed out of them. They asked me what I did and whether I liked sassafras tea and how many others I'd brought with me in the RV. Plus they knew a dude who died horribly and was from a state with the same name as the river I grew up by, and I'm not the type who questions that sort of thing. [20]

Here, the contact with young believers that Sullivan was not able to make online appears as a gift, an act of pure kindness as Sullivan appears to do nothing other than appear vulnerable.

The narrative about how Sullivan produces the experience at the Christian rock festival in the first place is, then, already one of collective action that stands in sharp contrast to the idea of the writer as an individual genius, who both intentionally researches and tells a good story. Sullivan clearly characterizes himself as a lowly, comparably powerless medium, one who is dependent on the help and even the initiative of others, such as his editor, the RV renters, volunteers, and other festivalgoers. The communal experience he has at the festival is not the result of intentional planning, but of human collaboration, kindness, and, ultimately, the collective will to prevent an accident. This makes Sullivan appear as an ironically passive observer, who diverges from the stereotypical journalistic objectivity that observes and records like a camera, unconcerned with its own influence on reality. As a medium, Sullivan is highly aware that he influences and, to a certain degree, produces the experience of reality he needs in order to tell a good story. At least initially, his account of incompetently stumbling into the experience becomes the story and sets the tone for the narration of the experience of the festival itself.

The Accepting Writer Anticipates a Doubtful Reader

In contrast to this meta-plot, Sullivan describes the experience of attending the festival itself as more actively produced by himself and through his mere physical presence. Reflecting upon the sensory perceptions that form his experience, Sullivan generally appears to have confidence in his senses and, hence, in his own raw or technical abilities as a medium. Nevertheless, he emphasizes how his senses are still mediated by his will and, thus, how his mind and body are

---

20   Sullivan, 14.

interconnected. More specifically, reflecting on his own mediality, he describes the material making of reality as rather reliable, compared to the more complicated symbolic workings that mediate it. It is not that his eyes or ears might betray him, but that the workings of his senses are directed and given meaning by himself; whether or not he tells a story about reality, in turn, is dependent on whether the reader trusts him.

To begin with, Sullivan repeatedly reflects on how his will determines his experience, and thus how the story he tells is ultimately anchored in his own subjectivity. As an example of the power of his will to perceive, he foregrounds his perceptions as potentially unwelcome and hints at the possibility of blocking them out, thereby signaling their actively selected character to the reader. For instance, during the handover of the RV, Jack, the lender, gives him a tour of the vehicle, which Sullivan describes as disturbing:

> We toured the outskirts of my soon-to-be-mausoleum. It took time. Every single thing Jack said, somehow, was the only thing I'd need to remember. White water, gray water, black water (drinking, showering, le devoir). Here's your this, never ever that. Grumbling about "weekend warriors." I couldn't listen, because listening would mean accepting it as real, though his casual mention of the vast blind spot in the passenger-side mirror squeaked through, as did his description of the "extra two feet on each side" – the bulge of my living quarters – which I wouldn't be able to see but would want to "be conscious of" out there.[21]

Here, Sullivan hints at a connection between will and consciousness, almost casually arguing that his paying attention is, at least in this case, intentional and that whatever is being said could also simply be ignored. Later on, shortly after having met the West Virginia guys, he hints at a similar connection between his own will to perceive and the consequences of this perception. Writing about the walk to the first concert at the festival, Sullivan states: "I suspect that on some level – the conscious one, say – I didn't want to be noticing what I noticed as we went."[22] Once again, Sullivan casually connects his own consciousness with both a will to notice and the consequence of what he notices. In both instances, he has to deal with unwanted perceptions. Yet, in neither case does he attribute

---

21   Sullivan, 7–8.
22   Sullivan, 16.

2.4 The Incapable Medium in John Jeremiah Sullivan's "Upon This Rock" (2012)

any agency to the senses, concentrating it rather in his will. Thus, he emphasizes that his sensory perceptions are actively selected. While this exhibition of self-reflection makes his judgment appear weak, he raises consciousness to the rank of master selector, which not only selects, but also reflects on what is not selected and why.

In a similar way, Sullivan casually comments about how his assertions about reality are also, in turn, influenced by other impressions and thoughts. For instance, he characterizes one member of the group, Ritter, as a guy who "could burst a pineapple in his armpit and chuckle about it (or so I assume)."[23] This active declaration of his own statement as mere assumption similarly weakens the force of his judgment. Of course, the use of the subjunctive already indicates that it is an assumption, making it appear to be mere irony. Once again, the cluster of similar asides suggests a more conscious emphasis on self-reflection. Only a few lines later, Sullivan writes about another boy, Darius, that the: "projection of his jaw from the lump of snuff he kept there made him come off a bit contentious, but I felt sure he was just high-strung."[24] Sullivan here attributes his own assertion about Darius to a mere feeling. Towards the end of the text, Sullivan overtly acknowledges that such descriptions of characters are mainly based on his own feelings and, more basically, his will to feel:

> I sat in the driver's seat and watched, through tinted glass, little clusters of Christians pass. They looked like people anywhere, only gladder, more self-contained. Or maybe they just looked like people anywhere. I don't know. I had no pseudo-anthropological moxie left.[25]

By basing his judgment on "moxie" and actively refusing to judge, due to a lack of energy, Sullivan once again attributes the main agency in his perception of reality to his will. Here, however, he goes even farther. He signals that even his description of reality is dependent on his fundamental will to describe, and ultimately on his physical energy. In conclusion, he paints himself as the teller of a story, whose coherence is provided simply by the very body of the teller himself. While this may make it unique, it also places the story—a story that,

---

23   Sullivan, 13.
24   Sullivan, 13.
25   Sullivan, 35.

after all, is supposed to be about a real experience of reality—on a supposedly flimsy evidential basis.

It only matters that when Sullivan describes himself as weak, but is also accepting of this weakness, he in turn anticipates a reader who will doubt these assertions. Addressing the reader directly, Sullivan signals that he also understands the relationship with him or her to be based on a mere will to interact and believe. For instance, while waiting in line next to a pickup truck with teenage girls, Sullivan makes an observation that he anticipates the reader might not believe:

> Their line of traffic lurched ahead, and an old orange Datsun came up beside me. I watched as the driver rolled down her window, leaned halfway out, and blew a long, clear note on a ram's horn. I understand where you might be coming from in doubting that. Nevertheless it is what she did. I have it on tape.[26]

Similar to other passages that have been quoted, this one has an ironic undertone, because the blowing of the horn that Sullivan purports to have witnessed and claims to have on tape is rather unspectacular. By contrast, Sullivan narrates a much more dramatic event—the death of a man standing next to him—in a rather straightforward way, without commenting on the plausibility of the episode for the reader.[27] Hence, Sullivan's assurance that he has a recording of the scene appears quite out of proportion and rather makes fun of its potential epistemological function as evidence.

However, the direct reader address can also be read as a casual reminder that the reader is more generally dependent on Sullivan's word. Throughout the text, Sullivan inserts similar comments and interjections directed at the reader. For instance, when he tells the reader about first driving through the festival grounds, Sullivan notes: "It's hard to put across the sensory effect of that many people living and moving around in the open: part family reunion, part refugee camp."[28] Later, Sullivan makes a similar aside about the difficulty of conveying a particular perception, when he tells the reader about how a speaker yelled out from a stage: "If I were to try to convey to you how loudly he

---

26   Sullivan, 9.
27   Sullivan, 36.
28   Sullivan, 11.

shrieked this, you'd think I was playing wordy games."²⁹ Elsewhere, Sullivan also comments on potential contradictions in his story when, after having given a report of tensions involving the West Virginia guys, he acknowledges that the reader might be put off by his account: "I admit that these tales of the West Virginia guys' occasional truculence might appear to gainsay what I claimed earlier about 'not one word spoken in anger,' et cetera. But it was playful."³⁰ Taken together, these comments directed at the reader all come across as clues from Sullivan that he is aware of his role as medium and especially his transmitting function. This self-reflection in turn signals to the reader that he or she is merely reading the produced account of a medium struggling to put his experience into words, and not an immediate, unambiguous representation of real events.

Past and Future to Make Sense of the Present

Sullivan extends his self-reflection to encompass how he makes sense of the experience. And just like the material making of the experience itself, this symbolic making of meaning by way of imagination and memory is ultimately anchored in his body. In part, the experience at the festival draws Sullivan away from the present, as it prompts him to remember the past and to imagine the future. In place of a detailed rendering of his personal experience at the festival, Sullivan mainly tells the story of why he cannot be a true Christian himself, via what he calls a "memory voyage"³¹ into his youth. Similar to the story about how the experience was accidentally produced, he expands on how his making sense of the experience is anchored in his very personal and subjective memory, being produced internally. In a similar way, Sullivan inserts hypothetical prolepses, imagined future events that might be seen as potential consequences of his actions in the present that provide meaning to his experience.

Sullivan's flashback plays a key role in his sensemaking. It works as a reference for the narrative of the experience at the festival, as there are clear parallels between the two. In both cases, Sullivan tells the story of his being attracted by a group of young believers. The reasons for this attraction are similar. First

---

29   Sullivan, 36.
30   Sullivan, 23.
31   Sullivan, 26.

of all, the groups are both characterized as authentic by way of their unapologetic self-awareness as passionate believers. When he first meets the group at the festival, for example, Ritter says that they were: "just a bunch of West Virginia guys on fire for Christ."[32] Later, Darius asks Sullivan to write in the text: "that we love God."[33] Sullivan elevates this self-characterization toward one of the clearest and simplest points he makes in the text, when he adds that: "I would have said it even if Darius hadn't asked me to, it may be the truest thing I will have written here: they were crazy, and they loved God."[34] When looking back at the group he joined in his teenage years, Sullivan similarly states he was drawn to Evangelicalism because of the sense of zeal it exuded: "The sheer passionate engagement of it caught my imagination: nobody had told me there were Christians like this. They went at the Bible with grad-seminar intensity, week after week."[35]

Another attractive quality of both groups to Sullivan is their appreciation for good music. Sullivan writes how he is dazzled by Darius' piano skills[36] and how the communal play in his RV during a rainstorm tightened their bond.[37] In similar ways, Sullivan attributes a key role to music in his affiliation with the evangelical group of his youth. He notes that he swapped music tapes with the group's leader[38] and that there was a bonfire after prayer sessions where the guitar "went around."[39] Music also serves Sullivan as a means of illustrating the tolerance for difference exhibited by both groups, when he writes that the West Virginians at Creation "were up for secular stuff."[40] Additionally, the fact that they find out rather early on that Sullivan is on a professional assignment, but still unconditionally welcome him into their group, marks them out as tolerant. Sullivan also explicitly characterizes the group he belonged to as a teenager as tolerant, when he notes that "they were accepting of every kind of weirdness"[41] and that they respected his reasons for ultimately leaving the group.[42] Thus,

---

32   Sullivan, 13.
33   Sullivan, 40.
34   Sullivan, 40.
35   Sullivan, 27–28.
36   Sullivan, 24.
37   Sullivan, 39.
38   Sullivan, 27.
39   Sullivan, 29.
40   Sullivan, 39.
41   Sullivan, 27.
42   Sullivan, 32.

Sullivan's memory voyage adds argumentative fodder to his narrative of his experience at the festival and strengthens his characterization of a particular branch of Evangelicals as passionate, tolerant humans.

However, the retrospection also works on a formal level, as a comparably solid point of reference for the complicated meaning that Sullivan constructs at Creation. Compared to the metatextual passages filled with irony analyzed above, Sullivan's voice here appears clear, unequivocal, and self-assured. The few instances in which Sullivan employs metatextual comments are the result of a concern for the privacy of the characters in the story[43] and to avoid boring the reader with too much information.[44] Nowhere does Sullivan comment on the nature of memory itself or lament an inability to remember. Notably, however, he admits on one occasion that his memory is incomplete, when referring to an event at the festival itself.[45] Thus, he also asserts his memory as a reality on a formal level. Similar to his trust in his own senses then, the attribution of meaning to his memory appears more interesting than the identification of its fundamentally aesthetic quality, because the authority ascribed to it affirms its embodied materiality.

However, Sullivan does not just draw on past, remembered experiences to make sense of the present ones. Twice, he imagines future, hypothetical consequences of his present actions. Like his memories, these fictional, imagined scenarios illustrate the highly mediated emotional process of giving meaning to present experience. When given a tour of the RV prior to his drive to Creation, for instance, Sullivan has a foreboding vision of: "my loved ones gathered in a mahogany-paneled room to watch this footage; them being forced to hear me say, 'What if I never use the toilet – do I still have to switch on the water?'"[46] In a comparable passage, referring to the near-accident, Sullivan imagines that his having rented the big RV would have terrible consequences: "Laid out below and behind me was a literal field of Christians, toasting buns and playing guitars, fellowshipping. The aerial shot in the papers would show a long scar, a swath through their peaceful tent village."[47] In both passages, of course, Sullivan anticipates his present actions as having sinister consequences. Could he really have felt so pessimistic and afraid? Again, to read both passages as mere

---

43   Sullivan, 26.
44   Sullivan, 29.
45   Sullivan, 12.
46   Sullivan, 8.
47   Sullivan, 12.

irony serving to signify the author's weakness would miss half the point. On a meta-textual level, the acts of cautious or fearful presaging also draw attention to themselves as acts of narrative sensemaking in respect of the present. In both cases, Sullivan imagines potential events in the future as reference points, in order to give meaning to feelings prompted by his experience at the festival.

In Sullivan's piece, then, both remembered past and imagined future narratives are used to comment on the central narrative about the writer's experience at the festival. They add to the impression of the text as both a commentary on an experience of Evangelicalism and a commentary on the very construction of a commentary on the experience of Evangelicalism. Furthermore, as a human medium's self-reflection, they also emphasize a human medium's distinct qualities of embodied memory and imagination.

Strong Weakness

As I have sought to demonstrate, Sullivan's narrative of an experience of Evangelicalism, as well as his meta-narrative, are by no means cleanly separable, because they are embodied in Sullivan's persona. If, on a meta-narrative level, Sullivan portrays himself as weak and unable to produce meaningful experience, then it is this exact weakness that enables him to make the connection with the West Virginia guys in the main narrative. It also signifies the aestheticization of weakness that he claims to admire in Jesus, when he states that not in: "what conquers, not in glory, but in what's fragile and what suffers – there lies sanity. And salvation."[48] In the text, this fragility is manifested in the different narratives Sullivan draws upon to make sense of his main experience, until he stops and designates one of them as basic and referential. It is also displayed in a use of irony that has a distancing effect, as Sullivan employs it to keep the realities of both his festival-going and the reader at arm's length. Sullivan's main concern is not with reality and its material objects, but with the symbolically negotiated relationships between them. Just as Evangelicalism is a story full of stories that believers tell themselves about reality, Sullivan's narrative about Evangelicalism is a story full of stories that he tells himself and his readers.

Similar to his view of Jesus, Sullivan aestheticizes his own weakness precisely by basking in his inability to believe in God in the same way as the fes-

---

48 Sullivan, 33.

tivalgoers do, but he does not revel in mere irony. The weakness he aestheticizes through his use of irony or the rendering of his inability to make and execute a plan has the potential to turn into a strength, because it opens the possibility for connection and collaboration. Towards the very end of the text, adding yet another form of narrative to make sense of the experience, Sullivan quotes a poem by the Polish writer Czeslaw Milosz that celebrates believers. "If one could only say it and mean it," Sullivan comments, thereby placing himself right outside of the circle of believers he has just spent time among, looking at them with an understanding that is grounded in an understanding of his own nature. Standing there, Sullivan is personating the position of a medium who has experienced not just in order to experience, but also in order to tell—possibly to believers.

Sullivan's very self-reflection as human medium illuminates the function of common belief in human communing that connects what is radically uncertain. As Sullivan ponders his own very human mediality not predicated upon religious belief, which seeks to make and transmit sense of reality alongside the experience of highly religious Evangelicalism, he maps out the need for an alternative kind of belief that potentially connects himself with his readers. His consolatory and nevertheless appreciative assessment of the believers at the festival illustrates the possibility of communing without religious belief as it stakes out a tolerant ethics of common fragility.

2.5 Uncertainties and the Negotiation of Trust in Communing

In all three texts the writers' reflection of their own material experience points to the core issue of common belief—or trust—in communing. The writers thus also point to parallels between the uncertainties involved in communing and this communing's symbolic meaning communicated to readers. The relationship between writer and reader is one of fundamental asymmetry. Because the writers' experience cannot be repeated by the reader, any "transmission of knowledge is only possible with the help of the social bond of trust."[1] This reliance on reader trust as consequence of fundamental asymmetry, which is at the core of reportage, corresponds to the fundamental uncertainty at the core of communing more generally. In the texts analyzed, this uncertainty is bridged by way of commonly accepted narratives of belief in the benefits of consumerism and religion. What makes everybody—precisely except David Foster Wallace—have a good time on the cruise is the commonly accepted and therefore authentic consumerist narrative of the hard worker who deserves to be pampered. Foster Wallace criticizes this belief as fantastically inauthentic and seeks to demonstrate in his text a sincerity he has not found on the cruise. What keeps George Saunders from decrying Dubai as a global consumerist dystopia is his belief in the human potential to do good that is kindled by fantastic authenticity despite the glaring evidence of material inequality. What conciliates John Jeremiah Sullivan with Evangelicals—despite their different taste in music—is their common celebration of authentic human weakness.

In all three cases then, writers critically replace the narratives of pre-fabricated touristic experience that aimed to define the experience's meaning as certain with new narratives of uncertainty. These narratives make new sense by way of incorporating and making transparent the function of belief in human

---

1 Krämer, *Medium, Messenger, Transmission: An Approach to Media Philosophy*, 149.

communing as a necessary symbolic instrument to address the fundamental uncertainty of communing itself. Thus, touristic experience is characterized as respite from critique in which pre-fabricated trust (by way of PR brochures, luxury architecture, preaching) is ritually performed. The authorial reinterpretations, in contrast, insist on the existential meaning of trust in communing and simultaneously incorporate this awareness into a narrative of said experience that seeks to be more sincere.

In this existential function, then, intersubjective trust undermines the technological reproducibility of communal meaning. It insists that, ultimately, in communing, individual humans interact materially and symbolically. The increasingly important role of technological mediation in mediatized societies, however, can only reflect this in a reduced way as it promotes simplified senses of meaning that must remain technologically reproducible and therefore certain.

3 On Real Bodies: Mediating Other Human Media

3.1 Reflexive Subjectivities and Their Differences

Although it may fittingly serve to illustrate human experience in modern mediatized Western societies, the human medium of course is not alone. The reporter or writer is certainly not the only type of human subject affected by technical media's spatializing or compartmentalizing forces. Rather, human subjects, who can function as human media themselves as well, affirm themselves in ways similar to reporters. Therefore, it is in texts that rub up against the journalistic genre of the profile,[1] which have particular human beings as their main subjects, that writers consider the reflexive (and hence contingent) formation of their own subjectivity as human media by way of examinations of other, different human media.

For instance, if reporters react to technological developments that bolster the reproduction of human experience with increased displays of self-reflection, this might also apply to other human subjects. And, conversely, if such displays of self-reflection illustrate the uncertainties and possibilities of self-creation in contemporary societies, this could also apply to the professional roles of writers or reporters. In contrast to the texts on human communing then, the three texts analyzed are concerned with issues of specific subjectivities rather than human interaction.

Still, they exhibit the same sensibility of human subjectivity's existential contingent reality that challenges technology's semblance of immediacy, reproduction and possible commodification. Rather than highlight the ways in which human communing is mediated by getting individual subjects to coordinate, they examine the possibilities and limits of individual subjects to mediate themselves. Consequently, rather than the possibilities of human interaction apparent in the analyzed case studies of reportage concerned with ex-

---

1   An extensive analysis of the profile as journalistic genre is, i.e. Joseph and Keeble, *Profile Pieces: Journalism and the "Human Interest" Bias*.

periences of community, writers foreground the possibilities of intrapersonal action. That is, they inspect the uncertainties and thus possibilities of human self-making particularly in the ways in which this reflexive making of subjectivity is affected by the mediating functions that the portrayed humans can attain. It is no coincidence then, that the writers of these texts are more pressingly concerned with their own roles as human media than in the texts on communing.

The three texts analyzed in this chapter, then, all emphasize the contingencies in the self-affirmation of human media and an interplay that is marked by difference. In these texts, writers emphasize their own mediating capacities while observing the distinct mediating possibilities of other human subjects. Thus, they identify and promote the very human aspects of subjective knowledge more generally as rooted in the capacity for self-reflection. In "Buddha Boy", for instance, George Saunders examines his own functioning as a human medium while inspecting the possibility of a fasting teenage bodhisattva's radical individuality. In "Getting Down to What is Really Real", John Jeremiah Sullivan pitches the self-aware characters of a reality TV show against the commercialization of TV and his own public performance. In "Delusion is the Thing With Feathers", Mac McClelland investigates the possibilities and pitfalls of two self-sacrificing male ornithologists against the backdrop of her difference in gender and sex that very much shapes her experience.

In these instances the affirmation of human subjectivity and this affirmation's conjunction with individual human agency and power is crucial. More basically, this affirmation manifests the complex crystallization of existential questions pertaining to issues of human subjectivity that integrate both material and symbolic acts of making.

It is this integration or entanglement of material and symbolic action of individuals in social contexts that makes for the complexity and intrigue of the human subject as basic theme of these texts. According to Peter Zima, a subject is a: "dialogical being whose development depends on its interaction with others and with alterity in general."[2] Every subject's nature is transitory, and linguistically and culturally formed, and as such, highly contingent.[3] Furthermore, a subject is typically only considered a subject if it is conscious of itself.[4]

---

2   Zima, *Subjectivity and Identity: Between Modernity and Postmodernity*, 51.
3   Zima, 6.
4   Zima, 15.

Especially with to the self-affirmation of human media against technical media such as the computer, then, this self-awareness is a crucial characteristic that might singularly mark a human medium.

Importantly, this marker is existential as the capacity for self-reflection extends to the many ways of subjective self-making. This critically enhances the very complexity of a human subject further and requires some unpacking. In Zima's theoretical conception following Paul Ricoeur, the individual subject is: "a dynamic, dialogical synthesis of individuality and subjectivity."[5] Whereas individuality refers to the very basic social physicality of a human's body among others and, as such, a mere potential, subjectivity is this potential's realization in action, speech, or thought. Consequently, individuality and subjectivity presuppose one another in the formation of a dynamic dialectic.[6]

Of particular interest for this study, however, are the ways in which individual subjects—including then writers themselves—form their identities as they think, feel, act and speak and thus realize their individualities. Essentially, then, subjectivity can be considered: "as a dynamic synthesis of individuality and identity, for only somebody who has *acquired* a psychic, social and linguistic identity is recognized by others as a feeling, speaking and acting subject."[7] Thus, while human subjects in modern Western societies like the U.S. might experience freedom and a sense of agency in these processes of self-formation, they are also necessarily constricted by, for instance, bodily preconditions, social norms, material circumstances or their surroundings. The subjectivities expressed in these texts—again including the writers themselves—then, could be viewed as manifestations of contemporary subjects who: "construct identity as a tenuous and fragmentary structure that is inherently social and therefore subject to the political conflicts of its cultural location."[8]

Still, the very social and reflexive character of their acts of construction takes center stage in all three texts. In the reportage of George Saunders, the central conflict is one of belief in the possibilities of self-making. John Jeremiah Sullivan describes how mediatization affects the very awareness of the subjective making of identity that turns into performance. And in Mac McClelland's reportage the writer brushes up against the limits of a specifically masculine ideal of identity construction.

---

5   Zima, 15.
6   Zima, 15–17.
7   Zima, 17.
8   Malpas, *The Postmodern*, 73.

Such conscious instances of identity constructions must be viewed in light of the comparably recent pressures of globalization. In the 1990s, social scientists such as Anthony Giddens, Ulrich Beck or Scott Lash posited that in the accelerated, connected Western societies that leave no time to rest the individual makes his or her own identity inevitably in such reflexive ways.[9] Reflexivity means that the individual's construction of identity is continually created in dialogical exchanges with oneself, others, and the world.[10] It is thus integral to how such acts of construction have necessarily social aspects while, at the same time, they also inevitably are individual projects. This conflict of reflexivity has long been at the heart of identity construction. In pre-modern times however, it simply did not amount to a problem. Rather, then, according to Giddens or Beck, the unsettling forces of globalization and mediatization, importantly including a disembedding of identity construction from situations of physical co-presence, have radicalized reflexivity. Thus, reflexivity has turned from an incidental to the constitutive part of identity construction.[11] This also decisively affects our experience of society. For Giddens, for instance, self and society are thus interrelated for the first time in human history.[12] Furthermore, change is experienced as conforming neither to human expectations nor to control.[13] For Ulrich Beck, this amounts to a shift to a risk society in which the self attains a new quality that acknowledges that control is impossible.[14]

That reflexivity takes on this prime position in texts concerned with postmodern identity construction, then, is no coincidence. These acts of (self-)construction can be interpreted as bold acts of self-affirmation and hence repudiations of the stable, monadic, and bourgeois idea of modern subjectivity.[15] As such, furthermore, they can also be read as analyses of contemporary social realities. Different postmodern scholars have emphasized that the increasingly dominant role of (media) technology in postmodern societies has affected the ways in which humans recognize themselves as humans and more freely turn against social or even physical constraints on their own identity construction.

---

9 Lemert, "A history of identity", 32–33.
10 Chaffee, "Reflexive identities", 119–120.
11 Chaffee, 121.
12 Giddens, *Modernity and Self-Identity*, 32
13 Giddens, 28.
14 Chaffee, 125.
15 Malpas, 73.

Thinkers such as Jean-François Lyotard or Gianni Vattimo have presented optimistic theories of postmodern subjectivity that go beyond pointing out the constructed character of subjectivity. Lyotard identifies a potential in human subjectivity to be transformed and surprised by possibilities that systems of reason based on technology cannot. Viewed from Lyotard's perspective, the different gaps—which he calls no-man's land, the unrepresentable, or the sublime—would thus correspond to these possibilities, expose them as fundamentally human, and employ them as a force of resistance against capitalist and technological limitation.[16]

For Gianni Vattimo, the postmodern decisively refers to a: "society of generalized communication... of the mass media."[17] This environment of mediatization creates complexity and chaos and makes human emancipation possible in precisely this way.[18] Vattimo credits the emergence of media technology to the public dissemination of an unprecedented diversity of worldviews, which make it difficult to speak of reality in the singular. The postmodern subject, thus, experiences reality in a state of continual disorientation or oscillation that makes it aware of its own contingency of being enacted in dialogue and presents: "an opportunity of a new way of being (finally, perhaps) human."[19]

However, it is important to bear in mind that such exercises of reflexive freedom are always contingent upon existing material dispositions and structures of power. These structures—as will partly be shown in the final cluster of analyses of reportage on violence—are themselves reflexive and can be negotiated in ways that are less appreciative of free individual self-making. Furthermore, reflexive self-making is also subject to emotional and unconscious processes that cannot always be explained in logical analyses.[20]

The three texts analyzed all acknowledge such opportunities and limitations in different ways. They detail specific possibilities and limits of self-conscious individual identity formation in human interactions which are in turn affected by religion, media technology, and gender—all in unique and different, but similar ways as they juxtapose the contingent subjectivities of the writers and the other humans they interact with. Thus, these descriptions mirror

---

16 Lyotard, *The Inhuman: Reflections on Time*; Malpas, *The Postmodern*, 76–77.
17 Vattimo, *The Transparent Society*, 1.
18 Vattimo, 4.
19 Vattimo, 11.
20 Chaffee, 127–128.

the writers' own constructed subjectivities as specific human media and comment upon the contingent character of subjective knowledge more generally. Taken together, they make a case for fundamental human sameness in fundamental co-existence and difference.

3.2 The Mysterious Medium in George Saunders's "Buddha Boy" (2007)

Like "The New Mecca," George Saunders originally wrote "Buddha Boy" for GQ, which published the text in 2006. Saunders included an amended version of the text in the essay collection *The Braindead Megaphone* (2007). In this text, Saunders describes being confronted with the rumor of a Buddhist boy named Ram Bahadur Bomjan who had allegedly been meditating for seven months straight without eating or drinking.[1] He travels to Nepal to see the boy for himself and explores the possibility of the Buddhist teenager's superior powers of mind control. In contrast to the approach that he adopted in "The New Mecca," Saunders is not much concerned with the communal making of meaning. Rather, he is interested in the fundamentally subjective workings of interpretation that are practiced in Buddhism. More to the point, he is intrigued by the cognitive functions and possibilities of a human medium that triggers questions of religious self-creation.

Saunders mirrors the monk's reflexive performance in the multi-faceted self-reflection of his own subjectivity as human medium that creates itself more or less consciously. For instance, Saunders characterizes his experience in Nepal as being the result of a will that is motivated by bare human curiosity. Furthermore, he describes his experience as decisively mediated by his own mind, whose desire for cognitive closure he meticulously documents, analyzes, and questions. Thus, he explicitly portrays the narrative of his experience as the product of an interpretative process wrung from his own body.

---

[1] Bomjan started meditating in May 2005 but disappeared from the site visited by Saunders in March 2006. He has since been seen repeatedly at different sites but his story has changed dramatically as he has been accused of violence, rape and incest. Saunders's early fascination with the boy's meditating powers has therefore been called delusional. Burnett III, "The Dark Secrets of Nepal's Famous Buddha Boy."

In his telling of the story however, Saunders also comments on religion's persisting function for the self-making of the individual human subject. Kieran Flanagan has argued that religion: "constitutes the problematic many thought had dissolved into history, assassinated by reason and buried in the spirit of secularisation."[2] However, particularly if the human subject increasingly constructs itself reflexively, it is forced to confront its own contingency and to ask itself questions also related to ambiguity, enchantment and mystery.[3] The anthropologist Clifford Geertz has argued, rather broadly, that religion represents the human capacity to give meaning to reality and signifies a "metaphysical grounding" of social values.[4] As such, it influences social and personal identity. Even more generally, scholars have posited that spirituality fulfills similar functions, particularly in terms of the meaning, purpose, unification, or integration of personal identity.[5]

George Saunders's "Buddha Boy" prominently features Buddhist concepts of both self and subjectivity. Faced with the metaphysical and unfathomable subjectivity of a young monk, he emphasizes the limits of his own ability to make sense of his experience rather than foregrounding the monk's miraculousness. Importantly, Buddhism is dominated by a deeply skeptical view of the human subject. For instance, Buddhists reject the existence of an enduring or substantial self. For them, our sense of self is more like a cognitive illusion necessary to reify self and world. "On this view", Matthew MacKenzie argues:

> the sense of self arises from an on-going process of appropriation (upādāna) of the embodied stream of experience into a self-model that 'perfumes' all further cognitive operations. Moreover, it can change and even perhaps drop away entirely in certain types of experience (pathological or meditative).[6]

The basis for this self-model, then, is a kind of: "egoless streaming of reflexive awareness"[7] that can be perceived as a permanent self although it is, fundamentally, continuously (re-)created and its substantiality is an illusion. Here it is very much the inner dialogue between individual subject and identity that

---

2   Flanagan, "Religion and Modern Personal Identity," 250.
3   Flanagan, 255–256.
4   Geertz, *The Interpretation of Cultures*, 131.
5   Hill et al., "Conceptualizing Religion and Spirituality: Points of Commonality, Points of Departure."
6   MacKenzie, "Reflexivity, Subjectivity, and the Constructed Self: A Buddhist Model," 289.
7   MacKenzie, 290.

presents opportunities for subjective formation and, as will be shown in the following analysis of Saunders's text, fundamental considerations of self-reflection.

Mysterious Motivation

To begin with, Saunders characterizes his own role as performed. His concern with the decisive power, exercised by cognition on the writer's part, extends to the frame narrative. Here, Saunders displays an awareness of the importance of the professional context in which his experience in Nepal is produced. Saunders's trip cannot be viewed as an ordinary journalistic assignment, and hence professional necessity, but as the product of a mysterious inner drive. Saunders makes clear that he was initially approached by his editor to write about a meditating boy. "Last December," he writes in the opening line of the piece, "I got an email from my editor at GQ."[8] Although the editor explicitly asks him to look into the Buddhist boy's story, Saunders declines:

> I e-mailed my editor back: I was pretty busy, what with the teaching and all, besides which Christmas break was coming up and I hadn't been to the gym once the preceding semester, plus it would be great to, uh, get an early start on my taxes.[9]

As grounds for declining the offer, Saunders lists reasons—such as other professional duties—that might otherwise have prompted him to take the job. The fact that he would be paid to travel to Nepal, for instance, is never discussed once.

Rather, Saunders explicitly presents his experience as highly specific and subjective. Rather than invoking a professional or financial reason related to the capitalistic incentives of professional journalism, Saunders instead describes his motivation to travel to Nepal as originating in a reaction against the media's tendency towards prejudice and his own personal curiosity. However, he cannot "get this boy off [his] mind,"[10] and so Saunders confronts his friends with online accounts of the boy's story. Both these accounts and his

---

8   Saunders, "Buddha Boy," 211.
9   Saunders, 212.
10 Saunders, 212.

friends' reactions were, Saunders notes, marked by speculation and prejudice. "Skeptics said," he writes, with reference to his online research, "he was being fed at night behind a curtain, that his guru was building himself a temple, that his parents were building themselves a mansion, that the Maoist rebals, in on the hoax, were raking in tens of thousands of dollars in donations."[11] Saunders observes a certain tendency to judge the story in a polarizing way. On the one hand, certain people deem it impossible for the boy to still be alive. Saunders recounts: "One type of American—let's call them Realists—will react by making a snack-related joke... and will then explain that it's physically impossible to survive even one week without food or water, much less seven months."[12] On the other hand, he observes that certain people want to believe. "A second type—let's call them Believers—will say... they wish they could go to Nepal tomorrow."[13] Without explicitly taking sides, Saunders situates his decision to travel to Nepal in the context of these prejudiced views. He states: "What I said, finally, was: This I have to see."[14] Hence, Saunders establishes an early distinction between explicitly professional and mysteriously human motivation for inquiry.

This is further manifested in his preference of the rather general role of the writer over the journalist. Saunders characterizes himself merely as a writer with a distinct sensibility. This is particularly apparent in his repeated references to notetaking—a very concrete and physical manifestation of the act of writing. On the way to see the meditating boy, for example, Saunders mentions that he is unsuccessfully trying to take notes: "Beyond the staging area, the road goes single-vehicle, double rutted. I try taking notes, but the road is too bumpy. *CRWLFF!* I write, *FHWUED??*"[15] Elsewhere, while waiting to get closer to the meditating boy, Saunders merely imagines himself taking notes: "I sit on a log. What I'll do is hang out here for an hour or so, get my bearings, take a few notes on the general site layout."[16] During the night that he spends at the meditation site, Saunders writes about trying to take notes in the dark:

---

11   Saunders, 211–212.
12   Saunders, 212.
13   Saunders, 212.
14   Saunders, 212.
15   Saunders, 222.
16   Saunders, 225.

> From inside the Enclosure, or maybe the far side of it, I hear what sounds like a cough. Sound is traveling strangely. Was that the boy? Did the boy just cough? To note this possible cough in my notebook, I devise a system: I take out my mini-flashlight, mute the light with my hand, so as not to disturb the boy, record the time, make my note.[17]

In all of these cases, notetaking cannot simply be read as a mere vehicle for a writer's self-characterization. It also embeds the writer's processing of the experience through the taking of notes within the produced experience itself, insofar as it is affected by the quality of a road, is imagined as an effect of the experience, or is itself capable of altering the experience. Notetaking attains the status of an actively produced experience.

At least once, however, Saunders's idea of himself as a writer processing and storing his experience by means of a notebook is at odds with the sensory experience itself. When Subel, his guide and translator, calls him over to take a picture, Saunders hesitates at first:

> 'You have to,' Subel says. 'That's how they know you're a journalist.'
> I hold up my notebook. Maybe I could just take some notes?
> 'They're simple people, man,' he says. 'You have to take a photo.'[18]

In this passage, Saunders paints a clear picture of journalism as being in tension with writing—and with himself. However, this tension is due not to Saunders's own values or practice, but to a narrow understanding of journalism as being essentially visual that is held by "simple people." Saunders clearly does not see himself as a journalist; it is just a role that he occasionally has to play to please others. Elsewhere, for instance, when he is told the story of a snake that bit the meditating boy, he plays his part reluctantly:

> 'What kind of snake was it?' I ask, trying to be journalistic.
> 'It was... a big jungle snake,' Subel translates.
> 'Ah,' I say.

Being "journalistic" here clearly does not help Saunders. The question of what kind of snake it was is obviously not significant to the story. Hence, being a journalist, or even just acting like one, reflects a rather narrow idea of self for

---

17 Saunders, 234–235.
18 Saunders, 228.

Saunders. A writer, by contrast, cultivates an open-minded sensibility, rooted in the inexplicable personal, merely human curiosity of his self of which he cannot be fully aware.

The Master Mediator

In congruence with Buddhist philosophy, his mysterious openness and curiosity lead Saunders to perceive experience as being ultimately mediated mentally. In Saunders's depiction, however, the mind never works independently; it is connected to other media within or outside the body, such as the body's sensory organs, or other major characters, such as Saunders's translator or the a young monk called Prem. On the one hand, the mind's ultimate superiority as a medium is manifested in the minor role assigned to the mediation by way of the body's sensory organs. On the other hand, the mind's constant reflection upon the mediation performed by other media reveals its ultimate power to impose meaning upon reality.

In line with his depiction of experience, as mediated by the body in "The New Mecca," Saunders only rarely questions sensory perception. In "Buddha Boy," at least under normal circumstances, reality just *is*. In Kathmandu, for instance, Saunders comes across what later turns out to be a soup kitchen:

> Off to one side of the road is a strange sunken hollow – like a shallow basement excavation – filled with rows of wooden benches on which hundreds of the dustiest men, women, and children imaginable wait for something with the sad patience of animals. It's like a bus station, but there's no road in sight. Several Westerners huddle near a gate, harried-looking, pissy, admitting people or not. A blind man is expelled from the lot and lingers by the gate, acting casual, like he was not just expelled. What is going on here? Three hundred people in a kind of open-air jail, no blind guys allowed.[19]

Despite his obvious difficulties in making sense of the place, Saunders appears to fully trust his senses here. What he experiences is real; the question of whether or not his senses might be playing tricks on him is not raised. Furthermore, Saunders perceives primarily by means of his eyes and does not refer to other possible—and possibly intense—forms of sensory perception,

---

19   Saunders, 217.

such as smell. Saunders invites the reader to experience what he experiences much more rarely than he had in "The New Mecca". In these instances, reality appears rather simple. For example, in one episode that occurs on the night he spends close to the meditating boy, Saunders ponders the effect of the silence surrounding him: "In this quiet, even the slightest posture adjustment is deafening. If a tiny breeze picks up, you notice. If a drop of moisture falls, you jump."[20] Here, it is the lack of stimuli that gives the experience its appearance of simplicity. Similarly, shortly before Saunders sees the boy for the first time, he assertively describes the scene as if the reader were seeing what he sees, because it appears so straightforward:

> The first impression is zoolike. You are looking into an Enclosure. Inside the Enclosure are dozens of smallish pipal trees festooned with a startling density of prayer flags (red, green, yellow, many faded to white from the sun and rain). This Enclosure also has a vaguely military feel: something recently and hastily constructed, with security in mind.[21]

Framed by the zoo metaphor, the content of Saunders's experience is almost exclusively visual. Through a rather simplistic interpretation, the scene resembles an interchangeable object that Saunders thinks would be experienced in exactly the same way by the reader.

This situation changes when things start to get a bit more complicated for Saunders, regarding both his perception of reality and in terms of the zoo metaphor. In the following paragraph, Saunders switches subjects, turning back to himself, while his eyes assume greater agency:

> I scan the Enclosure, looking for That Which Is Enclosed. Nothing. I look closer, focusing on three or four larger trees that, unlike the smaller trees, have the characteristic flaring pipal roots. This too feels zoolike: the scanning, the rescanning, the sudden sense of Ah, *there* he is![22]

In this passage, although it is not stated explicitly, his eyes are more directly connected to his mind, as they search for the boy. The description of his visual searching, thus, takes on a much more subjective quality. This kind of searching, Saunders appears to suggest, is more contingent than the impressions

---

20 Saunders, 235.
21 Saunders, 224.
22 Saunders, 224.

that he had described previously. It is primarily the control of the mind, not the particular workings of the senses, or aspects of external reality itself, that signals a high degree of subjectivity—and not just in this paragraph.

In "Buddha Boy," the mind, rather than any particular sensory organ, appears to be the master-mediator of experience. It is the mind that is characterized as the engine of sensory experience and its interpretation, especially when the body as a whole is challenged. At the very beginning of Saunders's nocturnal camp-out, for instance, he hears a weird noise: "At 7:20, oddly, a car alarm goes off. How many cars in deep rural Nepal have alarms? It goes on and on. Finally it dawns on me, when the car alarm moves to a different tree, that the car alarm is a bird."[23] In this case, Saunders initially mistakes a bird for a car-alarm, as the result of a mistaken mental attribution of the sound. In a similar way, Saunders describes his mind as playing tricks on him, when—as suggested by nearby monks—he believes himself to be witnessing a miracle, as he sees colored sparks emanating from the boy's forehead and hears his inhumanly loud heartbeat:

> I look through the binoculars. Yes, red and blue sparks, yep, and now, wow, green. And orange. Then suddenly, they're all orange. They look – actually, they look like orange cinders. Like orange cinders floating up from a fire. A campfire, say. I lower the binoculars. Seen with the naked eye, the sparks look to be coming not from inside the Enclosure but from just beyond it. Slowly, a campfire resolves itself in the distance. The heartbeat becomes syncopated. The heartbeat is coming from off to my right and behind me and is actually, I can now tell, a drum, from a village out in the jungle.[24]

Here, Saunders arrives at a more sober conclusion about what he has seen and heard, because he keeps an open mind and ultimately interprets his perceptions differently—after having let some time go by and used binoculars. Hence, in both cases, it is the mind that decisively classifies what he initially sees and hears.

However, Saunders does not set up an opposition between body and mind. Their relationship is, rather, circular or dialogical, given that the body influences the interpretations produced by the mind and vice versa. For instance, when Saunders's body is challenged, his mind is challenged too. As Saunders

---

23   Saunders, 235.
24   Saunders, 236.

suffers while trying to fall asleep at the meditation site, he writes about how suffering affects the mind. Having initially been able to convince himself of the importance of not losing his calm[25] and even playing devil's advocate,[26] his mind struggles to make sense of reality when he realizes that the white flecks he saw were an optical illusion:

> Oh man, I think, I have no idea what's going on here. The line between miracle and hallucination is all but gone. I am so tired. The center is not... What is it the center is sometimes said not to do? Hanging? Having? The center are not hanging.[27]

Challenged by sleep deprivation and the extreme cold, Saunders loses the ability to clearly perceive reality, a condition that he expresses through a joking reference to the famous line from William Butler Yeats' poem *The Second Coming* (1920).[28] But even here, as he finally reflects in writing upon his earlier inability to think clearly, Saunders marks out the mind—in this case, explicitly the writing mind expressing itself in prose—as the ultimate master-mediator of experience.

Apart from the role played by his body, Saunders describes his experience as being mediated by other human beings, such as his translator Subel, or the young monk Prem. Subel, in particular, whom Saunders explicitly characterizes as "media savvy,"[29] repeatedly influences Saunders's experiences. For instance, Saunders uses Subel to illustrate the critical political state of Nepal as a country, when he narrates how Subel tearfully told him stories about a woman who was unable to get medical treatment or about the arrogance of soldiers.[30] However, Saunders interprets these stories for himself, explicitly concluding that: "[p]olitical pragmatism exhausted, they're looking for something, anything, to save them."[31] It is a friend of Subel's who tells Saunders: "he hopes the meditating boy will do 'something good for this country,' meaning, to my ear, *something good for this poor, beaten-down country which I dearly love.*"[32] In both

---

25   Saunders, 239.
26   Saunders, 241.
27   Saunders, 245.
28   Yeats, *The Second Coming*.
29   Saunders, "Buddha Boy," 220.
30   Saunders, 220–221.
31   Saunders, 221.
32   Saunders, 221.

cases, Saunders describes his experience as being mediated by another human being. Nevertheless, the meaning assigned to the experience is, ultimately, determined by Saunders's own mind. In the latter case, that of Subel's friend, this is even explicitly signaled by the italicization of Saunders's mental interpretation of what was already a literal quote from the friend.

Along the same lines, Saunders narrates his first encounter with Prem. When Prem lets Saunders into the meditation site, Saunders describes their interaction as follows:

> The young monk looks me over. He's not suspicious exactly; protective, maybe. He makes me feel (or I make me feel) that I'm disturbing the boy for frivolous reasons, like the embodiment of Western Triviality, a field rep for the Society of International Travel Voyeurs.[33]

Although Saunders does not explicitly identify the interpretation of the encounter as his own, he nevertheless raises the possibility that his mind might be decisively affecting his own feelings. Thus, while leaving the source of interpretation open, Saunders's subjective feeling is characterized as a product of both the monk's behavior and his mental interpretation of the monk's behavior. Saunders once again plays up the power of his mind to shape not only his interpretation of experience, but also his emotional response thereto.

Through this depiction of the writer's mind as the master-mediator, Saunders explicitly locates the power to assign meaning within himself. As he turns this power into the object of his text and story, he communicates a self-awareness of his role as a producer of meaning, who actively produces experience and, at the same time, is decisively involved in the interpretation of this experience. He, thus, champions a radically subjective form of knowledge, rooted almost exclusively in the human mind and will.

The Buddhist Base

As detailed previously, this radical subjectivity is based on a Buddhist philosophy of the self. Still, among the powers assigned to Saunders's own mind, we find the capacity to accept meaning originating outside of Saunders himself. He bases his interpretation of the experience in Nepal on rather general

---

33   Saunders, 225–226.

premises about human nature that are, in turn, undergirded by conclusions drawn from specific experiences, much like the belief in human sameness that Saunders expresses in "The New Mecca". In "Buddha Boy," Saunders explicitly lays out his most basic convictions that shape the story as influenced by Buddhist thought. Saunders ponders the first general premise on the flight to Kathmandu:

> The mind is a machine that is constantly asking: What would I prefer? Close your eyes, refuse to move, and watch what your mind does. What it does is become discontent with That Which Is. A desire arises, you satisfy that desire, and another arises in its place. This wanting and rewanting is an endless cycle for which, turns out, there is already a name: samsara. Samsara is at the heart of the vast human carnival: greed, neurosis, mad ambition, adultery, crimes of passion ... and all of this takes place because we believe we will be made happy once our desires have been satisfied.[34]

In this passage, Saunders declares his firm belief in the basic power of desire to drive human behavior. However, he also simply acknowledges a Buddhist concept that he has come to accept. Notably, this general passage about desire comes right after he has described how he was unable to articulate his own desires on the plane:

> I decide to close my eyes and sit motionless, to make the time pass.
> Somebody slides up their window shade and, feeling the change in light on my eyelids, I am filled with sudden curiosity: Has the shade really been lifted? By someone? Gosh, who was it? What did they look like? What were they trying to accomplish by lifting the shade? I badly want to open my eyes and confirm that a shade has indeed been lifted, by someone, for some purpose.[35]

Here, Saunders presents experience, interpreted in a specific way, as personal evidence for the general assertion stated above. He also expands his idea of desire to include curiosity, understanding it as a desire to know. In so doing, he ties the concept of desire to the larger story of the genesis of the article itself, which, as detailed above, is rooted in mere curiosity, as a response to the media's tendency, or desire, to judge prematurely.

---

34 Saunders, 214–215.
35 Saunders, 214.

Samsara is not the only general idea about humankind that he explicitly imports from Buddhism. Having come across a soup kitchen, on his walk through Kathmandu, Saunders concludes by introducing another Buddhist concept closely related to samsara:

> Life is suffering, the Buddha said, by which he did not mean *Every moment of life is unbearable* but rather *All happiness/rest/contentment is transient; all appearances of permanence are illusory*.[36]

In this paragraph, Saunders even gives more details about his understanding of the idea attributed to the Buddha by contrasting two possible interpretations. Furthermore, through the use of italics, he highlights the fact that both of these are personal interpretations of possible readings. He emphasizes the fundamentally temporary nature of happiness in human life. Understood in this sense, suffering could be interpreted as not yet satisfied desire. "Not so fast," Saunders seems to say, as he immediately provides a specific, yet different interpretation of his walk through Kathmandu:

> The faceless woman, the odd-toothed woman, the dusty elderly people with babies in their laps, waiting for a meal, the blind guy by the gate, feigning indifference: In Nepal, it occurs to me, life *is* suffering, nothing esoteric about it.[37]

Saunders adopts a literal interpretation of the Buddha's statement that he rejected previously. By its nature, however, the suffering that he experiences in Nepal is still temporary; it simply appears unlikely that it will end soon.

Later on in the text, Saunders makes another explicit reference to suffering that more explicitly evokes the temporal meaning of the saying. During the cold night that Saunders spends at the boy's meditation site, he physically suffers as he freezes:

> Time slows way down. I wait and wait to check my watch. Three hours go by, slow, torturous hours. It is now, I calculate, around three in the morning. Excellent: Next will come predawn, then dawn, then the minivan, the hotel, America. As a special treat, I allow myself to check my watch.

---

36 Saunders, 217.
37 Saunders, 217.

3.2 The Mysterious Medium in George Saunders's "Buddha Boy" (2007)

> It's 12:10. Fifteen minutes — fifteen minutes? ... Dammit, shit! I find myself in the strange position of being angry at Time.[38]

Of course, as he indicates here, there is the prospect of an almost certain end to the suffering in the morning. This is why time becomes his focus, which matches the more specific meaning that he attributed to the Buddha's saying.

In a third instance, Saunders articulates another general premise about human nature that shapes his interpretation of reality in Nepal. Having prayed for loved ones at a stupa in Kathmandu, Saunders, a practicing Buddhist, elaborates on the role of fear in human existence:

> Today at the stupa, it occurs to me that this low-level ambient fear constitutes a decent working definition of the human: A human being is someone who, having lived awhile, becomes terrified and, having become terrified, deeply craves an end to the fear.[39]

As Saunders's argument outlines, his interpretation of the centrality of fear—along with desire and suffering—includes a temporal dimension that reflects the nature of human life from a Buddhist perspective. In the text, Saunders explains this general assertion in greater detail in a passage that contains the specific narration of his praying at the stupa.[40] Through prayer, Saunders locates his power, that resides in mere belief, to positively affect the future as well as to avert the harm that he fears. He also observes this faith in the power of belief in the Nepalese people's will to believe in the meditating boy's powers:

> The country is scared, wired, suffering, dreading an imminent explosion that will take a catastrophically poor country and turn it into a catastrophically poor country in a state of civil war. In Katmandu it seems everybody knows about the meditating boy, follows news of him avidly, believes he's doing what he's said to be doing, and wishes him luck. They feel him, you sense, as a kind of savior-from-within, a radical new solution to festering old problems.[41]

---

38   Saunders, 238–239.
39   Saunders, 219.
40   Saunders, 218–219.
41   Saunders, 221.

In contrast to Saunders's prayer, however, this belief in the boy's powers almost appears to be a human necessity. Faced with a catastrophic reality, people look outside of it for reasons to hope, to what *might* only be real.

The general Buddhist premises that Saunders draws on in order to make sense of his experience in Nepal, therefore, only work in concert with specific phenomenal experience. Furthermore, the connection between the general and the specific is produced and maintained by and within Saunders, and is thus marked out as both subjective and arbitrary. It is described as a product of a human mind that is aware and that understands itself as having the desire to form concepts in order to sate its desire for meaning, while, in the process, coming to understand its own function as the maker of such concepts.

Mysterious Mind-Control

The central treatment of authorial self-awareness in the text occurs in Saunders's implicit linking of his own activity of making sense with the boy's performance. While Saunders describes the workings and power of his own mind at length, as it decisively produces, processes, and interprets experience, he juxtaposes it with the possible workings of the boy's meditating mind. Ultimately, Saunders is unable to determine how the boy manages to keep up his months-long meditation process, seemingly without support. However, Saunders has arrived at the point at which he is able to assert that the boy has turned into a human medium and attained a certain imaginative power that affects how Nepali people think about reality.

By reflecting on his own mind, which exercises a similar function as a human medium, Saunders foregrounds the possibility of a human mind that is able to perform the kind of body control that the boy appears to be capable of. Saunders locates the similarity between himself and the boy in their shared humanity and its supposedly common impulse to sate physical desire, which he describes as a fight against the physical. During the night he spends at the meditation site, Saunders asks:

> What if the boy is making this fight in a new way, by struggling against the thousands-of-years-old usage patterns of the brain? What if he is the first of a new breed – or the most recent manifestation of an occasionally appear-

ing breed – sent to show us something new about ourselves, a new way our bodies and minds can work?[42]

As Saunders puts it, this mere entertainment of the possibility that the boy could be an utterly different kind of human being is itself the result of fundamental human reflexivity; it is a cognitively activated will to believe in this possibility. In the text, then, it is Saunders's awareness of the capabilities and limits of his own mind that leads him to the conclusion that the boy's story is "pretty damn mysterious."[43] This also means, however, that the decision about whether to reject or accept the possibility of the boy's being fundamentally different is entirely up to the imaginative powers of his own mind. By engaging in such an extensive display of self-reflection, Saunders emphasizes the function of religion in the subjective, but nevertheless shared human aspects of imagination at work in the complex assignment of meaning to unfathomable reality.

---

42 Saunders, 243.
43 Saunders, 244.

3.3 Aware Media in John Jeremiah Sullivan's "Getting Down to What is Really Real" (2011)

John Jeremiah Sullivan's playful "Getting Down to What Is Really Real" (2011)[1] treats the mediated self-awareness of another human being as its central topic. The text, like "Upon This Rock," was first published in *GQ*. It appeared in 2005 under the title "Leaving Reality." Sullivan then included an amended version of it, entitled "Getting Down to What is Really Real" in the 2011 essay collection *Pulphead*. In this piece, Sullivan meets with former cast members of the reality TV show *The Real World: Back to New York* (2001) and describes how their self-awareness of their status as media affects their behavior. The format, whose first season was broadcast in 1992, has arguably contributed to the popularization of self-disclosure and self-branding in Millennial youth culture.[2] Particularly in later seasons like the one written about by Sullivan, its formula shifts to a more consciously self-reflexive play with the fourth wall as producers more actively and transparently influenced the plot and characters.[3] In his piece, Sullivan contrasts the cast members' performances in reality and on TV with his own performing for readers. Having explicitly situated the cast members in a communicative relationship, Sullivan himself forms a similarly complex subjectivity. He characterizes his experience as being shaped by an inner tension between his fandom and his professional role as a writer, blurring the line between the physical experience mediated by his body and the experience of watching TV. He, thus, explicitly places the former *Real World* cast members' behavior in the context of a mediatized society and culture. At the same time, he locates within himself the urge for acknowledgment and acceptance that

---

1   Sullivan, "Getting Down To What Is Really Real."
2   Klein, "'This Is the True Story . . .': The Real World and MTV's Turn to Identity (1992 –)," 59.
3   Klein, 84–85.

he observes in cast members. In this mélange of performed identities, then, Sullivan identifies a critical potential for self-emancipation.

Technical Media and Human Plasticity

Sullivan's perspective is backed by findings in media and communications studies. Importantly, the inventions of media technologies, such as the videocamera or the computer, have contributed to the idea of a kind of plasticity of human subjectivity because, in mediated interpersonal exchange, subjectivities are performed rather than explored. The idea that human subjects develop their identities in social contexts that are akin to the performer-audience relationship in theatre goes back to American sociologist Erving Goffman's book *The Presentation of the Self in Everyday Life* (1959).[4] Goffman argued that humans play different roles depending on the social context, and distinguishes between public and private selves that are performed in order to negotiate identities. Nick Abercrombie and Brian Longhurst have extended the key distinction between audience and performer to include performances that are mediated by technological mass media. Unlike simple performances, where audience and performer are physically present, mediated performances are: "elongated in time and space and fragmented" and are marked by a different performative aesthetic based on construction.[5]

The possibilities for such mediatized performances to shape identities depend, in part, on the media technologies used. In 1995, sociologist Sherry Turkle, for instance, argued that the computer brought about the culture of simulation that Fredric Jameson had associated with postmodernism because—among other things—it created spaces for the construction and reconstruction of human identity. "In simulation", she wrote, " identity can be fluid and multiple, a signifier no longer clearly points to a thing that is signified, and understanding is less likely to proceed through analysis than by navigation through virtual space."[6] More specifically, this culture of simulation

---

4   Goffman, *The Presentation of Self in Everday Life*.
5   Abercrombie and Longhurst, *Audiences: A Sociological Theory of Performance and Imagination*, 62–63.
6   Turkle, *Life on the Screen: Identity in the Age of the Internet*, 49.

manifested itself in the possibility that humans could play different roles as virtual personae while online.[7]

Reality TV is a specific example of how technological media illuminates the performative character of identity construction as an: "extreme form of this everyday role-playing".[8] Annette Hill has argued that, more specifically, in reality TV: "producers, participants and audiences co-create cultural experiences, events and trends."[9] Hill bases her approach on sociologist Viviana Zelizer's work on connected lives and understands this co-creation not as co-operation, but as a: "mingling of economic activity and social relations."[10] This mingling is marked by people's constantly on-going acts of testing, challenging, maintaining, or reinforcing relations to each other.[11]

As performances, participants' acts in reality TV formats are mediated via camera and transmitted to viewers whose reactions are anticipated.[12] Abercrombie and Longhurst have argued that this pervading performativity has created a modern society of narcissism that treats the self as spectacle. However, these performances can also illuminate the contingencies and ambiguities of contemporary subjectivity and spark change. For instance, Beverly Skeggs and Helen Wood have argued that: "reality television makes conscious the unconscious iteration that holds the inequalities of class and gender in place"[13] because performances of personhood let audiences take on the roles of judges and critics. This "invitation to the viewer to unpack person performance" creates "moments for critical attention" and consequently "enables audiences to see how utterly incoherent, contradictory and unstable the production of subjectivity and normativity is".[14] In short, it is precisely performativity made particularly palpable by mediatization that potentially raises the awareness of postmodern subjectivity's contingent character.

---

7   Turkle, 260.
8   Hill, *Reality TV*, 52.
9   Hill, 7.
10 Hill, 8.
11 Hill, 8.
12 Hill, 52–79.
13 Skeggs and Wood, *Reacting to Reality Television: Performance, Audience and Value*, 222.
14 Skeggs and Wood, 222.

The Viewer Versus the Writer

In this piece, Sullivan appears as an intra-diegetic narrator who actively produces the experience with a very particular subjectivity. Sullivan acts both as a writer with his own intentions and as an uncritical viewer, thereby locating one of the narrative's main tensions within himself. As a writer, Sullivan explicitly states that his intention is to write about a particular social and cultural sphere that is shaped by media technology and the laws of capitalism: [T]his thing I'd heard rumors of, what I'd come to get a peep at: this little bubble economy that *The Real World* and its less-entertaining mutant twin, *Road Rules* (essentially *Real World* in an RV), have made around themselves."[15] Apart from his thematic focus, Sullivan also mentions that he actively gathers material as he concedes that his being present during his main subject's club appearance: "wasn't enough, reporting-wise."[16] As a writer moving about within a particular economic system, Sullivan also follows its rules in order to gather the material that he needs. He asks his subjects out to dinner, in order to interview them, and reports that he bought tickets for a cruise with other *Real World* personalities, although it was ultimately canceled.[17]

Apart from Sullivan's role as writer, it is also his self-characterization as a fan that is described as affecting the experience. In other words, Sullivan situates himself explicitly as viewer/voyeur and, thus, as part of the audience for whom reality TV is produced and performed. Importantly, as this kind of observer, he takes part in the validation of cast members' subjectivities.[18] For instance, Sullivan recounts that the text's main subject, a *Real World* cast member nicknamed the Miz:

> would write in his online diary that he'd been nervous, for the simple reason that I [Sullivan] was there, with my notepad and my judgments and my dubious but sincere claim of being a 'hard-core fan' of MTV's *The Real World* and its various spin-off reality series.[19]

Here, Sullivan indicates that he is not only present as a writer, but also because he is a dedicated viewer of the TV shows in which the Miz appears. Sullivan

---

15   Sullivan, "Getting Down To What Is Really Real," 91.
16   Sullivan, 100.
17   Sullivan, 100–101.
18   Hill, *Reality TV*, 64–66.
19   Sullivan, "Getting Down To What Is Really Real," 90.

even emphasizes his fan knowledge and, thus, his self-characterization as a dedicated viewer, when he recounts how he knows the name of an unpopular female *Real World* cast member, whom not even the Miz could recall.[20] Furthermore, when Sullivan takes the reality TV stars out to dinner, he tells them about his favorite moments from the show, some of which they do not even remember themselves.[21] Sullivan consequently integrates two aspects of his character that appear contradictory at first glance. On the one hand, he is a writer who needs to come up with something interesting to say about reality TV. On the other hand, Sullivan is a fan of the shows and he has watched them avidly down through the years, which makes him appear uncritical and hence unprofessional.

Indeed, these two roles are at odds in the text. On several occasions, Sullivan describes himself as being unable to perform the actions that his role as a writer demands from him, precisely because he is also a viewer. When Sullivan meets the Miz, Coral, and Melissa for dinner, for example, he describes how his excitement about actually having the opportunity to meet them in person gets in the way of his professional duties:

> I was curious to see if they were real. If all those years spent being themselves for a living had left them with selves to be, or if they'd maybe begun to phase out of existence, like on a *Star Trek* episode. But then I got distracted.[22]

The distraction, Sullivan later admits, has emotional roots:

> It took me about twenty minutes to put together what was off about our interview: I was enjoying it. Ordinarily, one is tense interrogating strangers, worried about freezing or forgetting to ask what'll turn out to be the only important question. But since we'd all sat down, I'd been totally, totally at ease.[23]

As he notes here, Sullivan feels more comfortable in his role as a fan viewer than as a professional reporter getting the material that he needs for his writing. He uses the access to the more natural or human side of his subjects as grounds for

---

20   Sullivan, 96.
21   Sullivan, 100–101.
22   Sullivan, 100.
23   Sullivan, 101.

abandoning his original intention of finding out whether the reality TV stars were still real.

Sullivan's preference for a more human role manifests itself in his refraining from actions that might otherwise be deemed as belonging to his professional duties. During the same dinner scene, for instance, when the Miz complains about viewers' lack of restraint when they approach him, even when he is eating in a restaurant, Sullivan holds himself back:

> I was about to point out to the Miz that he might seem less approachable to folks like me if he'd quit taking money to party with us at places like the Avalon Nightclub, but that seemed like a real dick thing to say to a guy who's given me so much joy over the years.[24]

Once again, Sullivan justifies his lack of professionalism by appealing to the positive feelings the Miz has produced in him. Sullivan appears even more unprofessional when he concedes that he did not conduct any further research even though it would have helped to shed further light on his subject. After being told that MTV has a psychologist on staff, who contributes to fomenting drama on set, he remains passive:

> I'd suspected there were puppeteers involved in *The Real World*, invisibly instigating 'drama,' but to think that the network had gone for it and hired a shrink? ... Turns out Dr. Laura is a psychologist, not a psychiatrist, which is better, when you think about it, because psychologists don't have to take the Hippocratic oath, and she's definitely, definitely done some harm. No chance I was going to call her.[25]

Here, Sullivan willfully ignores the fact that the self-conscious fakeness that so fascinates him about *The Real World* might have negative consequences worthy of further investigation.

Hence, it is Sullivan's own subjectivity that reveals the article's stance with respect to *The Real World*. As the joy produced by fake reality interferes with Sullivan's own reality, namely his job as writer, he willingly sides with the fake over the real, which at the same time, suggests that they might ultimately be two

---

24   Sullivan, 101–102.
25   Sullivan, 107.

sides of the same coin. In other words, in a mediatized culture the rather basic enjoyment of relatability and mere connection appear more humane than existential investigation.

The Reality of Emotion

The blending of reality with fiction is also manifested in Sullivan's depiction of experience as both primarily visual and mediated by the mind. As a viewer, Sullivan sees reality, rather than perceiving it with different sensory organs. However, it is the human body that ultimately functions as the mediator of experience as it processes perceptions through the mind and undergoes emotional responses. When Sullivan first encounters the Miz, for instance, he describes how his own perception of him was likely wrong:

> It was maybe an hour before midnight at the Avalon Nightclub in Chapel Hill and the Miz was feeling nervous. I didn't pick up on this at the time – I mean, I couldn't tell. To me he looked like he's always looked, like he's looked since his debut season, back when I first fell in love with his antics.[26]

Here, in his article's opening passage, Sullivan observes the person standing next to him in a nightclub as if he were watching him on television. Furthermore, he associates television with a kind of permanence of impression and superficiality. Sullivan describes how the Miz: "looked so utterly guileless and unselfconscious as to seem incapable of nervousness,"[27] which indirectly suggests that TV communicates a lack of self-awareness and might produce the impression of confidence. However, as hinted at above, Sullivan is contradicted by the Miz, who later writes in an online diary that Sullivan's presence made him nervous. In any case, Sullivan chastises neither TV for affecting reality negatively nor the Miz for acting. Instead, he blames himself for having drawn a conclusion about the Miz' feelings from how he looked. Experience exclusively based on visual impressions, Sullivan seems to suggest, is prone to misconceptions. Similar to the situation with Saunders in "Buddha Boy," then, Sullivan's mind acts as the main mediator of experience.

---

26   Sullivan, 89.
27   Sullivan, 90.

This agency of the mind is repeatedly emphasized—particularly with regard to the interpretation of mediated experience. It is Sullivan's mind that determines whether it is important that reality and TV be kept apart. During the dinner interview scene, for instance, it is precisely the blending of TV and reality that made him feel at ease:

> Then I saw that this light, this tremulous, bluish light playing over their faces, was the very light by which I knew them best. I'd instinctively brought them to this place in Beverly Hills, Blue on Blue, that has open cabanas around a pool, and we were lounging in one, and the light was shining on their amazing, poreless skin. How many times had I sat with them like this, by pools and Jacuzzis? How often had we chilled like this, just drinking and making points? Thousands of times. My nervous system had convinced itself we were on the show.[28]

It is Sullivan's perception of the light—once again an exclusively visual perception—that is described as making him think that he is on the actual TV show. As he makes clear in the final sentence, TV and reality blur because his nervous system—not his eyes—cannot keep the two apart.

In the text's final scene, Sullivan similarly portrays the blurring of TV and reality as being primarily visually mediated and emotionally positive. Following his rejection of the idea of calling the TV show's psychologist, Sullivan shifts his focus:

> No, I'll picture the Miz instead, and see him as he was when I was walking out of Avalon, when we said goodbye. He was dancing with that girl whose breast he had signed. They were grinding. The night had gone well. He saw that I was leaving and gave me a wave and a look, like, 'You're takin' off?' And I shouted, 'Yeah, gotta go!' And he shouted, 'Cool, bro!' and then he went back to dancing. The colored lights were on his face. People were watching.[29]

Here, too, Sullivan mainly describes the scene in visual terms and compares the dance floor to a TV set, where the actors are turned into watched objects. As in the earlier restaurant scene, however, this state of being the object of attention and special lighting is accompanied by a positive feeling. Whereas there Sullivan had described himself as feeling at ease, here he sees the Miz as being

---

28   Sullivan, 101.
29   Sullivan, 107.

in a certain state of joyful connection. Furthermore, the reality of the dance floor, as Sullivan suggests, is at least in part pleasurable for the Miz because it is TV-like. Once again, Sullivan links the processing of visual perceptions by the mind—this time merely the imagined experiences of the Miz—with a positive emotional response.

In sum, Sullivan investigates the connections between mainly visual experience with positive, emotional senses of connection and acknowledgment. In these processes, his human body functions as the master mediator, producing thoughts and emotional responses to the visual impressions. It is the quality of these responses that Sullivan uses to measure and to judge experience. Again, the questions of whether this highly mediated experience is authentic or whether reality itself might even be fake are of little interest to him.

The Fiction Within

In depicting the processing mind as the master mediator of experience, Sullivan occasionally also elaborates on its workings as a sense-maker. In these instances, he describes his mind as employing fiction either to make sense of or to communicate reality. He locates the source of the meaning of his experience in the particular consciousness of his subjectivity as a writer. In this text, this state of affairs is manifested in the different ways in which Sullivan uses imagination to round off a certain narrative or provide closure to himself. For instance, Sullivan uses it to fill in the gaps in his journalistic research as he invents quotes to capture the critical debate surrounding reality TV that serves to contextualize the argument of his text:

> There was a time when people liked to point out that reality TV isn't really real. 'They're just acting up for the cameras.' 'That's staged.' 'The producers are telling them what to do!' 'I hate those motherfuckers!' and so forth. Then there was a sort of *deuxième naïveté* when people thought, Maybe there's something real about it. 'Because you know, we can be narcissistic like that.' 'It's our culture.' 'It gives us a window onto certain...' And such things. But I would argue that *all* these different straw people I've invented are missing the single most interesting thing about reality TV, which is the way it has successfully *appropriated reality*.[30]

---

30 Sullivan, 96–97.

By admitting that he has merely invented "straw people," Sullivan mockingly draws attention to a certain formal requirement for the story to feature real people who are able to provide context for a debate. Technically, then, this invention is a means of avoiding research that Sullivan simply does not view as being necessary. As he positions himself in this imagined conversation, he downplays the need to make a clear reference to reality. In this narrow aspect, he outsources the production of a connection between text and reality to his readers, implying that they are familiar with arguments like these made by real people. Using the fictional voices of his "straw people," Sullivan's mind imaginatively—and at least partly ironically—fills in an evidentiary gap in the meta-argument about the meaning of his experience.

Elsewhere, Sullivan uses imagination in a similar way in order to ironically provide closure for an imagined story of unity. This occurs after having established the various ways in which former cast members of *The Real World* series still profit from their experience, both economically and socially. Since they seem to never leave *The Real World*, even after they have already left, Sullivan literally imagines them all together in a picture:

> A whole little picture bloomed in the mind, of all those former cast members out there, a Manson family with perfect teeth, still hanging out, still feuding, still drunkenly hittin' that (a bunch of them even lived on the same block in Los Angeles, I'd been told), all of them just going around being somebody who'd been on *The Real World*, which is, of course, a show where you just be yourself. I mean, my god, the purity of that...[31]

In this paragraph, Sullivan pokes fun at his own "whole little picture" in at least two ways by ironically claiming purity for his act of imagination. On the one hand, he critically comments on the idea of a unified body of former cast members, all just continuing their lives as if they were still on the show, doing the exact same things. On the other hand, he mocks the general idea of the "whole" image that he himself came up with, in order to get a clear, rounded sense of the story. It is significant that Sullivan, as a writer, refers to his imagination as a: "whole little picture," thereby characterizing it as closed-off, visual, and faintly ridiculous. He implies the existence of parallels between his own mental production of an image, as a reaction to the desire to find closure, and the production of images by other media, such as TV producers. However, as he

---

31   Sullivan, 93.

gently ridicules the products of his imagination, he suggests that discerning different qualities of fiction is more appealing to him than merely acknowledging their existence.

In a third case, Sullivan uses his imagination for two ends: to provide closure to an episode that almost occurred and to illustrate the strangeness of his admiration for Big Ran, a former cast member of *The Real World*. After telling the Miz, Melissa, and Coral over dinner that a cruise with other former *Real World* stars had been canceled, Sullivan imagines the possibility of a different outcome:

> They canceled the cruise. I don't know if it was for the lack of ticket sales or what, but for a brief period, I wondered if maybe I'd been the only person to purchase a ticket. And then I imagined a scenario in which, for some nitpicky contractual reason, the cruise line had been forced to go through with the package anyway, and it was just me, Big Ran, and Trishelle out there on the seas, drifting around on our ghost ship, eating foam from the chaise cushions. Sure, there'd have been some tears, some wrestling and whatnot, but in the end...[32]

Here, too, Sullivan imaginatively completes a story that, in reality, was left incomplete. Moreover, by gently ridiculing his own vision of this completion, he shifts the focus to a larger issue. Of course, the scenario of him and two former *Real World*-ers being the only people on the cruise, even having to eat cushion foam, is overly surreal. Consequently, Sullivan makes fun of his own desire to spend time with the two under any circumstances. Sullivan's imaginary scenario also ridicules his own prediction that they would all have a good time, because it is shown to be based on the assumption that he could determine the quality of his social interactions with another real human being based solely on the latter's performance on a TV show. Sullivan depicts himself as unrealistically naïve and asserts the existence of an inevitable difference between reality and reality TV, without clearly stating what this difference consists of.

To conclude, Sullivan's descriptions of the workings of imagination present a kind of closure, precisely by making fun of the idea of closure. While revealing a self-conscious desire on Sullivan's part to fill the gaps in his narratives, they also comment on their own psychological function as processes of assigning meaning to reality. Marked out as inevitably human, these reflexive func-

---

32 Sullivan, 100–101.

tions of fiction, which comment upon the workings of the medium itself, are then positioned as reflecting a core difference between human media, such as a writer, and technical media, such as a video camera. Moreover, despite all of the power that Sullivan ascribes to reality TV, they also position human consciousness as something possessing decisive and powerful agency when it comes to the representation of reality. Drawing on the powers of fiction, Sullivan's mind is described as capable of occasionally illuminating what is real, by also adducing precisely what is not.

Text As Reality Show

Sullivan's self-characterization as a self-conscious medium goes beyond mapping the workings of his inner mind; it also includes a particular concern with the performativity inherent in the communicative relationship with readers—or his own audience—that he is engaged in as writer. This concern is illustrated by his playfully colloquial voice, which seeks to communicate various senses of community between writer and readers, akin to those that exist between viewers and stars of reality TV shows. Sullivan inhabits various roles that can be situated on a spectrum stretching from a rather serious writer to someone on the brink of being smarmy with another human being. His narrative voice contributes to Sullivan's styling of the text as a performative reality show that is aware of the communicative similarities with reality TV.

At his most distant, Sullivan plays the role of a writer who mainly emphasizes that he shares a cultural background with his readers. For instance, having claimed with regard to reality TV that: "the increased awareness of complicity in the falseness of it all"[33] has made characters more real, Sullivan simply asserts: "This is where we are, as a people."[34] Here, he imagines a bigger cultural community with readers—"a people"—based on the shared experience of a reality changed by reality TV. As Sullivan goes on to observe, however, this larger community extends to include a certain communal behavior. Having described the behavior of the shows' stars—their fighting, their crying—he once again refers to the "people" he sees himself as a part of:

---

33   Sullivan, 98.
34   Sullivan, 98.

3.3 Aware Media in John Jeremiah Sullivan's "Getting Down to What is Really Real" (2011)

> Are we so raw? It must be so. There are simply too many of them – too many shows and too many people on the shows – for them not to be revealing something endemic. This is us, a people of savage sentimentality, weeping and lifting weights.[35]

In contrast to the passage above referring to consciousness, Sullivan includes himself—only reluctantly and because of its sheer size—in the same community of "people" as the cast members of reality TV shows. Nevertheless, it is a community that he imagines both himself and his readers to be a part of. For Sullivan, the distanced writer, the community not only shares a consciousness and certain behaviors, but is also rooted in the shared experience of watching reality TV. Having claimed that the demographic of the cast has changed, for instance, Sullivan asks his readers: "But now – have you watched television recently? From what can be gathered, they're essentially emptying group homes into the studio. It has all gotten so very real. Nobody's acting anymore."[36] By addressing readers directly, Sullivan rhetorically asks for reassurance that readers share the same experiential basis—having watched particular TV programs. This communal experience is even presupposed in a later passage, when Sullivan introduces a former cast member, Melissa, whom he meets for dinner with the Miz and Coral: "Melissa was on the New Orleans Season. She's the one we all saw go off on Julie that time, for the speaking-engagement shadiness."[37] Once again, the community Sullivan points to and includes himself in is a community of watchers who cannot help but identify with the people they watch and thereby have their awareness transformed.

In another, more playful role, Sullivan communicates a narrower sense of community between writer and reader that more explicitly revolves around the shared cultural experience of writing and reading the text at hand. Here, as a writer, Sullivan plays with anticipated reader response and, hence, communicates an awareness of how the roles of reader and writer are themselves performed. When Sullivan introduces the concept of *The Real World/Road Rules Challenge* shows, for instance, he starts his account with by addressing the reader in the following way: "I don't know how ready you are to admit your familiarity with the show and everything about it, so let me go through the

---

35 Sullivan, 99.
36 Sullivan, 99.
37 Sullivan, 102.

motions of pretending to explain how it operates."[38] The behavioral dynamic that he confronts here as a writer is the same one that he sees at play in reality TV. It is not that the reader might not have had the experience that Sullivan expects; it is rather that the possession of this experience in any form can be viewed as a performative act of self-fashioning. This also holds for Sullivan's interjection towards the end of his presentation of the show's overarching concept. Instead of naming the things that the candidates compete for, he simply interrupts himself with the exclamation: "oh, fuck it! You know how it works."[39] Once again, Sullivan imagines that readers might judge him for explaining himself, possibly deeming it a pedantic performance by a self-absorbed expert. In a third instance, Sullivan explicitly makes fun of readers for potentially having an expectation he does not fulfill. When Sullivan asks the Miz whether his clubbing has taken a toll on him, and the Miz merely answers that he tried not to mix drinks, Sullivan pretends to dig deeper:

> 'But what about your soul?' I said. 'Does it take a toll on your soul?' He looked down at his drink.
> Psych! I didn't ask him that.[40]

Sullivan even teases his readers here, by referring to the performativity of their role. While insinuating that they might potentially be interested in the wellbeing of a cast member's soul, he openly admits that he himself is not, thereby raising the possibility that the readers might not really care about the question either. In all of these instances, Sullivan establishes a parallel between the communicative relationship of writer and reader and of reality TV star and viewer, thereby communicating an awareness of the possibility of complicity in the performances of all of these roles.

In a third role, Sullivan associates himself a bit more closely with the role of the viewer, a role that he potentially shares with his readers. In this role, he mainly emphasizes their shared desire to have fun together that he also observes in the cast members. This desire is mainly expressed in casual asides to the reader that communicate a sense of intimacy. On one occasion, for instance, he urges the reader to imagine how the cast members' awareness of

---

38   Sullivan, 92.
39   Sullivan, 92.
40   Sullivan, 95.

their income, as stemming from the simple act of being watched, affects their behavior:

> What if my job were to be on a reality show, being filmed, having you watching me, interior auto-mediation, and so forth? What if it were my reality, bros? Are your faces melting yet?[41]

Here, Sullivan addresses readers, as a community of reality TV watchers, in the second person plural as "bros," thereby indicating a certain familiarity that is exaggerated by his, ultimately joking, rhetorical question. Elsewhere, Sullivan positions himself more clearly in this community as a fellow fan. Having been told that a bar staffed by former cast members would open in Myrtle Beach, Sullivan jokingly states that: "I might just drop in here the little facty-facty that I live an hour from Myrtle Beach, so you all can sit on that."[42] Here, he teases readers as if he were part of a rival group of fans competing for the attention of *Real World* cast members.

In the text's final episode, Sullivan's three roles or personas merge, revealing the complex subjectivity of a medium inhabiting different perspectives. After seeing the Miz dancing with a girl and admitting that he found it hard to think critically of the Miz, Sullivan addresses his readers:

> Remember your senior year in college, what that was like? Partying was the only thing you had to worry about, and when you went out, you could feel people thinking you were cool. The whole idea of being a young American seemed fun. Remember that? Me neither. But the Miz remembers. He figured out a way never to leave that place.
> Bless him, bros.[43]

In this passage, Sullivan styles himself as a detached analyst conveying a thesis about the Miz's behavior. He again jokingly plays with reader expectation and ultimately addresses the readers as "bros" to signal their shared appreciation for the Miz. Here, a composite persona emerges between cast member and readers/viewers; Sullivan has become a conscious writer/fan, acknowledging the Miz's desire for the simple fun he gets from others' attention and the

---

41   Sullivan, 98.
42   Sullivan, 103.
43   Sullivan, 108.

community thus created. Like the Miz, he also primarily enjoys his freedom to shape his own identities.

Awareness of Self-Awareness

As his personas ultimately converge, in an accepting blend of a critic/writer/fan, Sullivan also resolves the tensions between the writer and fan within himself. After all, his ultimately accepting stance toward the Miz suggests that he deems it possible to play all of these roles at once. The solution appears to reside in his awareness that his self-awareness is a conflicted medium that signals the end of the story. In accordance with the theoretical findings of Beverly Skeggs and Helen Wood,[44] Sullivan claims with regard to reality TV that a: "shift toward greater self-consciousness, this increased awareness of complicity in the falseness of it all ... made things more real."[45] In fact, Sullivan performs a similar shift toward greater self-consciousness within himself that not only makes way for the acceptance of his inner conflicts, but also works as the basis for the playful performance of different roles and for engagement in various forms of communication. Just like reality TV characters who are aware of the fact that they are performing for TV viewers, Sullivan knows himself to be a writer performing for readers. In order to be real in his corner of mediatized society, however, Sullivan turns his own self-awareness over to readers. The readers, in turn, are forced to reconsider their own awareness of the various ways in which they construct meaning themselves. This shared objectification of self-awareness then, like a common language, forms a common base for a shared understanding of mediatized reality.

---

44 Skeggs and Wood, *Reacting to Reality Television: Performance, Audience and Value*.
45 Sullivan, "Getting Down To What Is Really Real," 98.

3.4 Different Media in Mac McClelland's "Delusion is the Thing With Feathers" (2017)

In "Delusion is the Thing With Feathers" (2017),[1] Mac McClelland tells the story of a trip that she undertook with the two bird conservationists, Tim Gallagher and Martjan Lammertink, as well as a photographer to remote parts of a Cuban jungle in order to prove the existence of an exotic bird; namely, the ivory-billed woodpecker. McClelland reflects the different ways in which her female sex and gender strongly affect her experience of the dangerous expedition and her ultimate portrayal of both Gallagher and Lammertink. In the piece, McClelland describes the experience of the trip as an extreme physical and psychological performance that was driven by two determined scientists cultivating a self-sacrificing masculinity. McClelland juxtaposes the starkly diverging interpretations of the experience by herself and the scientists. She lays bare different levels of mediation as she communicates her self-awareness as a writer who intentionally produces disturbing experience in order to create a public representation of the work of two ornithologists. All the while, the scientists, in turn, intentionally produce experience to publicly assert the existence of a likely extinct bird.

McClelland was an award-winning freelance reporter whose work appeared in outlets such as *Mother Jones*, *Rolling Stone*, or *The New York Times Magazine*. Apart from the various features for which she garnered three nominations for The National Magazine Award, she was also known for the investigative undercover reporting she undertook in an Amazon warehouse, as well as the emotional exploration of her post-traumatic stress disorder after

---

[1] The story, a finalist for the National Magazine Award in Feature Writing, was originally published in the May/June 2016 issue of *Audubon Magazine* and is available online under a different title. McClelland, "Can the Ivory-Billed Woodpecker Be Found in Cuba?"

witnessing another woman's rape in her memoir *Irritable Hearts*.[2] As detailed in a 2019 feature in GQ,[3] McClelland began a sex reassignment therapy in 2018 and consequently identified as the male freelance reporter Gabriel Mac. In October 2021, his personal website read: "He formerly published under the byline Mac McClelland. He appears in a multitude of photographs online as a good-looking lady."[4] I herein stick to Gabriel Mac's former female identity as Mac McClelland because it is highly significant for the analysis of his text and because, in fact, the text was published under his former female name.

Mac McClelland's work has hitherto largely evaded the attention of scholars, much like John Jeremiah Sullivan, Michael Paterniti, and Rachel Kaadzi Ghansah. However, there are reviews of and interviews about her work that discuss its specificity as perhaps the unusually brave work of a female reporter who consciously experiences emotionally and physically difficult situations and addresses them with an uncompromising confidence and sincerity. In one discussion of McClelland's book on her PTSD, her former editor Ann Friedman calls her "badass":

> It's rare to look at someone whose chief qualities are measured thoughtfulness and open emotionality and declare her a total badass. As women carve out careers and comfortably adopt traits that were once considered "masculine," there's strong social pressure on them to mimic the stoicism that men have traditionally been expected to maintain in the face of hardship.[5]

By fearlessly acknowledging difficult experiences, and their physical and emotional consequences, Friedman argues that McClelland exemplarily emboldens other women (her readers) to act similarly. McClelland herself has admitted to consciously allowing herself to react emotionally to difficult experiences. Reacting to her characterization as "badass", she rejected the idea that this implied a repressed emotionality stating: "if you are doing these hard things but having feelings about it and processing it and like moving through it and moving on and admitting that you have vulnerabilities, I think that's more badass."[6] Elsewhere, McClelland stated: "When it comes down to it, everyone struggles,

---

2   McClelland, "Bio."
3   Mac, "The End of Straight."
4   Mac, "About."
5   Friedman, "On Being a Badass."
6   Gordon, "Love in the Time of PTSD: Mac McClelland's Irritable Heart."

so the fact that I'm saying it publicly isn't an issue if you have any sense of humanity or compassion."[7]

McClelland researched and wrote the story about the trip to Cuba on the basis of a commission by *Audubon Magazine*, where it was published in May 2016.[8] Her original assignment was to profile the two ornithologists. She was told beforehand that they would camp for five days and spend the rest of the nights in bed and breakfasts, which turned out to be untrue. Furthermore, the unsafe conditions on the reporting trip triggered a post-traumatic stress syndrome that McClelland had suffered from a previous trip to Haiti. Both the uncomfortable lodging and unsafe traveling contributed to a serious disagreement between Lammertink and McClelland who at one point seriously considered leaving the party.[9] In an interview, McClelland said: "I believe I'm generally considered cooperative and not that hard to work with, but when I'm disrespected in terms of very basic safety, because it is my life at stake, we argued a lot."[10]

Lived Bodies and Self-Sacrifice

In her text, the writer establishes her self-reflexive subjectivity in part against performed masculinity by exploring the tensions between the performativity of gender and physical realities not necessarily related to sex. Analyses of gender's fundamental contingency are typically based on the premise that gender is a construct that is deeply affected by social circumstances. In her landmark study *Gender Trouble* (1990), for instance, Judith Butler described individual gender as primarily the result of a repeated performance whose substance is only apparent: "a performative accomplishment which the mundane social audience, including the actors themselves, come to believe and to perform in the mode of belief".[11] This socially mediated individual performance of gender nevertheless always occurs in connection with the physical reality of an individual body. Therefore, sex and gender, material and symbolic categories, have

---

7 Savchuk, "Annotation Tuesday! Mac McClelland and 'Delusion Is the Thing With Feathers.'"
8 Gravitz, "Mac McClelland Tails Extreme Birders Through Cuba."
9 Gravitz.
10 Savchuk, "Annotation Tuesday! Mac McClelland and 'Delusion Is the Thing With Feathers.'"
11 Butler, *Gender Trouble: Feminism and the Subversion of Identity*, 192.

recently been conceived as integrated within the human subject. Iris Marion Young for instance, has argued that Toril Moi's concept of the lived body might be more useful for analyses of gendered identity construction because it constitutes a unified idea rather than a binary. As idea, a lived body is: "a physical body acting and experiencing in a specific socio-cultural context; it is body-in-situation."[12] On the one hand, this subject is always faced with the material realities of his or her body. On the other hand, it is also always actor in a specific social setting featuring certain constraints and a freedom to act. In this conceptualization, gender becomes a feature of social contexts rather than individual subjects. As such, it is, Young argues: "a particular form of the social positioning of lived bodies in relation to one another within historically and socially specific institutions and processes that have material effects on the environment in which people act and reproduce relations of power and privilege among them."[13]

In McClelland's reportage, the context in which lived bodies interact is scientific field research—a historically deeply gendered activity marked, made and accompanied by masculine privilege.[14] For instance, in the 19th century, discoveries and explorations of nature turned the latter into gendered spaces made accessible by way of specifically masculine scientist subjectivities.[15] Towards the end of the century, exploration became an iconic undertaking in which real men iconically countered the growing popularity of civilized urban lifestyles and mechanization by way of embodying a certain ideal of natural manliness.[16] However, this reactionary ideal of masculinity was at odds with scientific inquiry when it emphasized manly competition—in particular in polar exploration.[17] Michael Robinson has documented how the concepts of antimodern manliness and scientific inquiry had to be carefully connected and mediated by explorers. For example, in order to support the claim that he was the first person to discover the North Pole in 1909, Robert Peary contracted the female journalist Elsa Barker as a ghostwriter to tell his story more convincingly.[18]

---

12   Young, "Lived Body vs. Gender: Reflections on Social Structure and Subjectivity," 415.
13   Young, 422.
14   Milam and Nye, "An Introduction to Scientific Masculinities."
15   Reidy, "Mountaineering, Masculinity, and the Male Body in Mid-Victorian Britain"; Robinson, "Manliness and Exploration: The Discovery of the North Pole."
16   Robinson, "Manliness and Exploration: The Discovery of the North Pole," 94–95.
17   Robinson, 90.
18   Robinson, 99–103.

Conversely, science and manliness were also connected in the crafting of the figure of the self-sacrificing explorer. Fearless men's long, precarious forays into untamed wilderness were thought to foster a deeper kind of self-knowledge of humanity at large. For instance, following his first attempt at climbing Mount McKinley, the mountaineer Robert Dunn claimed in 1907 that explorers were:

> human beings tamed by the centuries, then cast out to shift for themselves like the first victims of existence—they must offer the best field of all to help this knowledge of ourselves. He knows life best who has seen it nakedest, and most exotic.[19]

This shaping of an ideal masculine subjectivity in the service of a greater human cause required a great deal of sacrifice. As science had become professionalized by the last quarter of the 19th century, exploratory methods that caused physical or material suffering gained traction in scientific circles. The popular method of exploration among male scientists, Rebecca Herzig has argued, entailed: "an ability to suffer social isolation, financial impoverishment, even physical pain."[20]

Importantly, for white men, suffering also served an epistemological purpose. As the documentation of discoveries proved insufficient or even fallible, concerns with explorers' sincerity and trustworthiness grew, and their bodies stepped in as evidence. "The visible evidence of the experience of physical hardship", Herzig writes, "helped to assure the trustworthiness of the explorer and generate assent to his assertions."[21] Although, in large parts, it might have been constructed reflexively, the subject of the self-sacrificing discoverer, then, was never constructed independently. Still, it is one of McClelland's main points that self-sacrificing scientists are unique enough subjects—and the specificities of their performed identities intriguing because they also carry a potential for change.

---

19 Dunn, *The Shameless Diary of an Explorer*, 3–4.
20 Herzig, *Suffering for Science: Reason and Sacrifice in Modern America*, 71.
21 Herzig, 79.

The Different Professional

McClelland establishes this perspective in part via the tensions with her own subjectivity. As the grim natural environment constantly reminds the party of writers and explorers of their shared humanity, McClelland distances herself from the two scientists as she asserts her own subjectivity as female writer. In this self-positioning, however, her different sex is secondary as it appears only as a feature of her, more generally, different body in a specific situation shared with other bodies. This construction of an alienated subject is emphasized in the text in which McClelland even self-distancingly she refers to herself in the third person. She makes the conditions of her produced experience transparent, reflects on her eventual writing about the experience and distinctively sets herself apart as the party's only female member. Taken together, these facets of her distinct professional subjectivity create the impression of a particular human medium, different from the scientists producing experience in order to eventually communicate it in written text. McClelland characterizes herself as having a clearly defined assignment and, consequently, as producing the experience intentionally. However, she is not alone in having the job to document the two birders' actions. As she repeatedly mentions, McClelland is accompanied by a photographer. At one point, she even explicitly refers to herself and the photographer as "the media".[22] Occasionally along with the photographer, McClelland describes the media as carrying out a job that is markedly different from that of the two scientists. For instance, she narrates how her preparation for the trip differed from theirs when they were preparing to camp at the Cuban national park's visitor center in Taco Bay:

> Everyone, even the birders, hated the bathroom, a multiperson outhouse that did not enjoy much in the way of maintenance. When the supply of potable water they'd hauled in ran out, the writer taught herself how to use the $ 250 worth of water-filtration and UV-sterilization equipment she had bought before embarking (she and the photographer, who are accustomed to hardships but of a different kind, have discovered they are wearing matching new pairs of technical wicking antimicrobacterial quick-drying underpants). Gallagher helped her purify water for the group, impressed with how much more convenient it was than a camping straw, which filters

---

22 McClelland, "Delusion Is the Thing with Feathers," 8.

bacteria one sip at a time and does not filter viruses and which was all he carried in his bag[23]

By detailing how the water filter she brought on the trip was different from Gallagher's device, she communicates the professional awareness that she expected the trip to be a particular kind of work that required certain equipment necessary to performing the job. Furthermore, the mention that she brought the same pair of underpants as the photographer associates her equipment needs with his. Together with her aside, which they both were accustomed to a different kind of hardship, her selection of equipment characterizes herself as having a profession with distinct requirements. This self-characterization is sharpened by McClelland's more personal interpretations of her professional role. For instance, McClelland explicitly ties her judgment of the travel conditions in the group's rental car to her job:

> At breakfast the writer again expressed her wish that there were seatbelts, which she generally tries to secure on work trips when she is in charge of logistics; while the photographer kindly validated her feelings by saying this was a normal human desire, Lammertink did not deign to respond.[24]

Similar to her comment about the equipment, McClelland here mentions her desire for certain safety measures in order to counteract the trip's uncertainty. As she mentions that she generally secures seatbelts on work trips, she also hints at the potentially hazardous nature of her job in general. As the photographer shares her concern, while Lammartink ignores it, their belonging to separate professional camps is established.

McClelland further marks her subjectivity as professional with the different types of research that she performs. Apart from the trip to Cuba, she also produced material relevant to the story through various reporting activities. For instance, she visited the Cornell Ornithology Lab, where Gallagher and Lammertink provided several stuffed ivory-billed woodpeckers: "for the writer to inspect before heading to Cuba."[25] She also mentions that she talked to other expert ornithologists.[26]

---

23 McClelland, 6.
24 McClelland, 4.
25 McClelland, 9.
26 McClelland, 14–15.

However, McClelland also explicitly characterizes herself as a writer whose job it is to process experienced reality in ways different from the scientists whom she accompanies. When the group spends a rainy night in a Cuban military outpost, McClelland comments on the connection between experience and storytelling:

> 'This will be a great story to tell later,' he [Gallagher] keeps saying. He's been saying this for six days. He will continue to say it for eight more. But the writer is in no mood to agree with the principle that a good story is better than a good time, partly because she has become afflicted with diarrhea – the group has concluded that there must have been an accidental ingestion of a drop from the Bahia de Taco vat of river water – but also because people (read: men) who constantly tell stories of bad times are tedious, and she is basically certain she could write an equally compelling scene if this Cuban restricted-jungle military outpost in the mountains above Guantánamo had turned out to be home to a team of scrappy dogs attired in miniature formalwear and trained to serve cocktails – which would be a good time[27]

What stands out in this passage is McClelland's clear differentiation from the researchers regarding the basic component of her job, namely storytelling. The writer McClelland makes clear that she does not share the premise that only bad experiences make for good stories. On the one hand, she associates this rejection with confidence in her storytelling skills as a writer who is supposed to turn all kinds of experience into a compelling textual product. On the other hand, she also explains her stance with her sex and gender as she associates the penchant to put oneself in danger in order to brag about it with a certain kind of masculinity that is connected to the ornithologist's professional identity. Ultimately, it is the combination of professional conventions, personal role interpretation, and physical difference that clearly characterizes McClelland's lived body as being different from the male researchers whom she accompanies.

Mediating Body and Mediated Bird

As her concern with safety indicates, McClelland describes their human experience on the birding trip as physically wrested from the natural environment.

---

27 McClelland, 14.

This physical act is performed by the human body, which assumes presence in a particular place and consequently endures its conditions. In the narrative, this physical presence is rooted in the performing subjects' physical strength and willpower. Importantly, however, McClelland does not scrutinize the particular physical mediation of the human body through its sensory organs in these moments of endured presence. She appears more interested in the mere willingness to experience, which occupies the text's central focus. Hence, she narrates how the physical difference of her female body potentially affects the mediation of experienced reality, given that her mere willingness and capability to experience reality differ from the birders' experience. In addition to the human body, however, reality is also described as mediated by media technology, which offers further possibilities to objectify nature by way of storing and reproducing experience. This is demonstrated via the ultimately unfound bird, whose potential existence can—apart from the oral testimony of human witnesses—mainly be accessed through photographs, sound, and video recordings.

As hinted at above, McClelland characterizes her writer persona as having a different body, which results in her perceiving reality as being more precarious or dangerous. This difference is established in an early scene in which McClelland lays out the driving conditions on the trip. After having expressed her desire to wear seatbelts, as discussed above, McClelland is made aware that she has different physical needs by Gallagher.

> Gallagher, maybe a bit tipsily, had slapped her knee and laughed about it the night before as their young driver sped the proto-jeep away from the airport around the proliferation of horse-drawn carts on the street in the dark. Now, as they prepared to drive the first three of the many, many hours they'd spend on Cuban roads over two weeks, Lammertink invited the writer to cram herself into the only place she would fit, between him and the driver. 'It'll just be much more fatal in an accident,' he said of sitting in the front, then laughed.[28]

McClelland, being laughed at for her differing safety demands, describes herself as subject to the paternalism of Gallagher and Lammertink, the men in power. Consequently, as she suggests here, her femininity might not be the only reason for her craving of seatbelts, but also the very reason for why her

---

28   McClelland, 4–5.

demand is not met. She further designates her body as less resilient than her travelers' bodies as she is the only member of the group who comes to suffer from diarrhea.[29] Partly, this leads to her particular need for privacy when she observes that their place to spend one of the first nights, a simple room in a military outpost, contains: "a toilet that in addition to being The Worst has no door to separate anyone who's using it from her comrades."[30] McClelland further designates the diarrhea as the cause for a further weakening of her body. She narrates that, following the night at the military outpost, the: "writer, who has been ingesting food but has effectively not eaten in two days because of the diarrhea, becomes too weak to stand; they put her on a mule."[31] Despite the reality of her female sex she, nevertheless, rests at observing a mere difference in resilience or tolerance for suffering between herself and her co-travelers. This difference is never explicitly attributed to her difference in sex. Moreover, it is due much more to the scientists's performance than McClelland's. Simply put, they appear much more masculine than McClelland female.

In contrast to her own body, McClelland paints the bodies of her male co-travelers as resiliently enduring hardships imposed on them by nature. These characterizations result both from observations on the trip itself and from historical episodes relayed to McClelland. On the trip itself, McClelland explicitly refers to the birders' physical strength. Sixty-five-year-old Gallagher is characterized ambiguously. On the one hand, McClelland paints Gallagher as enduring when she describes his behavior on the drive to Farallones. In the car, she writes that he: "bounced his old bones about in the back with zero complaints and inhuman patience". On the other hand, she also notes that, just like herself, he had to be put on a mule because he was "growing increasingly tired".[32] McClelland only alludes to Lammertink's physical condition once, towards the end, when McClelland notes in passing that he: "can endure almost anything but cannot abide an unshaven face".[33] In general, both scientists appear to be more physically resilient, and thus capable of producing different kinds of experience, than McClelland herself.

These personal observations of male physical resilience are supported by narratives of male suffering, as McClelland tells historical episodes of the two

---

29 McClelland, 14.
30 McClelland, 14.
31 McClelland, 16.
32 McClelland, 16.
33 McClelland, 19.

birders' research trips. For instance, as they have told her themselves, they both took a birding trip to Mexico where they managed to both enter and exit an area violently dominated by a drug cartel virtually unscathed.[34] Furthermore, they also once went on a trek in Argentina where they were bit by mosquitoes carrying botfly eggs. McClelland relays:

> Lammertink said nothing about the pain but Gallagher caught him flinching once as one crunched away at the shoulder tissue under his skin. (Gallagher himself finally reached a breaking point and dug his infestation, and his skin and thigh tissue, out wholesale with a knife.)[35]

McClelland also notes that Gallagher has repeatedly suffered from diarrhea and, once in Mexico, even contracted Hepatitis A.[36] A "partial list of untreated-water tragedies" for Lammertink even includes the death of a field assistant from diphtheria.[37] Taken together, these episodes make the two birders appear to be almost heroically resilient. However, McClelland marks this resilience as a narrative construct only partially rooted in reality. Although never directly asserted, the sources of these episodes have to be Lammertink and Gallagher themselves. Through the narration of their experiences McClelland hints at the possibility that their remembered physical resilience is not a future given but, more likely, a psychological necessity. To make this case, she invokes another researcher, Saul Weidensaul. With reference to the dangerous night hike that they undertake in Cuba, he argues that: "part of that just becomes if you've gotten away with it in the past, you assume you're gonna get away with it in the future".[38] Seen from this angle, the past heroics Lammertink and Gallagher reveled in offer them justifications for taking risks in the present. Their bodies then, while being real physical media that make experience possible, are also contingent objects of narrative construction that inevitably differ temporally and qualitatively from their real referents.

This is also true for the object of their physical efforts itself, the ivory-billed woodpecker. In the evident absence of its real existence in Cuba, the bird is only present as a sign whose mediated relationship to its referent is utterly

---

34 McClelland, 6–7.
35 McClelland, 7.
36 McClelland, 6.
37 McClelland, 16.
38 McClelland, 15.

uncertain. There are, for instance, the several initially promising human witnesses who each ultimately turn out to be highly unreliable.[39] Even the different technologies used to objectively prove the species' existence carry the inherent uncertainty of media products. For example, McClelland observes that Martjan Lammertink has become doubtful of the hitherto most certain proof of the bird's existence in Cuba, namely photographs:

> But maybe, he thinks now, the birds weren't there then, in the few remaining patches of pine forest where American researcher George Lamb *definitely* saw (and obtained photographic proof of) them in 1956, the last such universally accepted records on Earth.[40]

The main tension in this passage rises from the juxtaposition of Lammertink's doubt with the italicization of *"definitely"* that suggests absolute certainty regarding the other researcher's early sighting. McClelland marks the truth regarding the sighting in the absence of concrete physical experience as necessarily contingent upon subjective belief in the photograph's authenticity. This is also the case for a sighting by Gallagher captured on video, which McClelland describes as being: "highly contested as proof"[41] and as a: "catalyst of the highest-profile birder fight in modern history."[42]

However, not only is the mediated bird the inevitable harbinger of uncertainty in the text, but it is also a means to access the possibly real woodpecker. This is illustrated in the researchers' use of Lammertink's hand-built double-knocker and a recording of the bird. After imitating the sound of a woodpecker with his device, Lammertink also plays a recording over the speakers.

> After ten double-knocks, he put the dowels down, picking up his MP3 player and speaker. He scrolled through his playlist, then pressed play, holding the speaker aloft as the recording of an ivory-bill, the only existing recording of an Ivory-bill, from 1935, played, underlain by heavy static. People say it sounds like a horn. Or a baby goat. *Kent. Kent-kent.*[43]

---

39 McClelland, 18.
40 McClelland, 10.
41 McClelland, 9.
42 McClelland, 21.
43 McClelland, 11–12.

McClelland describes the recording of the bird, although used as the most authentic means to attract a live one, as highly inauthentic partly because it carries an interfering trace of mediation. However, if mediated representations of its call cannot accurately represent the almost certainly extinct bird, this of course carries an upside. For there "have been times", McClelland explains:

> when Lammertink used the double-knocker in places where he knew for a fact *Campephilus* woodpeckers [a slightly different species] were nearby (-slash-existed), and they didn't respond. To get one to do so on this trip in a territory this large, he conceded to the photographer, would be very lucky. To not get one proves nothing.[44]

In the above passage, then, even technical mediation is described as inevitably ambiguous and contingent. It can itself neither fully prove nor exclude the existence of a bird because it can only function as a sign of the bird, not as the bird itself.

Consequently, the body of a human subject remains the main producer and mediator of experience. It is a human subject who exerts the agency over the technologies of mediation mentioned. It is a human subject who chooses to acknowledge or to discard their authenticity. It is a human subject who willfully exposes his or her body to the perils of the real world in order to create experience in the first place. In the text, then, the concrete qualities of human bodies matter precisely because there is nothing beyond physical human presence over which to assert knowledge. When Gallagher returns to McClelland's hotel room after unsuccessfully questioning the last witness, McClelland describes him as devastated: "I mean", he says, "I'm the most optimistic person in the world, and it was just ... inescapable to me. And I almost felt guilty, as though, like, me giving up made it so."[45] As long as there are no humans in Cuba to witness their existence, their hypothetical existence does not matter.

Between Cynicism and Necessity

More collective ethical concerns move into focus as McClelland anchors epistemological and ontological concerns in the individual human subject. The main

---

44   McClelland, 12–13.
45   McClelland, 20–21.

difference between McClelland and the birders as media is not the one between their bodies, but between their willingness to push their bodies in collective action. Consequently, one of the narrative's main tensions is located in the interpretation of the group's actions in Cuba. McClelland, on the one hand, describes her writer persona as reacting with cynicism to the birders' actions. The birders, on the other hand, initially view their actions as normal and necessary and only gradually open up to sharing the same grains of the doubt held by McClelland. McClelland is between the two extreme positions of necessity and incomprehension and by simply exhibiting this, she offers readers a potential sense or meaning in the group's efforts in Cuba.

Despite her inability to make sense of the two researchers' disregard for basic safety, McClelland's writer persona does not directly condemn their behavior. Instead, she expresses her disagreement in cynical passages that distance herself from the birders. Following the disagreement on the use of seatbelts mentioned above, for instance, she asserts her own position:

> Lammertink invited the writer to cram herself into the only place she would fit, between him and the driver. "It'll just be much more fatal in an accident," he said of sitting in the front, then laughed, the fact that car accidents cause the most American deaths abroad being funny.
> Ha!
> But of course, this is *birding*. Go dangerous or go home.[46]

McClelland here shows her disagreement with Lammertink's quip by first ironically laughing herself and then, again ironically, suggesting that birding is inherently dangerous. Thus, she questions the overall endeavor in which she nevertheless takes part because it makes her feel unsafe. However, McClelland also distances herself from behavior that only threatens the ornithologists' own health. When Gallagher helps her filter water, for instance, she notes how he was:

> impressed with how much more convenient it was than a camping straw, which filters bacteria one sip at a time and does not filter viruses and which was all he carried in his bag, though he has neither a naiveté about waterborne illness nor an ironclad digestive tract. A partial list of places where Gallagher has suffered severe gastrointestinal distress includes:

---

46 McClelland, 5.

Mexico, Costa Rica, and Peru. In Mexico, he also got Hepatitis A. Which is a virus.[47]

Here, McClelland cynically expresses her non-comprehension about Gallagher's lack of concern with his own health by simply juxtaposing his use of a straw filter, which is unable to filter viruses, with the fact that he had once contracted a virus. He appears simply unwilling to sufficiently care for himself.

Her cynicism also extends to the entire group's collective actions. When their jeep gets stuck, despite the warnings of national park staffers that it might not be able to complete a portion of their trip, they have to violently force oxen to pull the car out of the mud:

> After a couple of hours of this, Gallagher turns to the writer and remarks, "This gives you a little idea of how hard it is to study these birds. And why nobody's doin' it."
> It grows dark.
> It starts to pour.
> Really, she has no idea.[48]

McClelland here again reacts with irony to Gallagher's statement which, in the context of the predicted difficulty of the passage due to the jeep's apparently bad condition and the bad weather forecast, appears misplaced. Commenting on the same scene, McClelland even more explicitly questions the group's actions by way of the photographer. As they are witnessing the treatment of the oxen, the photographer asks her:

> "Do you ever wonder if this is all worth it? For a bird?" The two of them snickered darkly. Just moments before, a chunk of wood had cracked off an oxen-beating club as it broke over the animal's hide and shot past the photographer's head, missing him maybe by an inch. "One that almost definitely doesn't exist?"[49]

The question of the entire project's meaning looms large over all of the cynical passages and throughout the entire article. It expresses the main tension

---

47 McClelland, 6.
48 McClelland, 8.
49 McClelland, 14.

in McClelland's narrative. However, McClelland, with her irony, cynicism, and explicit distancing only raises the question without answering it and contrasts it with the two birders' largely uncompromising, determined actions.

In much of the text, Lammertink and Gallagher appear as archaic figures similar to the supposedly historical self-sacrificing explorers. They seem driven, almost obsessively, to find the ivory-billed woodpecker in Cuba. They seem willing to do whatever it takes, even risking their own lives. For instance, this is illustrated in their decision to make a dangerous hike downhill after the jeep has broken down:

> That night, after hours of human pushing and oxen pulling, the jeep is freed. And with more pushing and pulling, it is rolled backward, and pop-started. But it cannot make it up the now rain-slicked mountain rock, though the driver tries for a terrifying twenty minutes with all the equipment and group again loaded inside. There is a Cuban military outpost a ways back down; the group makes its way there in the downpour, in the dark, and begs a patch of concrete floor to sleep on in a dwelling containing what Gallagher will refer to for the rest of the trip and maybe the rest of his life as The Worst Toilet in the World.[50]

On the one hand, McClelland here only dryly describes the dangerous, albeit unnecessary in hindsight, collective actions of the group based on decisions made by Lammertink and Gallagher. On the other hand, she also breaks the hitherto painted image of Gallagher as an unfeeling, at times even unreasonable, research machine by showing that he hates the toilet. Even the birders, despite their obvious difference from McClelland, can appear aware of their own needs as humans. At this point, however, McClelland nevertheless reacts with irony to the birders' display of self-awareness. After a mule dies, McClelland describes Gallagher as tracking back his earlier claim about birding: "'This is not what normal birding is like,' Gallagher clarifies at some point to the writer, in case this has been lost on her."[51] She ironically acknowledges that Gallagher shares her interpretation, but she still distances herself from him. However, her distancing does not carry the pessimistic quality of much of her earlier cynical passages. Ultimately, when Lammertink admits to the riskiness of some of his work, adding that: "it's always for some kind of conservation project, and if

---

50 McClelland, 13–14.
51 McClelland, 16.

something goes terribly wrong, at least in my last moments, I know it was for some greater cause,"[52] she refrains from commenting at all, simply acknowledging his self-reflection.

While Lammertink and Gallagher ultimately appear more aware of themselves as humans, and are dedicated to a cause bigger than themselves, the distance that McClelland takes from their actions by showing her own ways of interpretation nevertheless opens a wide gap between the subjectivities of the female writer and the male researchers. This divergence between two kinds of aware subjectivities, with different ways of internal mediation sharing the same experiences, works to create a sense of sincere indeterminacy. After all, while criticizing the birders' concrete actions, McClelland never openly condemns their effort as being totally useless, but ultimately cautiously admits that the: "birders' passion does bring maybe balance but certainly conservation successes sometimes to this planet."[53] Furthermore, the divergence between the writer's and the scientists' subjectivities also works on the communicative level with readers, given that it marks the respective positions as ambiguous and utterly dependent upon both context and social interaction.

Productive Difference and the Possibilities of Delusion

Consequently, and despite the occasional cynicism, the difference that McClelland exhibits between herself and the birders, as two different kinds of human media, attains a productive quality throughout the text. It is precisely this difference that opens the possibility for mutual future understanding and acknowledgment as it sheds light on both subjectivities and marks them as both fluid and changeable. Despite their differences, MacClelland's self-reflection as medium also suggests basic, but clear similarities, between herself and the birders anchored in their shared humanity. Just like McClelland performs a specific kind of subjectivity to tell the public about the scientists' work, they themselves put in an effort to perform specific subjectivities affected by the conventions of their professional roles. McClelland merely acknowledges this similarity in difference. Elsewhere, she makes this point even more explicitly: "Nobody's right but nobody's wrong. People are just different. I think humans

---

52 McClelland, 19.
53 McClelland, 22.

are the most interesting thing of anything",⁵⁴ McClelland states in the interview on her birding story.

In the penultimate paragraph, McClelland writes that the photographer and writer: "don't understand, haven't understood, the risks the birders take. But one could argue that the writer and photographer do—that they are on this very trip doing—the same for their own work."⁵⁵ What is central here is her interjection "haven't understood", which signals the preliminary nature of the incomprehension that she claims for herself and on behalf of the photographer. Her awareness of the always only preliminary character of her own comprehension explains the site at which she draws parallels between her own work and that of the researchers. Just as the birders have not yet managed to ascertain the existence of the woodpecker, she herself has not yet been able to understand their actions. However, as Gallagher clarifies, invoking a fishing metaphor,⁵⁶ this does not mean they cannot succeed in the future. More existentially, the possibilities that are inherent in temporality apply to all of the text's reflexively produced subjectivities. Despite all of the irritation it begets, for McClelland, the masculine ornithologists' self-sacrifice is only a temporary trait of their reflexive identities that is not naturally connected to their bodies, but is an expression of their will to transform material reality. This interpretation of MacClelland's experience is further illustrated by the story's original title, which refers to a poem by Emily Dickinson. "'Hope' is the thing with feathers –", written in 1862, uses the bird as a metaphor to illustrate the aspiring character of hope.⁵⁷ With its reference to the poem, the title of McClelland's text suggests similar qualities in Gallagher and Lammertink's delusional undertaking. On a larger level, then, McClelland suggests that their temporary delusion carries the possibility of and signifies hope for a different future.

---

54   Gravitz, "Mac McClelland Tails Extreme Birders Through Cuba."
55   McClelland, "Delusion Is the Thing with Feathers," 22.
56   McClelland, 21.
57   Vendler, "314," 119.

3.5 The Possibilities of Reflexivity

It is the juxtaposition of the authors' specific reflexivities, and their human subjects, that makes for the central tensions in the three texts that were analyzed. As the writers as human media illuminate the equally mediate character of their human subjects, they thematize the very plasticity of human subjectivity. Thus, they unearth very specific possibilities and limits of reflexivity. In "Buddha Boy", for instance, Saunders ends up focusing on the will to control one's own desire which affects both his own and the boy's subjectivity. In "Getting Down to What Is Really Real", John Jeremiah Sullivan examines the very performativity that occupies the core of mediated human interaction, which increasingly spotlights the social component of reflexive subjectivity in mediatized cultures. In "Delusion is the Thing With Feathers", Mac McClelland unearths the performative, self-reflexive narrative justifications that inform both her own and her subjects' behavior under extreme circumstances.

The shared characteristics of the writers and their subjects in each case then, concern human nature rather generally. Each text could, thus, be read as an act of human self-examination that initially locates a fundamental similarity marked by performative self-making between writer and subject. This similarity's core characteristic, however, is an equally fundamental difference whose temporal nature carries the possibility for future change. These analyses of human subjectivity's core insight is the very contingent connection between any specific past, present, and future human subjectivity. As a consequence, any "objective treatment" of human subjects—be it by way of institutionalized behavior or technological standardization—that seeks to assert any kind of unity or certainty appears fundamentally futile.

However, in every text analyzed, this radical rejection of objectivity does not result in a sense of loss or nostalgia. Instead, all three writers seem to argue that the human difference also unearthed by the specific limits of reflexivity most fundamentally carries with it the possibilities for change. In Saunders's text, the asserted possibility that the boy could control his desires to such a large degree of course implies the possibility that any other human might be capable of the same. In Sullivan's piece, the mutual awareness of the differences and similarities between audience and performer carries the possibility for a deeper, more humane connection. In McClelland's reportage, the mere acknowledgment of the strong influence of mere narrative self-justification opens the door for more careful future action than the birders' current self-destructive behavior.

Furthermore, on a deeper level, this openness to possibilities for change fundamentally resists the reproduction of human experience. Thus established as singular, temporary and changeable, it also appears irreproducible. In the place of reproducibility as one of the main features of human experience affected by mediatization steps a willingness of the experiencing human subject to engage in a continuous dialogue about the meaning of performative self-making.

Different from the previous group of case studies on experiences of community concerned with the possibilities of change in groups of humans, writers here identify the main potential for such change in individual subjects keenly aware of their reflexive possibilities.

However, importantly, their optimism regarding these possibilities as well as their openness to playfully explore the freedoms of identity construction is contingent upon the material reality of the social world they choose to experience. This is shown in the upcoming final chapter of case studies. U.S. culture and society do not always present these possibilities for individual and collective identity construction. Certainly not by themselves and certainly not to everybody.

4 On Real Fragmentation: Mediating Violence

4.1 Material and Symbolic Violence

If individual and collective possibility makes up a central aspect of contemporary reality in the U.S., so does impossibility. Individual and collective freedom to make and change is not a given. To the contrary, a big chunk of journalistic work is concerned with stories of not primarily the human making or changing of connections but their violent fragmentation or breaking under the pressures of certain structures and abuses of individual and collective power. Ties can not only be strengthened or improved. It is also within the realm of possibility of human interaction that they worsen, and, in the case of violent death, are erased permanently.

The following case studies, then, take a closer look at authorial self-reflection in the face of different kinds of violence in contexts of power that address different degrees of individual and collective responsibility. The first text, by George Saunders, is concerned with the structural and collective yet not necessarily lethal violence of homelessness. The second text, Michael Paterniti's reportage, examines the nevertheless collective violence of singular acts of mass shootings. And the final text by Rachel Kaadzi Ghansah positions racial violence as a fundamental responsibility of White America.

As I will show, these texts have a lot in common with the ones previously analyzed, in terms of the self-reflection of the authors as human media. However, in many ways they can be set apart from the texts discussed in chapter two or three. Violence and death, the issues at stake, are more existential. Consequently, there is less room for the emphasis of play and free expression in language. In face of grave matters of existential material destruction, emphasis on the possibilities of symbolic self-making simply will not do.

Overall, compared to the previous six texts, we might observe a shift from the symbolic to the material that takes ethical matters more seriously. In these texts, it is certainly more relevant that the writers exist in reality; that they have themselves bodies that they put on the line. This does, of course, imply a shared humanity. But in these instances, this shared humanity is not cause for celebration but for the taking of responsibility. Language and mediation matter more in these texts, and it is evident that the connection of material worldmaking and symbolic sensemaking is emphasized with a different kind of urgency.

This is noteworthy, because, intuitively, the physical harming of others appears as entirely a physical matter. After all, the swinging of a fist or the pulling of a trigger are primarily physical acts. Words cannot break bones or pierce skin. However, crucially, every act of violence is also a communicative act that carries symbolic meaning tied to its material effect. Violence thus is a fundamental part of human experience as it influences both human cooperation and reflexive self-making. Importantly, as mediatization transforms human experience, it also affects the ways in which humans individually and collectively employ violence to shape individual and collective identity. "When one has been hurt by new technology, when the private person or the corporate body finds its entire identity endangered by physical or psychic change, it lashes back in a fury of self defense", Marshall McLuhan and Quention Fiore have argued. "When our identity is in danger, we feel certain that we have a mandate for war. The old image must be recovered at any cost."[1]

Furthermore, mediatization also affects the ways in which humans react to and make sense of acts of violence. If technical mediation lends its hands to spatializing and compartmentalizing forces, it might favor the interpretation of acts of violence as more narrowly mere physical acts and push their potential symbolic meanings into the background. The degree to which acts of violence are considered physical or symbolical matters is highly relevant to how a society reacts to past violence, and potentially informs future transgressions.

Writers consider these reciprocities as they reflect on violence in a mediatized society and culture such as the United States. The three texts analyzed in this chapter look at real manifestations of violence and process disturbing events in conjunction with writerly self-reflection to promote a specifically human mediation. Writers intertwine the material effects of physical violence with more abstract symbolic acts of mediation involved in the making of individual and collective identity in each of the texts examined. By way of displayed self-reflection, the writers exemplarily address real violence's material and symbolical causes and effects. Their texts are both evaluations of real physical violence and comments upon this same violence's very mediation, as well

---

1 McLuhan and Fiore, *War and Peace in the Global Village: An Inventory of Some of the Current Spastic Situations That Could Be Eliminated by More Feedforward*, 97.

as upon the ways in which material and symbolic aspects of meaning intersect in acts of violence. Thus, they again emphasize the singular and subjective human experience of violence and delineate their approach from any simplistic reproduction of violent experience associated with technological mediation.

In his piece of reportage, George Saunders connects the structural violence of homelessness to communication's social aspects. In his texts on mass shootings, Michael Paterniti considers the similarities between acts of deadly gun violence and industrial mass media's coverage of these acts. Rachel Kaadzi Ghansah explicitly understands her uncompromising profile of a racist mass murderer as a response to American society and culture's collective racist amnesia.

Perhaps somewhat paradoxically, violence involves the forceful restriction of certain possibilities of human interaction and self-making analyzed earlier. Nevertheless, as such, violence can also be an instrument of the reflexive personal or collective building and maintaining of identity. Broadly, it has been understood as: "violation of the self-same in its purity by an external other."[2] Based on the French philosopher Emmanuel Levinas' work, Hent de Vries argues more specifically that:

> violence can be found in whatever narcissistic strategy the self adopts to capture, thematize, reduce, use, and thus annul or annihilate the other. Violence can likewise be found wherever some otherness engulfs or seizes upon the self and forces it to participate in what it—in and of itself and, precisely, as other—is not.[3]

This spotlight on violence's universal character is important because it illuminates connections between the rather abstract acts of identity formation and the concrete acts involved in physical violence.

Despite violence's universal character, understandings of specific instances of violence differ in many respects. For instance, the World Health Organization (WHO) defines violence as:

> The intentional use of physical force or power, threatened or actual, against oneself, another person, or against a group or community, that either results

---

2   de Vries and Weber, "Introduction," 1.
3   de Vries, "Violence and Testimony," 16.

in or has high likelihood of resulting in injury, death, psychological harm, maldevelopment or deprivation.[4]

However, according to Toby Miller, there exist: "differences between state, collective, and interpersonal violence, between planned and passional violence, and between fatal and non-fatal forms."[5] Furthermore, he argues that non-physical forms of violence such as violence-inciting hateful rhetoric can also be counted as violence.

Some scholars also argue that violence does not have to be as directly perceived as, for instance, the blow of a fist swung into a man's head. As a constitutive aspect of the reflexive self-definition of contemporary Western societies such as the U.S. violence can also attain a collective, even normalized and generally tolerated character in the form of structural violence; in contrast to direct, intentional violence such as warfare, structural violence in part refers to unintentional actions by systems, structures, or institutions rather than human beings. In 1969, the Norwegian social scientist Johan Galtung wrote: "Violence with a clear subject-object-relationship is manifest because it is visible as action. ... Violence without this relation is structural, built into structure."[6]

Structural violence, he later elaborated, occurs in: "[s]ettings within which individuals may do enormous amounts of harm to other human beings without ever intending to do so, just performing their regular duties as a job defined in the structure."[7] It has to be understood as: "a process working slowly as the way misery in general, and hunger in particular, erode and finally kill human beings."[8] Although criticized for its wide, general scope, Galtung's distinction has made the violent workings of concrete institutions and social structures much more visible.[9]

Importantly, then, in democratic societies such as the U.S., structural violence refers to a certain collective abuse of power tolerated by a majority. This abuse of power infringes upon the freedom of certain individuals to make themselves reflexively in ways that other individuals can. Newton Garver for instance expanded a definition of violence to include structural violence as the

---

4   Krug et al., "World Report on Violence and Health," 5.
5   Miller, *Violence*, 6.
6   Galtung, "Twenty-Five Years of Peace Research: Ten Challenges and Some Responses," 171.
7   Galtung, 145.
8   Galtung, 145–146.
9   Roberts, *Human Insecurity: Global Structures of Violence*, 22.

violation of fundamental human rights. What he calls covert institutional violence "operates when people are deprived of choices in a systematic way by the very manner in which transactions normally take place".[10] Structural violence then can be viewed as the collective toleration of inequality in terms of, for instance, wealth, gender, race, ethnicity, immigrant status, sexual orientation, or class. While the concept may be a bit general to account for specific acts of indirect violence or the normalized abuse of power, it nevertheless serves to explore the connections between the social aspects of specific acts of such indirect violence and the social components of the making of meaning and identity.

As is apparent in George Saunders's reportage, distanced structural violence as the toleration of extreme poverty and homelessness can also contribute to more direct physical violence between individuals. In many ways, then, structural violence helps illuminate the perhaps less apparent connection between the real material conditions for collective and individual human self-making and their actual reflexive realizations of individuals. They are, even in a seemingly free society such as the U.S., inhibited or even made and kept impossible by collective (in-)action and repressions of the core social aspects of the reflexive construction of individual and collective identity.

The U.S. provides the specific social and cultural backdrop for the violence described in the three texts analyzed in this chapter. It is an extraordinarily violent country with by far the highest level of gun ownership in the world, the highest homicide rates in the Global North, and high rates of racially motivated hate crimes.[11] Furthermore, it also continues to feature a high rate of homelessness.[12]

It is therefore significant that all three texts analyzed connect the violence of this specific culture to a larger point about mediatization as they grasp violence's fundamental reflexivity in mediatized realities. As acts of individual and collective identity formation, acts of physical violence are always tethered to the negotiation of their symbolic meaning. Importantly, as I will show in the analyses, it is precisely the writer's own display of self-reflection that helps them to unearth the specific dynamics of violence's reflexivity in their respective texts. And this reflexivity, in turn, illuminates the specific qualities of human mediation in distinction from the capabilities of technological media.

---

10   Garver, "What Violence Is", 265.
11   Miller, *Violence*, 13–18.
12   "State of Homelessness: 2021 Edition."

4.2 The Fractured Medium in George Saunders's "Tent City, U.S.A." (2009)

George Saunders's reportage "Tent City U.S.A." explores the precarious conditions in a homeless encampment in Fresno, California. It was published in GQ in September 2009. Saunders briefly lived in the area himself for his research. In the actual text, Saunders analyzes how the area's inhabitants communicate and, consequently, how their linguistic expressions mirror their material and social circumstances. Faced with the occasionally shocking experience, Saunders extensively reflects upon his own role as a human medium on various levels. For instance, he makes his role as an external intruder clear, only temporarily living in the area in order to conduct research for a text. He qualifies his experience as decisively mediated by the utterances and narratives of his sources, namely the camp's inhabitants. He makes transparent his own process of trying to make sense of disconcerting experiences and mirrors the camp's fractured social relations and psychologies in his own narrative construct. Ultimately, his self-reflection contributes to an understanding of a similar reflexivity connected to mental health at the core of homelessness; namely, the ways in which the structural violence is evident in the homeless camp decisively shapes the sensemaking process of the very experience of homelessness.

Importantly, Saunders's approach has a long history. His method of participatory observation—championed by ethnographers and anthropologists such as Bronislaw Malinowski in the 19th century—has become the core of a journalistic genre that has been called stunt journalism or, more recently, immersion journalism. The point is to become the subject itself and thus experience the reality to be described firsthand as a simple, fellow human being. As repeatedly hinted at by Saunders, the entry barriers for this activity are very low. As James P. Spradley has noted in his landmark student handbook on participant observation in ethnography, anyone can easily engage in this kind of qualitative research. "Ethnography offers all of us the chance to step outside our narrow cultural backgrounds, to set aside our socially inherited ethnocentrism, ... and to apprehend the world from the viewpoint of other human beings who live by different meaning systems."[1] Recently, journalistic products that lean heavily on ethnography as method of research have attained the scholarly label "immersion journalism". Due to the centrality of the research method for the story told, immersion journalists actively make the story by becoming someone else. Chris Wilson has noted that, therefore, such texts typically reflexively point to their own making and "propose themselves as both accounts of *being* immersed and *how* such immersion was enacted."[2]

In particular poverty and its accompanying conditions of human life have repeatedly been journalistically documented by way of this intentionally experiential method of research. Early examples are, for instance, James Greenwood's "A Night in a Workhouse" (1866),[3] or Nellie Bly's "Ten Days in a Mad-House" (1887).[4] With his occasionally ironical self-parody, however, Saunders's text shows similiarities with Crane's "An Experiment in Misery" (1894).[5] For one thing, Crane also narrates his "experiment" in the distancing voice of a third-person narrator—a "youth"—that can appear ironic given the obvious fact that Crane refers to himself. Holly E. Schreiber has therefore considered the text as journalistic self-critique in the form of "a creative repurposing of an established genre with the goal of both celebrating the genre's strengths and exposing its weaknesses".[6]

The Structural Violence of Homelessness

The contemporary misery that Saunders immerses himself in temporarily is only slightly different from the housing of homeless in late 19th century New York described by Crane. Like then, today's homelessness is a typical example of structural violence in Johan Galtung's sense. As the ethnographer Vincent Lyon-Callo has pointed out, the increase in homelessness in the U.S. around

---

1   Spradley, James P. *Participant Observation*, vii–viii.
2   Wilson, "Immersion Journalism and the Second-Order Narrative," 347.
3   Greenwood, "A Night in a Workhouse."
4   Bly, "Ten Days in a Mad-House."
5   Crane, "Experiment in Misery."
6   Schreiber, "Journalistic Critique through Parody in Stephen Crane's 'An Experiment in Misery'," 31.

the millennium shift concurred with the widening gap between rich and poor.[7] It is the result of a concrete worsening of the historical and material conditions that determine income and housing costs for a wide section of people living in the U.S.A. In turn, these conditions were altered by a political and economic restructuring that prioritized free market forces and individual action.[8] In addition to contributing to homelessness, this neoliberal complex of policies and ideas also affected responses to and the public perception of homelessness as result of deviance or pathology. "A wide range of disorders is understood as contributing to making a person homeless", Lyon-Callo has argued, "but these are all understood as being within the bodies or minds of individual people."[9]

In particular, highly individual mental health issues have been tied to homelessness. About a third of the current homeless population in the U.S. suffers from a severe and disabling mental disorder. These people tend to stay homeless longer and are affected by additional health problems.[10] Their mental illnesses can be both cause and effect of homelessness. For instance, how the rising level of homelessness in the U.S. during the second half of the 20th century correlated with different reforms of the mental health care system that resulted in insufficient care for many people with mental health problems has already been carefully documented.[11] On the other hand, studies have suggested that counteracting the social isolation central to the experience of homelessness by way of community housing, for instance, also helps to alleviate the effects of mental illness.[12]

A Researcher Out of Place

In Saunders's text, the author-narrator's self-presentation attains a core function in the analysis of homelessness because it highlights ethical issues that

---

7   Lyon-Callo, "Homelessness, Employment, and Structural Violence: Exploring Constraints on Collective Mobilizations against Systemic Inequality," 295.
8   Lyon-Callo, 295.
9   Lyon-Callo, *Inequality, Poverty, and Neoliberal Governance: Activist Ethnography in the Homeless Sheltering Industry*, 13.
10 Caton, *The Open Door: Homelessness and Severe Mental Illness in the Era of Community Treatment*, vii.
11 Caton, *The Open Door: Homelessness and Severe Mental Illness in the Era of Community Treatment*.
12 Schutt, *Homelessness, Housing, and Mental Illness*.

are connected to the structural character of the violence at play. Furthermore, it situates the text's main focus on how the meaning of this violence is negotiated, rather than on the violence itself. Saunders styles himself as an outsider, a person who is different from the Fresno homeless. As such, he is present only in order to intentionally produce experience. Saunders fittingly refers to himself in the third person, as a researcher who conducts an "in situ study"[13] of the homeless in Fresno. This self-assigned role is highly ambiguous. On the one hand, it serves as justification for Saunders's presence in an alien space. On the other hand, he repeatedly comes across as uncomfortable with this role, which necessitates his voluntary presence in a place in which others live involuntarily.

Saunders's self-characterization is expressed by both his active selection of the encampment and his use of equipment for professional use. Even as early as in the first paragraph, he states that he intentionally conducted a "study" and that: "the objective of the Study was to explore this unusual community of homeless people and learn something of its inhabitants."[14] He also adds that he chose the camp due to the size of its population and grounds. Furthermore, Saunders writes that he went looking for a different homeless camp, because the one at hand did not correspond to his expectations.[15] He thus presents his choice of location—and hence experience—as being both highly subjective and intentional.

In addition to these disclosures of intention and objective, Saunders describes his author-narrator persona, the principal researcher (PR), as a professional who uses particular tools and devices to do a particular job. This clearly sets him apart from most of the other inhabitants of the encampment who are not there to work. In a general statement regarding his research method, for instance, he mentions that: "when use of a notebook seemed problematic, the PR would switch on a portable tape recorder."[16] Apart from the use of recording devices, which has the potential to be problematic because it marks him as an outsider, Saunders also refers to both his car and his tent as equipment necessary for his work. The mere possession of these goods signifies a certain difference from the area's regular inhabitants. In an early interaction with a woman named Wanda, for instance, she points to his car. "Wanda stated that the PR 'looked rich'. The PR protested that he was not rich. Wanda looked pointedly

---

13   Saunders, *Tent City, U.S.A.*, pt. 1.
14   Saunders, pt. 1.
15   Saunders, pt. 2.
16   Saunders, pt. 2.

at the project research vehicle, a late-model rental minivan."[17] Saunders's car here is clearly associated with its function of contributing to the study. However, it also signifies a certain wealth and difference. The same goes for Saunders's tent, which is also part of his project's basic and necessary equipment. Saunders writes that the:

> PR's tent was new. He had never assembled it before. All day he'd been worrying about this moment of confused fumbling, and now it was happening. Several more poles than expected tumbled out of the bag. The instructions were observed to be blowing away. The PR felt the eyes of the entire Study Area upon him.[18]

In addition to the car and the tent's mint condition, Saunders's apparent inexperience in setting it up here distinguishes him as an outsider.

Elsewhere, Saunders communicates such concerns more explicitly with his own appearance, in connection with his role as an outsider. Saunders is uncomfortable when he first enters the encampment, writing that he had to overcome "some initial fear-related resistance to exiting the vehicle."[19] Despite all of the professional goal-orientation at play in Saunders's role as a researcher, conducting a study of a previously selected area, he also notes the human elements, such as fear, have the potential to affect both the experience and his results.

This tension between the professional and the human in Saunders's researcher persona is negotiated through Saunders's own human body. This is particularly evident in a passage where Saunders observes a drug deal taking place right outside his tent. "Observing the illicit transaction," Saunders writes, "gave the PR a giddy, powerful feeling. The dealers didn't even know he was there, taking notes."[20] In this passage, Saunders connects the joy he feels with a certain sense of power he derives from being invisible to others, while simultaneously being able to observe them. However, Saunders is not too different from the people outside his tent, as he soon becomes "aware of an urge to urinate."[21] It is his basic human physicality, then, that forces him to leave his tent and take the risk of interacting socially, which might, of course, lead

---

17 Saunders, pt. 3.
18 Saunders, pt. 4.
19 Saunders, pt. 2.
20 Saunders, pt. 10.
21 Saunders, pt. 10.

to his identity being revealed. Tellingly, and in order to resolve this impasse, Saunders modifies his signifying body. "As the PR crossed the empty zone, he observed himself to be walking in a deliberately shuffling gait, with a slight fake limp, in an attempt to appear more homeless."[22] In order to be able to do his job as researcher, and to assume his presence in the encampment, Saunders suggests here that he needs at a minimum to project the appearance of having physical—not just professional—reasons to be present.

The deceptive resolution of this key tension between Saunders's appearance and his professional function paves the way for the narrative's conclusion. Although the revelation of his true reasons for being in the camp did not immediately foster resentment,[23] Saunders anticipates negative consequences:

> Enough was enough. He had a wife, he had kids. He had to get out of here before something bad happened. He was lying about who he was as much as anybody else in here, and it now seemed clear that the uncovering of this lie must lead to resentment, and resentment, in turn, to some retributive cost.[24]

As he makes clear in this passage, the resolution, for Saunders, lies in abandoning his role as a researcher and embracing his true self, as a man with a family, living and working elsewhere. Thus, the role of researcher is marked out not only as artificial, but even as an explicit lie, whose revelation could provoke physical harm. Notably, Saunders never justifies his becoming a researcher with any reason other than the mere production of knowledge about the homeless camp. However, this ending also suggests that this pre-condition of Saunders's presence in the camp could not only be seen as problematic, because the homeless are thereby dehumanized and reduced to mere objects of inquiry, but also because he himself is being objectified, as a mere means to a scientific end at odds with his more basic human identity. The temporarily experienced structural violence has a damaging effect even upon him: it makes him compromise his sincerity.

---

22   Saunders, pt. 10.
23   Saunders, pt. 29.
24   Saunders, pt. 29.

Aural Experience and the Discontents of Mediation

As a researcher, Saunders's task is to immerse himself in the life of the homeless in Fresno, to temporarily live like them, and to derive knowledge from this experience. One of the main characteristics of experience in the tent city is its aural quality, its condition as mediated sound. His perception of sound mediated in different ways serves Saunders as a particular illustration of both the connecting and separating potential of mediation in general. In terms of communication, Walter Ong has shown that the speaking medium typically remains a unified actor in oral cultures because actor and act typically inhabit the same space. In literacy however, actor (writer) and act (text) are typically separated and the medium split.[25] Consequently, in areas of predominantly oral communication, such as homeless camps, the separation of speaker and speech resembles a violent fragmentation.

This is most evident in passages in which Saunders either only perceives a sound, without seeing its source—for instance, from within his tent—or when he is confronted with gossip directed at him by the voices of the camp's other inhabitants. In these instances, Saunders points to the precarious status of sound as an indexical sign and the weakness of the link between sign and potential referent. He connects his experience of aural mediation with the overall fracturing of social life and to a sense of violence and strangeness in the homeless camp. Nevertheless, he also describes how sound, transmitted from one human being to another in the form of speech, carries the potential to connect the inhabitants.

The connection between violence and sound is established in Saunders's first mentions of aural experiences. For instance, Saunders links the fear that he felt in Fresno with the PR's perception that "[w]ild shouts could be heard."[26] And while Wanda—the first inhabitant that he meets—"exuded a wry joviality,"[27] on the visual level, what she expresses vocally is an unambiguous threat: "I'm a rape you."[28] The strangeness of this type of threat is also manifest in instances in which sound itself is dominant—and hence appears strange and potentially violent. Typically, these episodes occur at night in the absence of

---

25 Ong, *Orality and Literacy: The Technologizing of the Word*; van Loon, *Media Technology: Critical Perspectives*, 8–9.
26 Saunders, *Tent City, U.S.A.*, pt. 2.
27 Saunders, pt. 3.
28 Saunders, pt. 3.

visual perception, when, due to his particular situation, Saunders was limited to hearing the sounds emitted by other inhabitants of the camp. For instance, Saunders devotes an entire section of his text titled "LISTEN TO THE MUSIC OF THE NIGHT" to the experience of sound at night:

> The night was full of sounds. These included: the whoosh of traffic from Highway 41, sirens; the metal-on-metal sound of freight trains coupling and uncoupling, hammering sounds as several Study Area residents made nighttime improvements to their dwellings; a bullfrog in the junk pile next to the PRs tent.[29]

This list of fairly ordinary sounds is followed by a list of perceived utterances Saunders attributes to different voices. Although only a minority of the sounds he lists could be perceived as relating directly to violence—a male voice, angrily shouting into a cell phone "I don't like that! I don't know you! I don't like that!" for instance[30]—their mere existence at a time usually reserved for rest and quiet proves uncomfortable for Saunders. "It occurred to the PR," Saunders concludes the section, "that he was not the only person in the Study Area anxious for the night to end."[31]

This uncomfortable character of nightly sounds, perceived from inside a tent, is heightened when Saunders is unable to attribute a clear referent to the aural sign, and the sound consequently potentially represents a threat. The night after the revelation of his true identity, for instance, ends with Saunders waking up to an unsettling sound:

> The PR woke to the sound of a woman being fucked or hit, he couldn't tell which. Her cries were rhythmic and laden with sorrow. Woman, he thought, you really are the nigger of the world. Unless that is a pleasure sound. And even then, you still are. Because look where you are, and who you're getting that pleasure from, and at what cost.[32]

Here, Saunders is unable to tell whether the woman is being violently beaten or taking part in sexual intercourse. As Saunders has grown increasingly cynical at the time of this experience, however, not even the latter option could provide

---

29   Saunders, pt. 11.
30   Saunders, pt. 11.
31   Saunders, pt. 11.
32   Saunders, pt. 29.

any kind of reassurance. The mere perception of sound leads Saunders to assert that the encampment in general is a bad place for women. Ultimately, then, it is uncertainty concerning the origin of the sound that leads him to draw this sweeping, sad conclusion.

In a similar scene, described only a few lines later, Saunders hears the sound of fighting dogs "left on their own, to rend, tear, and kill one another."[33] He dozes off only to wake up again to the sound of a whistle coming from the freight yard:

> Then the whistle left off and there came the most complex exotic birdsong he'd ever heard, a sound made more beautiful by its occurrence in such a godforsaken place, as if the bird did not discriminate but made beauty wherever it went, just because it could, a song that then resolved itself into what it actually was: the yelp of a dog in pain – kicked, maybe, or wounded in a fight, or just tied too long to a fence by its absent, wasted master.[34]

Here again, the sound that Saunders hears has an uncertain, and hence ambiguous, source. This initially even leads Saunders to wrongly perceive it as the song of a bird, before soberly declaring that it comes from a wounded dog. In these instances, then, the perception of mediated sound without its emittent is described as fostering an uncanny feeling, whether because of its untimeliness, because of the uncertain relationship between sign and referent, or because of its role as a conveyor of indications about the encampment's precarious state of affairs.

Furthermore, Saunders describes mediated sound as problematic when he perceives it in the form of talk or gossip by the homeless. In these instances, in a way analogous to the disconnect that he experiences in the tent, he either has no means of verifying the link between sign and referent or there exist multiple, contradictory links. For instance, one inhabitant's story about the origins of the encampment is contradicted by a woman named Large Jo;[35] the conflict between Valerie, her jailed husband Pablo, and Rusty is subject to different interpretations;[36] Saunders relays the false, wild tales of a former soldier,[37] and

---

33 Saunders, pt. 29.
34 Saunders, pt. 29.
35 Saunders, pts. 6–7.
36 Saunders, pt. 20 + 33.
37 Saunders, pt. 17.

reveals that "even sweet, broken Ernesto"[38] lies. In general, regarding the stories he acquires by way of hearing, Saunders states:

> truth was relative within the Study Area. Truth is relative everywhere but was even more relative within the Study Area. Anything anyone ever claimed during the Study was, at some point, directly contradicted by something someone else claimed. Stories within the Study area... were rife with exaggeration, omission, or fabrication.[39]

Of course, the connection between this relativity of truth and its mediation in sound is one of correlation, rather than causation. Saunders points this out himself when he attributes the prevalence of falsity and contradiction to mental illness and to the camp's dire material conditions.[40]

As Saunders suggests in the text, however, relativity and uncertainty are inherent characteristics of mediation in general, not specifically of sound. This point is illustrated in the final scene when he sits and talks with Rusty, who is dying of bone cancer. Rusty tells him a story about how a little girl was brutally punished for having interacted with him during a CIA mission in El Salvador. The punishment is so brutal that it appears hard to believe, which leads Saunders to ponder the more general value of his talk with Rusty:

> The PR realized he had reached an exquisite level of perfect Study Area immersion: He honestly didn't know if Rusty was lying or not. And he didn't care. It didn't matter. What mattered was the display. It was beautiful to hear Rusty, this dying man, this vanishing soul, say the crazy things he was saying, whether they were true or not.[41]

The inherent indeterminacy regarding the truth of Rusty's speech does not provoke desperation in Saunders. Instead, he acknowledges the value of the fact that the conversation is taking place at all. Thus, he shifts the focus from the separating aspects of mediation to its connecting function, ending on a hopeful note.

---

38   Saunders, pt. 28.
39   Saunders, pt. 7.
40   Saunders, pt. 7.
41   Saunders, pt. 33.

Disclosing Soliloquy

When faced with this relativity of truth, the encampment's bewildering violence and the fractured social relations, Saunders seeks certainty within himself. Frequently, the interpretation of his experience takes on the form of a soliloquy that attains a stabilizing function, given that it helps him to judge present reality and to find a foundation for future decisions. Thus, he describes his actions as mainly being influenced by his own personal interpretations of reality and takes responsibility for them. In these instances, a large part of the mediation occurs within Saunders as a human medium. In the form of soliloquies, Saunders exhibits this mediation as produced by himself in reaction to his disconcerting experience in the camp. In the section aptly titled "A MORAL INQUIRY," for instance, Saunders questions his own morals in relation to a girl," possibly a prostitute, who is supposedly being held by a man in a tent. The man had offered the girl to Saunders. Later, Saunders reflects on his personal obligation to help the girl and other residents, given the fact that he has personally witnessed their living conditions. On the one hand, he thinks that any action on his part would be like "a single shot from a gun being fired into a massive orbiting planet."[42] On the other hand, he thinks:

> what would happen if he decided to abandon the Study and commit all his resources to the sole purpose of extracting the white girl with red hair from that tent and getting her into whatever treatment program was required? Wasn't it possible – wasn't it, in fact, likely, given his resources – that he could effect a positive change in the life of the white girl with the red hair? And if so, wasn't it, at some level, a moral requirement that he do so? That is: By continuing down G Street, the white girl with the red hair becoming less real with his every step, was he not essentially consenting to her continued presence back there in the tent, waiting to be sold, by the tall man, to anyone who happened by? Wasn't he, in a sense, not only allowing that to happen but *assuring* that it would happen?
> Yes.
> Yes, he was.[43]

In this passage, Saunders reflects not only upon the possible plight of the girl but, more urgently, on his own moral position with regard to the girl's

---

42   Saunders, pt. 15.
43   Saunders, pt. 15.

living situation. What begins as mere self-interrogation concludes with a clear answer: a repeated and thus emphatic "Yes". Saunders traces his thinking here, which ultimately leads him to an unequivocal conclusion that puts him into a quandary. He fails to act immediately and abandon his study to help the girl, instead prioritizing his role as a researcher over his identity as an ordinary human being. By making his motives transparent and acknowledging the dilemma, however, he nevertheless takes responsibility for this failure to act. Thus, he advances a display of awareness of his ethical position as an observing researcher as potential solution, or relief, to the inner tension that his witnessing causes.

In another instance, Saunders similarly engages in a soliloquy in response to a quandary, giving it the form of a dialogue of an inner voice making different contradictory points. Having decided to leave, Saunders intends to give away his belongings, but is faced with another dilemma. Who should he give his tent to?

> First he'd give away all his stuff: his sleeping bag and pad, his little light, the tent itself. Wanda had been asking for the tent. Valerie had advised him against giving the tent to that little crackhead Wanda. He'd also considered giving it to Suzanna, a lost soul just out of jail, stranded here in Fresno with no tent of her own, also a crackhead, but a crackhead more adrift than Wanda, who, though a crackhead, was also well connected and fat and slothful, always begging and playing the angles. Per Wanda, Suzanna had sold her jail-issued train ticket for crack; why give a brand-new tent to someone like that? By rights, Valerie should get the tent. Valerie was his pal. Valerie was no crackhead. Valerie was a grandmother of seven and a half. Then again, Valerie already had like five tents. Why did she need another one? Arguing in Wanda's favor was the fact that she had been hit by a train and could barely walk and was awfully genial and forgiving for someone so down on her luck.
> Jesus, he couldn't wait to get out of here.[44]

Here, Saunders maps his thinking process against the backdrop of his observation that nobody's talk could be trusted, and that truth was highly relative in the camp. Of course, this consideration complicates the entire passage, because the potential grounds for giving the tent to one person or another, which

---

44 Saunders, pt. 29.

4.2 The Fractured Medium in George Saunders's "Tent City, U.S.A." (2009)

Saunders can appeal to, cannot be trusted. Despite asking himself and weighing different points, he does not come to a clear conclusion. Instead, he merely acknowledges the difficulty of the decision with which he is faced. It is also this difficulty concerning the ethical position that he finds himself in that contributes to his desire to leave the camp. Once again, the soliloquy serves to clarify his interpretation of an experience—in this case, the experience of uncertainty—that complicates his own decisions and actions.

In a third scene, Saunders justifies his own acceptance of being extorted, when he reasons himself out of a quandary by way of a soliloquy. When he observes that Rusty has taken his tent, because Saunders has not paid him to stay in what Rusty claims to be his area, Saunders finds himself at a crossroads again:

> The PR was flustered. Rusty was basically extorting him. Rusty had kidnapped his tent? His poor loyal tent lay there like a bug on its back, a humiliated hostage. This was too much. But what was he supposed to do, fight Rusty? Kick the ass of a guy three inches shorter than him who was dying of bone cancer? Or, conversely, get his ass kicked by a guy three inches shorter than him who was dying of bone cancer?
> His impulse was to pull out his wallet and just pay the five bucks. But if he pulled out his wallet and Rusty saw all the money in there, Rusty might increase the ransom, or grab the wallet.
> Buying himself a little time, the PR claimed his money was in his wallet, which was back in the van.
> ...
> Still, shit, was he really going to capitulate to that little asshole Rusty? Rusty had punched Valerie in the face. Jesse hadn't said anything about needing to pay Rusty. And he hadn't even needed Rusty's protection in the first place! He could have just stayed where he was and saved the five—
> Ah, fuck it, the PR thought. It's five dollars.[45]

In this passage, Saunders not only ponders his different options, but also imagines different outcomes based on his potential actions. When he imagines fighting Rusty, or the possibility that Rusty might ask for more money if he sees his wallet, Saunders displays the role of fiction in logical argument. His soliloquy here helps to shine a light on the dilemma that he is facing by simply trying to live in a tent in a potentially lawless area. Furthermore, it also

---

45 Saunders, pt. 32.

reflects upon the ways in which a human mind deals with such a dilemma and how it draws conclusions by weighing the potential consequences of different actions.

However, Saunders also employs the soliloquy in order to question the dichotomy of body and mind. The notion that experience is processed in a body simply working in concert with a mind is displayed in a passage in which Saunders imagines a part of his body—his penis—to be talking to him as a response to the experience in the camp:

> The first three nights of the Study, the PR woke in the night with a hard-on unique in that it felt completely devoid of sexuality. It was more like a fear hard-on. Its function seemed to be to wake the PR up so he could reevaluate his safety. Why are you sleeping? the PR's penis seemed to be saying. Shouldn't you be awake and watchful? His arms and legs would be freezing, but his cock would be hot and ready to flee. Was he horny? Did he want to masturbate? Ha ha. In here? No. He'd go back to sleep, but his penis would stay awake, complaining, at full attention, about the danger in which it had been placed so late in his life, having served so honorably for so long.
> About Day Four, the fear hard-ons ceased. The PR believed this to be related to a general evolving comfort with his surroundings.[46]

Here, Saunders employs a soliloquy in order to imagine how a body part might talk to the mind or how the body as a whole, not necessarily only the mind, might engage in an interior dialogue, in order to interpret experienced reality.

Consequently, the instances in which Saunders prominently employs soliloquies are instances in which the writer exhibits a particularly acute awareness of his reflexive qualities as a human medium. He indicates that his own actions cannot be separated from the experience of reality that he aims to mediate. The human body's interpretative workings in these instances, then, are part and parcel of the reality that is represented and communicated, as well as comments about reality as it is experienced. Through this ambiguity, they illustrate the anchoring of knowledge about reality in the relevant subject; in this case, Saunders and his body. As it carries a universally human meaning, this understanding of interpretative work also seems to apply to the other inhabitants of the encampment—despite the absence of any unequivocal example in the text.

---

46   Saunders, pt. 22.

The Active Role of the Passive Voice

The text can be read as an assemblage of different voices, talking with, to, or against one another, as Saunders's use of soliloquy, among other things, suggests. There are the voices coming from nearby tents at night,[47] the cynical collective voice of the camp's inhabitants,[48] different dialogues, such as the one between Ernesto, Brenda, Lyle, and Saunders's PR persona,[49] and the voice of Jesse expressed in a poem.[50] However, the voice that speaks most directly to the reader as an expression of Saunders's role as a human medium is the voice that narrates the story. It is in this voice that Saunders conveys his experience and, thus, most prominently fulfills his communicative function as a writer and as a medium. This voice of an omniscient, third-person narrator can be characterized as utterly passive and distanced, mimicking the tone of academic research reports. Notably, it is not attributed to the principal researcher's persona, but to an omniscient narrating entity. Similar to the narrative voice in Mac McClelland's reportage about the birding trip, it is a voice that—although it is styled as distanced—has insight into the deepest parts and workings of the researcher's body and serves to communicate the most concrete details that the researcher observed. It is this striking disconnect between narrative distance and epistemological proximity that serves to raise valid questions about the level of the communicative relationship between Saunders and his readers.

This voice inevitably appears ironic, because it reveals the separation of roles and personas in reportage as fictional. In reality, Saunders is both the producer of the experience in the camp and the text's named author. In the text, however, a zealous and distanced voice akin to that of an academic research report renders the insights of a researcher persona. At first glance, this might mark the out text as fictional. A second glance reveals, however, that it challenges the conventional separation of fiction and nonfiction, because it suggests that any narrative text has an author and a constructed narrative voice and that it is possible for the author to act as a narrative's main character and the producer of the narrative voice, while at the same time relaying a story referring exclusively to a real human being's actions and perceptions. Thus, this separation of roles ironically points to the fact that, in the reality of a reportage

---

47   Saunders, pt. 11.
48   Saunders, pt. 18.
49   Saunders, pt. 21.
50   Saunders, pt. 25.

text, they are simply different narrative functions employed by the same real person. The irony of this separation becomes apparent, in the first instance, in the clash of different roles. In the text's second section, having outlined the method and scope of the study, the passive narrative voice recounts that: "[i]t is difficult to convey the sobering effect of entering the Study Area for the first time."[51] While still maintaining a passive tone here, the narrative voice nevertheless clearly signals that it has its origins in a human subjectivity that not only actively feels, but that also reflects upon his or her own narrative function. The functions of the narrative voice and of the experiencing researcher persona converge in a singular way, revealing the voice's ironic quality.

This irony is further heightened as the narrative progresses and the voice's distanced tone is contrasted with the intimacy of the details regarding the researcher's experience that it communicates. For instance, following the PR's first exchange with Ernesto, the narrative voice states that the: "PR observed with some interest that his reaction to the clarification that Ernesto's friend had not been murdered, but had only killed himself in despair, was relief."[52] Here, the stylistically distanced voice narrates an observation of the PR that is concerned with the PR's self-awareness—and hence something which only the PR himself could possibly know about. Later in the text, revealing the same disconnect between narrative distance and epistemological proximity, the voice relays the contents of one of the PR's dreams:

> In his sleep, the PR dreamed he was a beautiful blond woman, like Sharon Stone in Basic Instinct, who possessed considerable confidence in her powers of seduction. The PR was naked, in a hot tub, surrounded by male inquisitors. The PR posed and preened in the hot tub, refusing to answer the questions. This approach, it seemed, had worked before. This part of the dream was seen from the point of view of the PR: He could feel his feminine power, sense the mounting frustration of his inquisitors.[53]

Here, the disconnect is even more striking, as the distanced voice passively refers to actions that were multifariously mediated and dreamed up by the PR, even as the PR as the main subject, or rather the only one, is occasionally obscured through the use of passive constructions.

---

[51] Saunders, pt. 2.
[52] Saunders, pt. 5.
[53] Saunders, pt. 12.

Since this narrative distancing comes across as highly ironic, despite the framing of the text as a report on a sociological study, the voice rhetorically invites readers to question its generally distanced stance. This occurs not only on the level of form and the narratological separations mentioned above, it also happens on the level of the researcher's methods and his own position vis-à-vis the objects of his inquiry. Are the PR's actions, in trying to produce knowledge about the homeless, credible and comprehensible? Does the distance that he maintains in his role as a writer or researcher appear productive for readers? Is he convincing when he fails to keep distance? Most of all, it invites moral questions: Is the distanced voice justified with regard to the human suffering that Saunders witnesses? How do readers personally relate to the homeless' plight? Ultimately, Saunders's ironically heightened self-awareness as author serves to productively reveal important issues about the very processes of experiencing and communicating homelessness as a privileged US citizen.

Storytelling, Materiality, and the Possibilities of Fragmentation

With regard to the entire text, then, Saunders effectively connects the symbolic and material aspects of his experience. The various splits in mediation, which Saunders's self-reflection symbolically discloses, correspond to the material effects of structural violence inflicted upon the homeless community and upon its inhabitants. On one side, the wild and utterly fractured storytelling occasionally associated with mental illness affects social relations within the homeless camp. On the other side, personal tragedies and social isolation correlate with the telling of stories that are "rife with exaggeration, omission, or fabrication,"[54] which the homeless tell about themselves and others. As mentioned previously, Saunders ascribes this to the material conditions themselves that prevail in the camp. By presenting his own narrative about these conditions in an ironically fragmented, multi-voiced way, Saunders ultimately acknowledges that his own storytelling forging relations with readers is carved out of the same wood as the storytelling that takes place in the homeless camp. He explicitly relates a social community's material conditions to the ways in which its members communicate.

He makes the case that homelessness is deeply affected both by the stories told about it and the material circumstances that invite this storytelling

---

54   Saunders, pt. 7.

in a manner not unlike scientific research on homelessness. This suggests that with the material conditions, the stories might also change and vice versa. As Saunders's own storytelling suggests, he grounds this possibility in the pillars of symbolic, material, and social self-awareness that form the basis for knowledge about the other in a highly mediated society. Ultimately, this suggests that the insincere narrative of homelessness as an individual problem is part and parcel of the structural violence inflicted upon the homeless.

4.3 The Atoning Medium in Michael Paterniti's "Should We Get Used To Mass Shootings?" (2016)

In April 2016, GQ published an exploration of the ubiquitous gun violence in contemporary U.S. society by Michael Paterniti's reportage, entitled "Should We Get Used To Mass Shootings?" Like John Jeremiah Sullivan or Mac McClelland, Paterniti is primarily known as a magazine journalist, who has written reportage, profiles, and criticism for mainly U.S. outlets such as *Harper's*, *Esquire*, or *GQ*, where he is a correspondent. With several nominations for the National Magazine Award, Paterniti is considered to be one of the pre-eminent current American narrative journalists. After Paterniti published a collection of his magazine writings entitled *Love and Other Ways of Dying*[1] in 2015, a reviewer called it: "journalism elevated beyond its ordinary capacities, well into the realm of literature".[2]

Similar to Saunders's text, Paterniti's reportage zooms in on the reflexivity of violence and the ways in which symbolic responses to gun violence interact with and correspond to its material causes and effects. Claiming to be making amends for his own past neglect, Paterniti tries to make sense of the violence by exerting presence in space and time; Paterniti does so by looking and listening closely at the crime scenes in particular. The resulting narrative's main tension can be located in Paterniti's display of his own dealing with violence, torn between the moral imperative to stay attentive and the psychological necessity to shut out the consequences of gun violence. Paterniti addresses the contradictions of the simultaneously engaging and paralyzing media coverage

---

1   Paterniti, *Love and Other Ways of Dying: Essays*.
2   Keohane, "Hurting for Words."

of these acts of violence in the self-reflective exhibition of his ambiguous workings as medium. This occurs mainly in three areas: His self-awareness as a human medium is manifested in his self-characterization as a human writer at odds with the technological production and transmission of experience in the media industry. It is apparent in his deliberate acts of remembering the past and imagining the future aimed at countering the ending or negligence of time through deadly violence and media coverage. It is also displayed in his engaging communication with readers imagined as being part of a community of sinners who need to change.

Not unlike the work of John Jeremiah Sullivan, Mac McClelland (Gabriel Mac), and Ghansah, Michael Paterniti's texts have largely escaped scholarly attention to date. Currently, there exists no critical scholarship with a specific focus on Paterniti's work—not even a paper or a book chapter. Passages of his stories have occasionally been used to analyze features of narrative journalism.[3] His work received the most scholarly attention in Norman Sims's book *True Stories*.[4] Sims lauded him as one of the pre-eminent, current American narrative journalists and marked his story of the 1998 Swissair plane crash in Halifax as a modern classic of the genre.[5] Paterniti has talked about his approach to reportage on different occasions. In these interviews, he repeatedly emphasized his specific interest in phenomenological experience as research method. For instance, he told a college weekly: "I don't have some strident message. My work is just to bear witness and tell the story."[6] And in the Longform Podcast, he stated: "I want to see it, whatever it is. If it's war, if it's suffering, if it's complete, unbridled elation, I just want to see what that looks like—I want to smell it, I want to taste it, I want to think about it, I want to be caught up in it."[7]

Still, with its decidedly declared intention to bear witness, "Should We Get Used To Mass Shootings?" appears as a fairly unusual text in the overall body of Paterniti's work, which usually consists overwhelmingly of profiles in which the author examines the inner world of his subjects, rather than his own. In his examination of gun violence, Paterniti visits some of the places where mass

---

3   Hartsock, "Exploring the Referentiality of Narrative Literary Journalism."
4   Sims, *True Stories: A Century of Literary Journalism*.
5   Paterniti, "The Long Fall of One-Eleven Heavy." The story was first published in print in the July 2000 issue of *Esquire* magazine.
6   Fosler-Jones, "Author Michael Paterniti Talks Process, Travel and Journalism."
7   Linsky, "Longform Podcast 93: Michael Paterniti."

shootings occurred in 2015. Then, over a stretch of ten days beginning in late November, the U.S. experienced 14 mass shootings across the country.

Mass Media and Mass Shootings

Compared to homelessness, the mass shootings thematized in Michael Paterniti's text are a more direct, yet no less specifically American, type of violence. More than 500,000 people have died in the U.S. through bullet wounds in the first two decades of the 21st century alone. In 2019, incidents of mass shootings with at least four persons killed reached a new high: 211 persons died in 41 shootings.[8] Although mass shootings occurred previously, they are largely an American cultural phenomenon of the 21st century that was defined in many ways by the 1999 shooting at Columbine High School. This incident was the first mass shooting to be covered live on cable news and it was—second only to the O.J. Simpson case—one of the biggest American news stories of the 1990s.[9] Definitions of mass shootings are ambiguous but typically refer to isolated attacks in a fairly public setting in which at least four people die.[10] In most cases of mass shootings, the shooters suffer from untreated mental health problems such as severe depression or paranoia. Furthermore, shooters are socially marginalized with regard to their masculine identity. In many cases, the shootings also have to be understood as suicide attacks in which the shooters themselves plan to die.[11] Most of the weapons used in mass shootings are legally purchased semiautomatic guns.[12]

In his text, Paterniti focuses on the formal and technical issues associated with live media coverage that has potentially anesthetic effects on viewers. Watching a live event, John Durham Peters has shown, amounts to a kind of passive witnessing that is highly entertaining because it draws on the uncertainty of the present, which is "catastrophic, subject to radical alterations."[13] There have been concerns, then, that live TV's highly entertaining quality normalizes the oftentimes troubling content of the broadcast because it first

---

8 Miller, *Violence*, 15.
9 DeFoster, *Terrorizing the Masses: Identity, Mass Shootings, and the Media Construction of "Terror,"* 44.
10 DeFoster, 46–47.
11 DeFoster, 47.
12 DeFoster, 48.
13 Peters, "Witnessing," November 1, 2001, 719.

and foremost assures the viewer of an access to truth and authentic reality.[14] "Instead of providing news that helps people to understand what happened and what it means", Susan Brockus has argued that "live coverage may force viewers to settle for seeing and hearing what is real and significant *for the moment*."[15]

Despite their frequency, most Americans experience instances of mass shootings mediated through news media.[16] Ruth DeFoster has claimed that the: "role of mass media in helping to perpetuate the conditions that continue to lead to these shootings is considerable and inescapable."[17] DeFoster mainly criticizes the coverage in terms of content as overly superficial for its focus on individualizing the shooters and trying to identify specific reasons why a certain gunman lost control. Such narratives, which emphasize individually troubling experiences of unrequited love or bullying, have tended to ignore the deeper issues such as easy access to weapons, untreated mental health problems, and toxic masculinity.[18] As mentioned previously, acts of mass gun violence and the ways in which the media cover them are deeply connected to America's own cultural identity.[19]

A Human Journalist and the Industrial Horde

Paterniti's self-positioning is absolutely central to the text's overall point. Paterniti styles himself as a human journalist motivated by an internal drive. He is straightforward regarding his motivation for creating the experience and hence determines it as having been intentionally produced. In the text, Paterniti admits that he had a clear idea of what he was doing:

> The idea seemed a little perverse, actually. Ten days in America tracking mass shootings from place to place. Hunting those who had been hunted, to understand that we are being hunted, too.
> Even my wife asked: Why? Isn't there a happier story?

---

14   Brockus, "Coming to You 'Live': Exclusive Witnessing and the Battlefield Reporter," 31.
15   Brockus, 40.
16   DeFoster, *Terrorizing the Masses: Identity, Mass Shootings, and the Media Construction of "Terror*," 7.
17   DeFoster, 203.
18   DeFoster, 50–52.
19   DeFoster, 59.

4.3 The Atoning Medium in Paterniti's "Should We Get Used To Mass Shootings?"

It worries me, she said.
It keeps repeating, I wanted to say, because we keep looking away. I was a main offender like everyone else.
So this was my making amends: ten days of mass shootings in America, which could be any ten days in America, really, which could be the next ten days before us, full of possibility, too.[20]

Here, even Paterniti states that he also followed an intention regarding the writing and communicating of the story. He intends to avert future harm simply by fully confronting past violence. Furthermore, he confesses that he feels he has not paid enough attention to past acts of gun violence and wants to make good. This confession clearly imbues the story with a religious component and establishes a central temporality along with a personal connection. By referring to his wife's reaction to his idea, Paterniti further characterizes himself as a human subject with a private life and claims a role beyond that of a journalist merely fulfilling particular functions within an industry. His impetus, it appears, inevitably combines ethical concern with a sense of epistemological obligation.

However, Paterniti does not fully break away from his professional role as a journalist, but instead enters into an ambiguous relationship with the identity that his stated intention carries with it. Just like the other journalists covering a shooting in San Bernardino, for instance, he attends the press conference. "I was there in time for the press-conference phase of assuage," Paterniti writes, "of tell-it-like-it-is, of aftermath and air-of-calm competency, of everyone-relax-situation-under-control."[21] Later, he assumes a more explicit responsibility as he associates with the other journalists present: "The horde, of which I was a part, fiddled with cameras, mics, pens, went straight to the regurgitation of details."[22] As he admits, Paterniti is aware that he is complicit in the established ritualization of the social processing of gun violence through his mere attendance at the press conference, which marks him out as a journalist. As such, however, he is inadequate. For instance, Paterniti admits that when he started traveling to the scenes of the shootings, he had: "wanted to go to all of them but [...] couldn't keep up."[23] Furthermore, he fails to get a man he calls

---

20   Paterniti, "Should We Get Used to Mass Shootings?," pt. 2.
21   Paterniti, pt. 3.
22   Paterniti, pt. 3.
23   Paterniti, pt. 4.

Ray, a witness to the shooting in New Orleans, to talk. "Two hours earlier, he'd had enough, wanted to stand up; now he wanted nothing to do with it, to make himself and his family invisible."[24] Although not explicitly described as manifestations of inadequacy or weakness, but presented rather as consequences of a reality which have simply become overwhelming, these instances designate him as different from the ordinary horde of journalists.

Throughout the text, Paterniti's distinguishing feature can be located in his very human capacity to experience, which he identifies as being at odds with the workings of the media industry. At the press conference following the San Bernardino shooting, for instance, he abandons the mode of immediate retelling, simply stating that: "someone else stepped to the bank of microphones, to offer a logistical update. All of it was uploaded instantly and beamed live; all of it scrolling across America's ticker with equal emphasis, the same valence."[25] In juxtaposition to this mechanical process of seemingly immediate dissemination, Paterniti focuses his attention as a human subject and medium interested in the most human consequences of the tragedy before him. He stays by the side of Lieutenant Mike Madden, one of the first responders to the emergency call, who has stepped back from the microphones:

> But Mike Madden, after stepping back, stood with his hands clasped. He made a show of listening, but wore a pensive frown. He seemed far away, in that unmendable room again. That was an image that stays with me, even now, months later: a man in a crowd, looking through the horde in front of him, to an unshakable memory. The horde, of which I was a part, fiddled with cameras, mics, pens, went straight to the regurgitation of details. Photos of the guns used by the killers were displayed – the two AR-15s, the semiautomatic nine-millimeter – as heads craned and cameras shuttered. At the end, someone yelled, "Can we get a closer look at the weapons?" A fellow officer put a hand on Madden's shoulder; he turned and walked away.[26]

Although part of the horde, as noted above, Paterniti cultivates a different kind of attention, focused on a human being in the background, rather than on the deadly technology in the foreground. He describes Madden's physical appearance, imagines his inner thoughts, and ultimately shows him in a comforting

---

24   Paterniti, pt. 4.
25   Paterniti, pt. 3.
26   Paterniti, pt. 3.

image physically connected to another human being. By contrast, the mass of journalists appears mechanically focused on the mere functional transmission of detail, rather than on human meaning. As he watches them crane their heads, they come across as mere tools performing a mechanical function, simply getting "a closer look."

Paterniti presents a more precise illustration of the mechanical character of mass media in instances when he himself acts as a media consumer and when a member of the mass media, a TV correspondent, describes the routines of the trade. Paterniti is on a plane when the shooting in San Bernardino happens. Still, he is able to follow the proceedings in California on television:

> By going to the CNN feed, and watching live, I could see the snuff in real time: Syed Farook, the 28-year-old Muslim father of a 6-month-old baby, sprawled on the street across from the vehicle, bleeding out, his long rifle flung nearby. I could watch when the police in the BearCat, thinking the whole SUV booby-trapped and ready to blow, dumped Tashfeen Malik, the 29-year-old mother, from the backseat of the vehicle onto the ground.[27]

In this passage, Paterniti describes, with a sense of estrangement, how live TV makes it possible for him to seemingly immediately—"in real time"—watch how real humans, a father and a mother, die. The mechanics of this kind of mediation uncouple time from space, thereby creating a technological experience of the event elsewhere.

As Paterniti describes it, this seeming transcendence of space is combined with a temporal selection based on predicted audience interest. When meeting a TV correspondent, Paterniti asks her to elaborate on the criteria for determining how much attention they pay to mass shootings. She answers that it is largely based on how quickly the assailants die or are imprisoned and how easy it is to determine a motive. "There is a formula," she writes, "sadly after the killer is gone or imprisoned, the flowers die at the memorials and the press packs up, these communities are widely ignored by the national media."[28] There is, as Paterniti indicates by means of her explanation, a particular, superficial, and predetermined narrative for the TV coverage of a mass shooting that isolates the actual crime and its perpetrators from the victims. Significantly, as the TV correspondent makes clear, this story is informed by the interests of both the TV

---

27 Paterniti, pt. 3.
28 Paterniti, pt. 8.

viewership and the networks. By making this TV narrative an object of his own narrative, Paterniti distances himself from this way of telling. He feels the need to view these events differently than TV viewers and to narrate them differently than the TV cameras, even though he is also part of the media—the horde.

Acknowledging Human Time

The entire thrust of Paterniti's text then, it could be argued, works against a particular, inhuman way of experiencing and processing gun violence that he deems complicit in the shootings themselves. Paterniti's own interpretation of the experience necessitates a more productive and preventive approach to narrating and experiencing. In his view, such approaches necessitate a broader awareness of the meaning of time in human existence. As I have sought to show, Paterniti describes live media as the creator of a particular kind of experience that disconnects time from space and that isolates moments of spectacular attention, that show a present without a past, future, or shared space.

However, human life is, as Paterniti writes, characterized by the very experience of time that creates a past, present, and future. Wanting to "raise an alarm, years past it mattering,"[29] Paterniti establishes this acknowledgment of temporality as the basic premise for the interpretation of his experience:

> We couldn't take back our past. Couldn't rewrite it. We couldn't teleport to that McDonald's in San Ysidro, 1984, to warn the 21 dead to flee as a 41-year old-father of two walks in, armed with an Uzi, pistol, and shotgun, and says, "I killed thousands in Vietnam, and I want to kill more." We couldn't go back to the University of Texas, in 1966, to warn the 14 dead about the unhinged engineering student, carrying an M1 carbine, who is perched in the clock tower about to fire. And we couldn't go back to that midnight show of The Dark Knight Rises in the Aurora, Colorado, movie theater, in July 2012, interrupted by a neuroscience Ph.D. candidate, who opened fire on the crowd, killing 12 and injuring 70.[30]

Paterniti emphasizes the temporality at the center of human life, and thus at the center of lethal violence, by declaring the fundamental impossibility to change the past and undo three past acts of gun violence.

---

29   Paterniti, pt. 3.
30   Paterniti, pt. 3.

4.3 The Atoning Medium in Paterniti's "Should We Get Used To Mass Shootings?"   245

In this way, he lays the groundwork for a framing of acts of gun violence as acts that, in their particularity, end time. A metaphor for this ending of time is the interruption of traffic in San Bernardino, where, right after the shooting, "everything was concentrated and frozen in that moment."[31] Paterniti observes a similar stasis in New Orleans, where violence caused a stoppage and the ensuing fear silences potential witnesses and disguises the potential existence of video evidence of the shooting. "We were in the middle of the city," Paterniti writes about sitting at the playground where the shooting occurred, "and yet nothing moved here."[32]

However, the ending of time also has a spatial component in Paterniti's interpretation. This is manifested in the ways in which Paterniti refers to death at least twice. In a summary of shootings, he mentions a deadly day in Chicago, where "three people are... shot dead/erased/vanished."[33] When remembering the shooting at Columbine High School, he writes that the victims: "had been erased/disappeared/vanished. There were the families now clustered around these sudden erasures and absences, and families gathered around those families gathered around the void."[34] Death creates not only a temporal stoppage, but also a physical void because the end of a human life time also means the end of a human body. Here, then, space and time are connected as they are both anchored in concrete human bodies that disappear, vanish, remember and mourn in Paterniti's transmission, where the human medium is different from live television.

Hence, to acknowledge time for Paterniti involves confronting not only its stoppage in the particular case of death, but also its continuation in the general processing of the particular. Continuation, in such a morally charged context as a mass shooting, means oblivion. If stopped traffic serves as a metaphor for death in the text, flowing traffic signifies forgetting. It is the restarting of traffic that bothers Brittany, the girl working in the hotel lobby in San Bernardino, because it makes her aware that the interruption was only temporary, that her life continues despite the fact that it has ended for others.[35] Paterniti emphasizes this metaphorical connection between traffic and forgetting as he devotes

---

31   Paterniti, pt. 3.
32   Paterniti, pt. 4.
33   Paterniti, pt. 6.
34   Paterniti, pt. 9.
35   Paterniti, pt. 1.

an entire section of his article, number 7, to this interpretation: "History evaporates, but here we are again. From the hotel desk, she can see the traffic moving. And that's when we begin to forget again..."[36] The traffic metaphor here serves to illustrate the basic ambiguity in the human perception of time that includes the possibilities of both ending and continuing, locating this connection in human consciousness.

For Paterniti, then, acknowledging time naturally points to the element of human agency in its perception. He emphasizes the human subject's agency while remembering the Columbine shooting and the various rituals of mourning and he concludes: "It seemed as if the traffic stopped for a long time, that first time."[37] Paterniti suggests that the length of time the traffic is stopped for, how consciously the dead are mourned, depends.

This emphasis on human agency in the perception of time consequently includes the agency of a human medium and in Paterniti's case can even be seen as a moral obligation. As such, Paterniti makes his point in passages in which he explicitly remembers the past, faces the present, and imagines the future. His making amends necessarily includes a confession of his past oblivion. When he reported on the Columbine shooting, Paterniti remembers: "I didn't just look away, I ran."[38] He confronts what he deems a past failure by remembering that he fled Columbine in order to be able to avoid having to face the grief of the victims' relatives:

> I now wonder if part of the reason I wanted to get out was to avoid the onslaught of their pain, perhaps a typical response/reflex. To avoid full responsibility. To remain untouched. To live my Manichaean illusion: There's good and evil, and the latter can be avoided.[39]

This remembering of past repression consequently necessitates the retroactive taking of responsibility.

So Paterniti does what he could not bring himself to do seventeen years previously: he visits some of those left behind. Looking closely at the present for him involves looking at a present that is affected by past gun violence and by its normalization. This is what he hears from the mother of one of the Columbine

---

36   Paterniti, pt. 7.
37   Paterniti, pt. 9.
38   Paterniti, pt. 9.
39   Paterniti, pt. 9.

4.3 The Atoning Medium in Paterniti's "Should We Get Used To Mass Shootings?"

shooters who "disagreed with the word 'epidemic' to describe these events. "It gives it a normalcy I think is dangerous.""[40] It is also what he concludes after visiting a father of a boy killed at Sandy Hook Elementary School. This shooting proves that shootings have become so normal that they can happen anywhere and even affect his own family: "My youngest son was in second grade at the time. That is, *we* were the Newtown parents, and they had been us, too, formerly."[41] Looking closely at the present also brings with it a moral necessity; if normalization of gun crime has fostered gun crime, then it is paramount not to normalize it, not to look away when it happens, but to keep looking. "He didn't take anyone's guns away," Paterniti writes referring to Mark Barden, the father, "he just wanted to make us look at what they'd done to us."[42]

These acknowledgments of past and present affect Paterniti's imagination of the future. This future also involves the possibility, hinted at previously, that we will be personally affected by gun violence. In section 5, Paterniti imagines this possibility, addressing not only himself, but also his readers:

> It began, begins, will begin again. With a sound, reported as a dull crack. A firecracker in the distance. A backfire, a chair tipped, hitting the floor. It's a shift of air, an exhale. It will begin with a thud, a whimper. On a robin's-egg-blue morning in my town, yours.[43]

In the entire passage, too long to quote in full here, Paterniti imagines the future as a possibility derived from the reassessed past and the unflinchingly confronted present. Consequently, the future as he imagines it is a collective one in which present collective inattention will lead to a collectively shared risk of being affected by gun violence. Paterniti also imagines, as a future consequence, the question about where the shooter got the gun from and the necessary answer: "[I]f answered honestly," Paterniti writes, "each and every time we'll realize that we gave it to the killer ourselves. By amnesia, inaction, or the true belief that every American should own a gun, if they want."[44] Citing amnesia or inaction as causes, Paterniti also presents, as a necessary cure to the problem, the simple acknowledgment of temporary dimensions and the activation of a memory that he is exercising as a writer himself.

---

40   Paterniti, pt. 9.
41   Paterniti, pt. 11.
42   Paterniti, pt. 11.
43   Paterniti, pt. 5.
44   Paterniti, pt. 5.

A Threatened Nation's Consciousness

The collective address is one of the text's key rhetorical characteristics. In his communicative relationship with readers, Paterniti explicitly affiliates himself with them as a fellow citizen as he sounds a call for a different kind of attention from an entire national community threatened by random gun violence. In his narrative, then, Paterniti communicates a sense of urgent national unity and connection on a personal level, while fragmenting his perception of live police radio in passages of montage that correspondingly make the experience appear strange.

As detailed above, Paterniti presents gun violence as a communal threat with the potential to affect both himself and his readers. In the text, this sense of community is gradually established, expanding outwards from Paterniti's acknowledgment that he is included in this threatened community to include his readers too. Paterniti begins this gradual expansion with an interpretation of an utterance by the girl working in the lobby of the hotel in San Bernardino. She tells him that she only had a breakdown when the traffic started moving again after the police barriers had been removed:

> I only realized later what she'd been saying underneath, about the cars and all.
> What she was saying was that she felt they were coming for her.
> What she was saying was: I don't know how to tell you this, but you're next, too.[45]

In these final lines of the text's opening section, Paterniti accepts the girl's sense of being threatened as threatening to himself, too. It appears to be an ethical move on Paterniti's part because he only acknowledges the threat indirectly, as his own interpretation of her confession about the breakdown related to traffic. To feel threatened, then, is something that he presents as an ultimately moral choice based on the acknowledgment of another's experience. This, of course, has the consequence that not only Paterniti, but also his readers, could make this decision and accept the threat if they were only willing to look at reality in the same way as Paterniti. In this initial passage, then, the reader's inclusion in the threatened community is only invoked through Pater-

---

45   Paterniti, pt. 1.

niti's embodiment as a stand-in for people not yet affected, but who are willing to pay attention if necessary.

This invocation turns more explicit as Paterniti's narrative progresses, explicitly designating readers as parts of a community, too. After listing the mass shootings that occurred in the span of just a few days, ultimately including the shooting in San Bernardino, Paterniti refers to a shared consciousness: "Of course, it's San Bernardino that will score the deepest mark on our psyche, that will force us to pause,"[46] he writes. The communal psyche he invokes here suggests that the community he is referring to inevitably includes readers. While on the plane, listening to the reports about the shooting in San Bernardino, Paterniti refers to this community again:

> The flight attendant was motioning. Coffee? Smiling, I mouthed the words "I'm good." But I was thinking the opposite. I wanted to raise an alarm, years past it mattering. That was the stark desolation of the moment we now found ourselves trapped in.[47]

This reinforcement manifested in the use of the inclusive "we" creates a sense of urgency and common experience. The community that Paterniti and his readers are parts of not only has a psyche, but it is also trapped in a moment of "stark desolation."

This sense of urgency is raised as Paterniti marks the community as national, directly addressing his readers as fellow citizens. After relaying the details of a shooting in Columbus, he writes: "We must consider this a historical event. But the novelty came in the details, not in the event itself. And indeed it had the staying power of dew in our national consciousness, which is to say none at all."[48] The communal consciousness appears not only as explicitly national here, but also as forgetting. Hence Paterniti, as mentioned above, takes it upon himself to refresh the communal memory and address his readership as a nation, concluding "there's your rough year, America."[49] As a human medium, then, Paterniti does not claim to be different from either the people he experiences in reality or the real readers for whom he writes. On the contrary, the

---

46   Paterniti, pt. 2.
47   Paterniti, pt. 3.
48   Paterniti, pt. 4.
49   Paterniti, pt. 6.

very point of his text is to lay claim to identity and an exemplary model for taking responsibility for it, since he views communal action as the way to change reality.

In Paterniti's model, this imagined change of reality involves a way of seeing reality that acknowledges its mediation. This is manifested in his use of montage to present the experience of police radio from live TV as strangely familiar. In part 3, for instance, he describes his westward flight:

> a normal flight – guy reading Clive Cussler, woman doing Sudoku, flight attendants shuttling up and down the aisle with fizzy soda – except I was listening via in-flight Internet to the disembodied, live streamed voice of the female dispatcher on the police scanner in San Bernardino, the call-and-response of various units, from three various crime scenes, crisscrossing over her[50]

What makes the normal flight strange, then, is Paterniti's own intentional experience of hearing the police scanner in San Bernardino that is juxtaposed with his experience of sitting on a plane, being on a "normal flight." In his narrative, Paterniti replicates this experience for the reader who is reading a normal text. Paterniti intersperses his own narration with unmediated excerpts from police radio transcripts that appear as intrusions from reality.[51] This juxtaposition reveals the existence of two different kinds of mediated reality: On one side, the experience of the reading of a written text about gun violence; on the other side, the grim experience of listening to people actually reacting to gun violence. Furthermore, as a consequence, the juxtaposition emphasizes the latter aspect and, thus, characterizes the experience of listening to police radio as unusual, making its very familiarity appear strange.

Human Memory and Attention Against Violence

Paterniti's text, then, can be read as the urgent testimony of a human medium who interweaves his experiencing and telling in a particular way of being in the world, based on his self-awareness of being human. Against the backdrop

---

50   Paterniti, pt. 3.
51   Paterniti, pt. 4.

4.3 The Atoning Medium in Paterniti's "Should We Get Used To Mass Shootings?"

of the threat of potential random gun violence is the fact of Paterniti's possession of a body, and consequently living and being vulnerable in time; this accounts for the text's urgency. This aspect is crucial because it positions the text in such a way that serves to illuminate broader discussions of genre and reference, of fact and fiction in the specific context of violence. John Durham Peters has argued that: "the boundary between fact and fiction is an ethical one before it is an epistemological one: it consists in having respect for the pain of victims, in being tied by simultaneity, however loosely, to someone else's story of how they hurt."[52] From this point of view, the ethical component of Paterniti's text derives from his own humanity. However, willingly choosing to pay attention to how others are hurting, as Paterniti does, also very much carries with it epistemological implications. By looking at the present grief of others, Paterniti drags the cause of this pain from the past into the present and, hence, frames it as worthy of our present attention. "Living people's pain is news, dead people's pain is history,"[53] Peters goes on to say. It is precisely the dead's pain that Paterniti seeks to save from history by confronting the present and by remembering the past.

The workings of history, collective consciousness, and attention are explicitly thematized in the text by way of Paterniti's references to a Milan Kundera novel that he reads and from which he quotes.[54] These references illustrate the core ambiguity in his own role as human medium that he seeks to overcome, because he sees it as the main reason for collective inaction on gun violence. The pace of events makes every shooting a historical, newsworthy event. As it becomes historical, though, the victims' pain recedes into the past, giving way to other events demanding our present attention. His role as a narrator of experience requires him to give an account of the past. His role as a witness requires constant attention in the present. As a narrator, he has to work against the forgetfulness of history. As a researcher immersed in experience, he has to resist distraction. As Paterniti suggests, both tasks are specifically human and cannot satisfactorily be delegated to media technology or to the industrial logics of mass media coverage driven by capital.

---

52 Peters, "Witnessing," 2009, 38.
53 Peters, 39.
54 Paterniti, "Should We Get Used to Mass Shootings?," 4.

4.4 The Resilient Medium in Rachel Kaadzi Ghansah's "A Most American Terrorist" (2017)

Rachel Kaadzi Ghansah's "A Most American Terrorist" was published in GQ in August 2017 and addresses a very specific kind of American mass shooting. Ghansah spent three months in South Carolina working on a profile of Dylann Roof, who shot and killed nine African Americans in a church in Charleston in June 2015, in order to write the text, for which she was awarded the Pulitzer Prize for Feature Writing in 2018.[1] Drawing on a very diverse set of research methods, Ghansah's text is the least typical reportage analyzed in this work. Ghansah interweaves instances of personal experience with the results of historical research or quotes from newspapers. In the story, Ghansah presents herself explicitly as being aware of her role as a female black writer, determined to hold Dylann Roof and White America morally accountable. As she paints a picture of Roof, as a product of unethical and incomplete human mediation, Ghansah also marks out her text as the product of a personally affected Black medium, reflecting on experience, interpretation, and communication from a decidedly Black-American perspective. She describes how her Black body affects her, very intentionally produced, experience. She also details how the production and interpretation of her experience are intertwined with her desire to fill the gap in Roof's identity, while she engages in the communal processing of grief in the Black community. Due to its subject matter, however, the text's display of authorial self-awareness does not manifest itself in playful reflections, but in a morally urgent production of experiential evidence and hence responsibility.

Ghansah, a freelance writer, had previously published profiles of African American writers, musicians, and artists, as well as excerpts from memoirs

---

[1]   The Pulitzer Prizes, "Rachel Kaadzi Ghansah, Freelance Reporter, GQ."

and cultural criticism in different US magazines.² As mentioned previously, Ghansah's work, which has not been published in book form and evades generic ascriptions more specific than 'essay', has been largely ignored by critical scholarship. There exists only a brief mention of her prized text on Dylann Roof in a recent book-long takedown of traditional journalistic objectivity. "She's not 'objective'", Lewis Raven Wallace has argued. "But 'objectivity' asks that we accept our current structures of dominance as inevitable."³

However, Ghansah has talked about her work in a few instances and elaborated upon her approach to writing reportage in general and her story on Dylann Roof in specific. In at least one of these instances, Ghansah has revealed an acute awareness of mediation. For instance, she explained how the assignment's economic frame can influence her ultimate product and that she had travelled to Charleston prior to the trial and reported a story about the victims before she contacted an editor at *GQ Magazine* because she wanted to interpret the event independently:

> I like the autonomy – that's my favourite word – I like the autonomy of figuring out the story for myself before I go to someone. And then, you know, maybe they start to conceive of it the way they want to. It was very important for me to conceive of it the way I thought it should be told. From my work and from what I saw.⁴

Furthermore, she repeatedly connected the emotional aspects of human mediation and symbolic sensemaking to the ethics of concrete deeds that have material consequences. Ghansah said that she felt a certain moral obligation toward the families of Dylann Roof's victims that was influenced by their shared skin color. She felt that she could fulfill this obligation by holding Dylann Roof's family accountable on a symbolic level:

> The ability to talk to them as Black people was different. And it made it different. It made me feel an obligation to them to do something... I felt like I want Dylann Roof to know that if you walk in a church and you kill Black people, someone will come to your parents' door and ask them to be responsible for your behaviour. And ask them: What did you do to raise a child with this little sensitivity and this much rage. I want these guys to know that they

---

2   The Pulitzer Prizes.
3   Wallace, *The View From Somewhere: Undoing the Myth of Journalistic Objectivity*, 175.
4   Linsky, "Longform Podcast 260: Rachel Kaadzi Ghansah."

will be implicated and indicted. And they won't have the right to control the narrative.

In the same interview, Rachel Kaadzi Ghansah also explicitly tied Dylann Roof's story to how the history of slavery in the U.S. has not been properly addressed, thereby revealing the story's larger, interpretive frame. Importantly, this framework itself is a story of insufficient or faulty (historical) mediation. For instance, Ghansah has stated: "I think until America grapples with the legacy of chattel slavery we're going to be in a bad place." As her main interpretative influence, she mentions William Faulkner's novel *Light in August* (1932) the first line of which she cites in her own text. "*Light in August...* is a perfect book because it does discuss, right, we don't have a clear understanding of how race works in America."[5] Fittingly, the evidence she deems to be the most convincing shows her that Dylann Roof "was a kid who couldn't make sense of things well... Dylann Roof and his dad did not go to school. They did not do their work. They're not invested in this country. Their only sense of belonging, the only right they should have to feel the way they do is because they believe their Whiteness means something."[6] We might say more generally, then, that the violence Ghansah writes both about and against results from a lack of self-reflection.

The Communal Violence of Lone Wolves

In the actual text, Rachel Kaadzi Ghansah reacts to the medial individualization and marginalization of racist mass shooter Dylann Roof that suggests reduced responsibility on the part of American society and culture. In recent American news media coverage, marginalized white men particularly, who have committed serious acts of mass violence, have repeatedly been labeled as independently acting "lone wolves".[7] This denominator, which has its origins in a militant White nationalist's essay from 1983,[8] has also been applied to

---

5   Linsky.
6   Linsky.
7   DeFoster, *Terrorizing the Masses: Identity, Mass Shootings, and the Media Construction of "Terror,"* 195–196.
8   Kamali, *Homegrown Hate: Why White Nationalists and Militant Islamists Are Waging War Against the United States,* 222.

perpetrators with a Muslim background whose acts were classified as terrorism. At the same time, American mass media has been very reluctant to call shooters, like the white supremacist in Ghansah's text, terrorists.[9] The findings suggest that subsequent mediation of the acts has gained an increasingly critical role, particularly in the cases of seemingly independent actors.

In fact, recent scholarship has argued that the very awareness of this symbolic meaning is central to such assailants' acts. In his analysis of three recent acts of racist mass shootings, similar to the one covered by Ghansah, Mattias Gardell claims that: "performative acts of weaponized whiteness do not only target the individuals they happen to kill, but the communities of racialized others their victims were forced to represent by being killed."[10] Gardell used extensive and multifaceted research to argue that the murders were essentially political, motivated by their expected symbolic meaning. They were "meant to amplify existing tensions in society, to ignite the apocalyptic race war through which the white nation would be born anew."[11]

This kind of violence always occurs against the backdrop of certain symbolically negotiated ideas of collective identity, such as White nationalism or White supremacy on the U.S. far right. While White supremacy refers to the idea that Whites are superior to what they call other races in terms of biology of culture, and they thus have the right to subjugate and control them, White nationalists like Dylann Roof desire to live in a purified state of only White people and, thus, justify the eradication of what they deem to be other races.[12] Related to these ideas is a treatise called "Fourteen Words", which argues that the coming extinction of the White race calls for violence to establish a White ethnostate.[13] Today, much of this symbolic negotiation of collective identities, such as Whiteness, occurs technologically and is mediated on the web. In her extensive study, Sara Kamali has argued that the internet has made it easier for extremists to find ideological and personal encouragement for concrete acts of physical violence to be undertaken. Furthermore, its global reach has given them a sense of both power and belonging.[14] Racist mass shooters such as Dylann

---

9   DeFoster, *Terrorizing the Masses: Identity, Mass Shootings, and the Media Construction of "Terror,"* 199.
10 Gardell, *Lone Wolf Race Warriors and White Genocide*, 3.
11 Gardell, 6.
12 Kamali, *Homegrown Hate: Why White Nationalists and Militant Islamists Are Waging War Against the United States*, 24–25.
13 Kamali, 236–237.
14 Kamali, 228.

Roof, or the ones analyzed by Mattias Gardell, reference each other and their convictions in their online manifestos. "The transnational nature of militant White nationalism", Kamali writes, "emphasizes how not alone these individuals are."[15]

At the same time, even acts of explicitly racist mass violence are also shaped by fantasies of individual identity and its perception within a collective, albeit more narrowly. In many cases, the actual shootings were preceded by active self-presentation on the part of the perpetrators.[16] Prior to his attack on the church in Charleston, for instance, Dylann Roof anticipated future media coverage and disseminated a manifesto with pictures online.[17] Gardell suggests that a mythic hero quest lies at the heart of such fascist lone wolf identities.[18] He refers to a fascist anthology of superhero narratives whose American authors argue in the introduction: "In a world where culture has been replaced by consumerism, where 'God is dead' and reality is experienced on a screen, the closest glimpse most people have on the sublime is a superhero."[19] Gardell's religious study fits psychologists' observations that mass shootings—especially those premediated by the shooter's publications of manifestoes—can be linked to narcissism. In fact, mass shooters have repeatedly referred to themselves as figures with outstanding capabilities in their manifestoes.[20] This has led psychologists in the U.S. to explain the rise of mass shootings in part with the increased observation of narcissistic tendencies among U.S. citizens. Brad Bushman recently argued, for instance, that: "if narcissism continues to flourish as a subclinical but influential personality trait of many members of the population, we may see even more narcissistic mass shooters in the years to come."[21]

A Black Medium's Intentional Presence

Ghansah's text pushes back against such individualizing psychological explanations. It has to be read as an utterly intentional answer to a specific lack

---

15 Kamali, 240.
16 Gardell, *Lone Wolf Race Warriors and White Genocide*, 6.
17 DeFoster, *Terrorizing the Masses: Identity, Mass Shootings, and the Media Construction of "Terror,"* 199.
18 Gardell, *Lone Wolf Race Warriors and White Genocide*, 85–86.
19 Johnson and Hood, *Dark Right: Batman Viewed From the Right*, 1.
20 Bushman, "Narcissism, Fame Seeking, and Mass Shootings."
21 Bushman, 236.

of collective and individual self-care that resulted in a heinous act of racially motivated gun violence with immense material and symbolic consequences. Ghansah explicitly and consequentially performs the split of the witness described in the analysis of Paterniti's text. She pays attention to the grief of others in the present while making sense of a historical event. Most importantly, she reflects on this dynamic and makes it transparent. Early on, framing the examination of Roof's identity that is to follow, Ghansah herself makes clear that she views the sensemaking as a consequence of the sorrow:

> I had come to Charleston intending to write about them, the nine people who were gone. But from gavel to gavel, as I listened to the testimony of the survivors and family members, often the only thing I could focus on, and what would keep me up most nights while I was there, was the magnitude of Dylann Roof's silence, his refusal to even look up, to ever explain why he did what he had done.[22]

In this early passage, Ghansah states that her initial intention to write about the victims was changed by her experience of the right to silence afforded to Dylann Roof by the justice system. Hence, she marks out her text as something produced intentionally by explaining the genesis of this intention. In addition, this change in direction implies that her work carries a heavier moral load than the mere execution of a journalistic assignment. Ghansah interprets Roof's silence as an evasion of responsibility. Hence, by prioritizing the attribution of responsibility for a horrific act of gun violence over the victims' stories, she imbues her project with a certain moral necessity and urgency that extend beyond the symbolic aspects of text.

Apart from being informed by this moral imperative, Ghansah's presence also has a physical aspect, marking her out as a medium with a distinct body and subjectivity. As a black writer covering a racist hate crime, Ghansah is neither an impartial onlooker nor a directly affected survivor. And yet she is, in a sense, both. As she criticizes the media coverage of the shooting, her change of intention appears at least partly affected by the color of her skin:

> Almost every white person I spoke with in Charleston during the trial praised the church's resounding forgiveness of the young white man who shot their members down. The forgiveness was an absolution of everything.

---

22   Ghansah, "A Most American Terrorist: The Making of Dylann Roof," pt. 1.

4.4 The Resilient Medium in Rachel Kaadzi Ghansah's "A Most American Terrorist" (2017)

> No one made mention that this forgiveness was individual, not collective. Some of the victims and their families forgave him, and some of them did not. Not one acknowledged that Dylann Roof had not once apologized, shown any remorse, or *asked* for this forgiveness.[23]

As Ghansah states here, the dominant framing of the shooting in the press reflected white praise of the victims' forgiveness, while leaving out the different manifestations of black anger. This interpretation frames the expression of forgiveness as conforming to white will, pushing the question of white responsibility into the background. As Ghansah describes her change of intention, she is committed to framing racial violence and racial responsibility in a way that, if not specifically black, is certainly non-white.

However, this commitment does not represent the narrow focus of an angry black subject who is out for revenge. Ghansah also pays close attention to how whites themselves suffer from Dylan Roof's racial violence. For instance, sitting behind Dylann Roof's mother, who had a kind of convulsion in the courtroom before a victim's testimony, she imagines the latter's inner turmoil:

> She trembled and shook until her knees buckled and she slid slowly onto the bench, mouth agape, barely moving. She said, over and over again, "I'm sorry. I'm so sorry." She seemed to be speaking to her boyfriend, but maybe it was meant for Felicia Sanders, who was soon to take the stand. A communiqué that was a part of the bond that mothers have, one that was brought up by the radiant shame one must feel when your son has wreaked unforgivable havoc on another mother's child.[24]

Here, Ghansah shows how Roof's mother apologizes for her son's actions, assuming the responsibility that he avoids for herself. Although it is unclear at whom the apology is directed, Ghansah speculates charitably that it might be Felicia Sanders, the mother about to testify. She views Dylann Roof's mother as a human being with a suffering body and tries to imagine the shame that she must be feeling. Hence, her moral stance is more broadly rooted in a belief in essential human sameness.

Yet, despite depicting the humanity of Dylann Roof's mother, Ghansah also indicates that, to her, racial difference makes for a more compelling story than

---

23 Ghansah, pt. 1.
24 Ghansah, pt. 1.

human sameness. Reacting once again to Dylann Roof's mother, she characterizes her own concern for her as misplaced:

> When Dylann Roof's mother fainted in the courtroom, a reporter from ABC and I called for a medic, and not knowing what else to do, I used my tissues to put a cold compress on her forehead and started dabbing it – before I felt out of place, or realized that I was too much in place, inside of a history of caretaking and comforting for fainting white women when the real victims were seated across the aisle still crying.[25]

Here, just like in the passage referring to the victims' families' expressions of forgiveness, Ghansah argues that the victims' pain cannot be compared to the pain of Dylann Roof's mother. This conclusion suggests the existence of a racial and moral framework that governs her experience. Ghansah bases her argument on her own feeling of being "out of place" or "too much in place," without explicitly referring to her own blackness. This interpretation is presented as the conclusion of both a logical argument and a moral choice, rather than a reactionary feeling. Still, in detailing how Ghansah feels about her own physical presence, she nevertheless acknowledges her argument's subjectives dimension, which is, after all, put forth by a black medium.

If Ghansah's intention is not explicitly described as being influenced by her own black body, her research nevertheless appears to be complicated by her own blackness. Ghansah first mentions her own skin color when she visits Dylann Roof's father late one evening:

> Wrapped in that moonless night, I knocked on the door of the yellow house, and in the confusion of having an unknown black woman at his door a few hours before midnight, wanting to talk about his son, Bennett Roof let me come in and handed me an ice-cold beer that tasted like relief in my paper-dry mouth, parched from my nerves.[26]

Here, Ghansah associates her blackness with the darkness of the night and imagines herself from the perspective of Dylann Roof's father. Her blackness consequently serves to explain both his confusion and her ultimate relief, when he welcomes her in. As such, Ghansah describes her own black skin as a potentially divisive force operating between herself and a white-skinned man in this

---

25 Ghansah, pt. 1.
26 Ghansah, pt. 2.

4.4 The Resilient Medium in Rachel Kaadzi Ghansah's "A Most American Terrorist" (2017)

passage. She initially imagines it as merely complicating matters and not, as their conversation ultimately shows, as making them impossible.

Later, she gives a more detailed account of the complex feelings that she experiences in exchanges with white Americans. As she visits the church of Dylann Roof's father and grandparents, for instance, she states:

> This black body of mine cannot be furtive. It prevents me from blending in. I cannot observe without being observed. At Dylann Roof's church, I was greeted warmly at the door by a young white woman and a middle-aged white man. But when I entered the chapel and was seated in a rear row, many eyes turned on me, making me feel like I was a shoplifter trying to steal from their God. Was it because I didn't know the hymns, because I didn't take Communion, or was it because I was black? I do not know.[27]

As a researcher, there is no chance for Ghansah to appear distanced and objective because—depending on the place she is in—her skin color designates her as an outsider and calls attention back to herself. As a black woman assuming a physical presence in white America, she necessarily appears as a subject, openly provoking interaction, rather than quietly observing. Consequently, the doubt that she admits to having about the possible reasons for the white churchgoers' paying so much attention to her indicates this interaction's complexity. Even if race does not divide, it certainly points to the bare possibility of separation, thereby sowing doubt and complicating social interactions.

Generally, even if she repeatedly refers to this possibility, Ghansah does not assume that she is treated differently due to the color of her skin. At least once, however, she imagines that her blackness makes an interaction with a white American impossible. When she tries to meet with white supremacist Kyle Rogers, his neighbor is the only person that she finds with whom to talk. When she asks him whether Rogers lives next door:

> he stopped smirking, and I started to suspect that I was being had and that we both understood what the deal was. It began to dawn on me that chances were he knew Rogers, he probably liked Rogers, and he probably did not want anyone, especially someone who looked like me, to bother his neighbor.[28]

---

27   Ghansah, pt. 5.
28   Ghansah, pt. 9.

Here, Ghansah infers from their interaction that Rogers' neighbor would not let someone who looked like a black woman make contact with Rogers. In contrast to her attitude in the passages above, here she only infers a slight sense of doubt and does not give any alternative reasons for his behavior. Here, then, it is the neighbor's racial prejudice, not Ghansah's, that prevents her from meeting with Rogers. While the black woman seeks to make an interaction possible, the white man is evasive, most likely due to her very blackness.

In sum, Ghansah cautiously details how the framing of her text on the shooting is produced as a story of white racial violence, rather than black victimhood. On the one hand, this production is based on raceless, logical questioning and empathy with the victims and their families. On the other hand, it is also shaped by the fact that Ghansah's own blackness forces her to assume her presence as a subject, because her research experience is affected by the difference in skin color between her and the white Americans with whom she interacts. A context that turns skin color into a matter of life and death necessarily has an effect on its witnesses.

Producing Responsibility

Ghansah considers this aspect in many ways. As noted previously, she states her intentions during the narration of her experience at Dylann Roof's trial, drawing upon her interpretation of his evasion of responsibility. This interweaving of interpretation and intention is one of the main drivers of the text's narrative and it presents Ghansah as a human medium who is producing meaning for others because it is her experience that is supposed to fill the gap in Roof's identity. However, her ongoing willingness to experience, in order to be able to say in a magazine article what Dylann Roof does not say in court, does not yield a definitive assessment of Roof's identity. Moreover, it consistently portrays Dylann Roof as disconnected and incomplete. Still, it also depicts him as human, thereby making a strong claim for white America's collective responsibility.

Although Ghansah begins during the part of the trial at which he was at least physically present, she characterizes Roof throughout the text as a blank or as absent, and thus unable or unwilling to interact. Even in court, she describes him as unwilling to listen to the testimony. "He didn't object often, but when he did it was because he was bothered by the length and the amount of testimony that the families offered. Could they keep their stories about the

4.4 The Resilient Medium in Rachel Kaadzi Ghansah's "A Most American Terrorist" (2017)

dead quick?"[29] Similarly, still at the trial, Dylann Roof appears unwilling to interact on a more fundamental level:

> After Roof was found guilty, they went up to the podium, one by one, when it was time for the victim-impact testimony, and standing near the jury box, they screamed, wept, prayed, cursed. Some demanded that he acknowledge them. "Look at me, boy!" one raged. He did not. Others professed love for him. He did not care. Some said they were working the Devil from his body. *Feel it,* they shouted. He did not appear to feel anything.[30]

In Ghansah's characterization of Roof's fundamental unwillingness to acknowledge any connection between himself and the families of the people he killed, he appears almost inhuman but certainly anesthetized; unable to have feelings. Still, Ghansah does not simply dismiss him as such, but rather interprets his behavior as an exercise in control granted to him by the American justice system:

> Roof was safeguarded by his knowledge that white American terrorism is never waterboarded for answers, it is never twisted out for meaning, we never identify its "handlers," and we could not force him to do a thing. He remained in control, just the way he wanted to be.[31]

Not having to answer for the killing of African Americans then, in Ghansah's interpretation, is the privilege of a white American. After all, and despite the strangeness of his behavior, Dylann Roof is portrayed as a human being.

As a human being, however, he has failed to connect with others. Having contacted some of Roof's former teachers, Ghansah states: "It is as if he floated through people's lives leaving nothing for them to recall. One teacher who spent time with him in her classroom every day says that she typically has a good memory, but she apologizes because she really can't remember anything about him."[32] Ghansah also presents an interpretation of a picture in a yearbook that she is shown by the former principal at Roof's elementary school:

---

29 Ghansah, pt. 1.
30 Ghansah, pt. 1.
31 Ghansah, pt. 1.
32 Ghansah, pt. 3.

The students were grouped together, with clear affection, elbows on each other's backs, almost hugging, giggling with ease. And then I found him. Off-center, straining at a smile, with sad eyes, standing to the side, in a natty-looking red jacket, with his bowl-cut blond hair, already looking like a boy apart.[33]

As Ghansah's research shows, Roof's birth was already marked by incompletion: "There was no birth announcement when he arrived. In fact, on his birth certificate, there is no father even listed."[34] She concludes that: "in the classroom and around town: He was an unmemorable ghost, until he wasn't."[35] Seen from the perspective of people who interacted with him, Ghansah concludes that Dylann Roof appears empty, his identity incomplete.

This emptiness is also manifested in Roof's behavior. For instance, Ghansah narrates how Roof fails to see either past or present clearly. She states that Roof denies history by claiming that he never had a black friend.[36] She describes him as carrying "the cognitive dissonance of a man looking for what never was,"[37] and to be a student of "false history."[38] Furthermore, Roof is also depicted as being "spaced or zoned out while working," falling "asleep virtually anytime he was stationary," and being "quiet, uncomfortably quiet, strangely quiet."[39] To conclude, Ghansah's research supports her impression of Roof in court. He is a nobody, unable or unwilling to assume productive agency in American society—but still a human being.

Consequently, Ghansah's research does not paint an accurate picture of Roof's individual responsibility. This is not because he is not also individually responsible, but because this would not be the whole story. She presents the argument for Roof's lack of individual agency even as she shifts the focus from individual to collective responsibility; she analyzes the hateful ideas and behavior with which Roof ended up identifying. She describes him as: "a child both of the white-supremacist Zeitgeist of the Internet and of his larger environment"[40] and according to Ghansah: "Roof is what happens when we prefer vast

---

33   Ghansah, pt. 3.
34   Ghansah, pt. 4.
35   Ghansah, pt. 4.
36   Ghansah, pt. 3.
37   Ghansah, pt. 4.
38   Ghansah, pt. 9.
39   Ghansah, pt. 6.
40   Ghansah, pt. 8.

4.4 The Resilient Medium in Rachel Kaadzi Ghansah's "A Most American Terrorist" (2017)

historical erasures to real education about race."[41] In order to hold these larger forces accountable, therefore, Ghansah also seeks to experience both the places and the people who represent them by confronting them with their connection to Roof.

This takes conscious effort on her part. Just like Ghansah's research experiences concerning Roof's individual responsibility, such as the visit with his father, these experiences are described as products of acts of will. For example, after recounting the rejection of a request for an official visit to a plantation where Roof posed with stuffed slave dummies, Ghansah tells her readers: "I am a black woman, the descendant of enslaved people, so I went anyway and walked along the same path that Roof did, where the quarters are set on something cheerfully marked as 'slave Street'."[42] The plantation illustrates the racist physical environment in which Roof grew up; by visiting it, Ghansah makes this physical reality at least partly responsible for Roof's deed. In a similar scene, she seeks to confront a representative of the white supremacist ideas circulating online in the person of Kyle Rogers, the head of a local white-nationalist organization. This experience, too, Ghansah writes, is the product of insistence: "because after Kyle Rogers refused to take my call, I went there one day and knocked on his door."[43] Although she does not end up meeting Rogers in person, her visit is an act of making him responsible *ex negativo*. It makes his active evasion of responsibility evident. Consequently, for Ghansah, responsibility is by no means a given component of reality, but rather the product of symbolic and material human action. If Roof's refusal to take responsibility for his heinous crime is manifested in his unwillingness to speak, then her making him and parts of white America responsible is embodied in her very presence and in her asking of questions, which literally force people to respond or to have their evasion of responsibility made public.

---

41   Ghansah, pt. 9.
42   Ghansah, pt. 8.
43   Ghansah, pt. 9.

Addressing Two Communities

Racist violence, like Dylann Roof's, always carries symbolic meaning tied to collective identity. Its meaning differs depending on the receiving communities. If Roof's violence symbolically addresses at least two different groups, most obviously kept apart by the color of their skin, then Ghansah's answer to his act of violence will have to do likewise. Therefore, as a narrative about the struggle to assign meaning to racial violence, Ghansah's text is addressed to at least two different communities with two different messages. As I have shown above, Ghansah very much assumes her agency as an experiencing black subject, if only because she feels personally threatened by Roof's crime, an act of racist violence. Despite this experience, her concern is not primarily with issues of personal feeling, but rather with collective identities that may be shaped by feeling. As a communicating medium, she addresses collective communities; as a witness, she has to address both general injustice and personal pain. The communities whom Ghansah addresses change over the course of the narrative, depending on these distinctions. Initially, Ghansah imagines her readership as a rather general public that witnesses injustice. When she describes how her intention has changed in the courtroom, she addresses a broad community similar to the American public in Paterniti's text:

> Over and over again, without even bothering to open his mouth, Roof reminded us that he did not have to answer to anyone. He did not have to dignify our questions with a response or explain anything at all to the people whose relatives he had maimed and murdered. Roof was safeguarded by his knowledge that white American terrorism is never waterboarded for answers, it is never twisted out for meaning, we never identify its "handlers," and we could not force him to do a thing.[44]

In this passage, Ghansah speaks of a community that asks questions, reminded by Roof of white America's privilege. Despite the obvious racial tension in this accusation, Ghansah, by referring to the justice system, does not explicitly speak only of a black American community, but rather of a larger society granting this privilege to whites like Roof. Ghansah speaks to this American community as a whole, as a representative and member thereof.

---

44   Ghansah, pt. 1.

Consequently, she implicates herself in granting Roof the privilege of silence and explicitly positions herself as unwilling to accept any opposition between black and white America.

However, toward the end of the text—and certainly by the end of her research narrative—this broad community has been narrowed down and Ghansah speaks to a community to which she relates to more emotionally. In the last section, having located the responsibility for his crime in white American society, and having "learned about what happens when whiteness goes antic and is removed from a sense of history,"[45] Ghansah explicitly addresses a more narrowly defined black American community that praises the example of the victims' families, which, as she writes:

> reminds us that we already know the way out of bondage and into freedom. This is how I will remember those left behind, not just in their grief, their mourning so deep and so profound, but also through their refusal to be vanquished. That even when denied justice for generations, in the face of persistent violence, we insist with a quiet knowing that we will prevail. I thought I needed stories of vengeance and street justice, but I was wrong. I didn't need them for what they told me about Roof. I needed them for what they said about us. That in our rejection of that kind of hatred, we reveal how we are not battling our own obsolescence. How we resist. How we rise.[46]

It is clear that her concluding invocation of African-American endurance is strictly communal, even while she framed the initial uncertainty about Roof's identity as a social concern. The victims' families' refusal of the hatred that Dylann Roof embodies mirrors her own way of identifying hatred and of making it responsible without giving in to its divisive effects. Ultimately, then, Ghansah argues that her concern is not with white America in general, but with white-American hatred in specific in her communicative framing of the narrative and in the address to her readers. As Michael Paterniti revealed in his text about mass shootings, such deadly hatred also attacks the notion of time, since it literally makes human beings into history. In order to counter deadly violence, therefore, Ghansah invokes the power of timeless nonviolent resis-

---

45   Ghansah, pt. 11.
46   Ghansah, pt. 11.

tance, of staying alive as a community, thereby embodying "the everlasting, the eternal."⁴⁷

Collective Identity, Collective Violence, and Collective Responsibility

Like the other texts analyzed, Ghansah's narrative points to its own distinct quality as a product of a human medium. Unlike the other texts, however, she only rarely reflects upon the act of production itself. Her self-assigned task feels too urgent to spend time on the phenomenal aspects of her experience or too obvious to display the inner workings of her process of interpretation. If society is a product of collective human action, then so too is the violence committed by Dylann Roof that results from real hatred. Emphasizing this assessment appears pointless in the face of his terrible crime, though. Instead, Ghansah highlights that the production of identity cannot be isolated and individualized. Much like Dylann Roof's identity, whom she describes as the product of his parents as well as his social and cultural environment, she acknowledges that her own identity is also affected by the experiences of her community and the meaning assigned to those experiences. For instance, as she fears for her black body or tells her own story of the prevalence of black Americans in the face of racial hatred, she sets an example for the creation of a resilient black collective identity in the face of violent threats by another group of people. Unlike Paterniti, then, her concern as a narrator is not with potential forgetfulness, but with a pre-dominantly white framing of a white racist's hate crime. Consequently, Ghansah repeatedly points to the production of her experience because this experience, wrung from a racist reality and against the backdrop of a heinous crime, already carries with it its own interpretation.

As such, it is also the most convincing evidence against the myth of Dylann Roof as a lone wolf. Her experience, be it in the form of a visit to a former plantation or her rejection by a White Supremacist, supports her claim of Roof's deed as being backed by a reduced and ignorant collective identity of White America. It is precisely its reduction of identity to mere skin color, and its lack of self-awareness thereof and its parenthetical lack of confidence, that makes White America continuously reaffirm itself by way of racist violence. Understanding violence as tied to misguided identity formation implies dismissing any individualization of a crime that has strong symbolic meaning. Ultimately,

---

47   Ghansah, pt. 11.

4.4 The Resilient Medium in Rachel Kaadzi Ghansah's "A Most American Terrorist" (2017)

it makes the murderer's criminal prosecution and individual sentencing appear reductive and insufficient. In part, Ghansah addresses this exact insufficiency with the example of her intentionally produced experience that raises the question of collective responsibility. At the same time, the example of her continuous self-reflection as human medium presents a counter-example to the root cause of White America's deluded collective identity and suggests a key measure to prevent future racist mass shootings: a more honest self-examination of America and its racist legacy as a kind of overhaul of its collective identity.

4.5 The Reflexivity of Violence

As we have seen, the self-reflection of the writers confronting violence reveals the deep connection between symbolic and material violence in all three cases. Just as violence is closely related to processes of individual and collective identity formation, so too does it have similarly reflexive functions. The writers of the three texts thematize this reflexivity in two main ways. First, concrete acts of violence always carry collectively negotiated symbolic meanings that deeply affect how they are perceived. As social transgressions, their meaning affects the possibility of similar acts of future violence. For instance, as George Saunders observes, homelessness is likely to amplify mental health problems, which make it more likely for a homeless person to remain homeless. As Michael Paterniti claims, previous acts of gun violence have the potential to foster a kind of trauma that leaves them unaddressed. This neglect makes it just as likely for mass shootings to happen again in the future. In similar ways, Rachel Kaadzi Ghansah argues that the insufficient cultural accounting for the legacy of racial violence in the U.S. contributes to future acts of violence against Black people.

Second, the production of symbolic meaning itself always resembles an act of violence. In all three cases, the writers explicitly consider the ways in which communication is connected to the physical violence under investigation. George Saunders, for instance, highlights how verbal threats and lies are rampant in the camp. In addition, he reflects upon how his mere presence, which involves the constant freedom for him to leave, resembles a kind of symbolic extraction of value on his part from the people who do not share this same freedom. Michael Paterniti is worried about not being able to muster the kind of attention deserved by the trauma that he aims to confront and to prevent. Furthermore, he thematizes the ways in which technological media's effects of immediacy shape the ways in which traumatic events are collectively addressed. Finally, Rachel Kaadzi Ghansah understands her production of symbolic meaning as a forceful kind of accountability that essentially questions certain ideas of identity. In addition, she points to the internet as media technology that carries the potential to empower evil.

In sum, the authors insist on the universal and integrated character of violence in their examinations. For them, any act of violence always works both physically and symbolically. Hence, the mediation of violence also points to the violence of mediation in their texts. This is to say that, just like violence, one function of mediation includes selective prioritizing and effectively choosing one meaning of combined form and content over other alternatives.

As the writers consider this interrelation, they effectively point to violence's existential aspects, the specifics of human perception and mediation, and indirectly address mediatization's dismantling character. When viewed in this way, the increased human reliance upon technological media resembles an act of self-harm. Consequently, their own proposed alternative ways of mediation are highly subjective and are laden with ethical considerations. They claim that violence is universal, constitutive to human identity and communication, and that confronting it unflinchingly in acts of human self-examination—doing precisely what technical media are unable to—is the human way to handle it.

In addition, against the backdrop of the acts of structural or physical violence described, questions pertaining to meaning more generally appear more urgent. It is apparent that the performed ethical considerations revolve around concerns like: Who gets to assert a certain meaning? How do personal, subjective meanings relate to the ongoing acts of intersubjective negotiations that occur in conversations? How does common meaning shape communities? In any case, the juxtaposition of real, physical violence with its symbolic meaning also casts meaning's material aspects and its relation to the unequal distribution of power and freedom into sharper relief. Thus, writers describe technological mediation with reproducibility as its main functional feature as complicit in acts of violence, because the very reproducibility of meaning potentially contributes to the normalization of mass violence.

Conclusion

The Possibilities of Human Media

Throughout this study I have framed the self-reflection, analyzed in reportage, as the reporter's existential self-affirmation as human medium who embodies both the material and symbolic making of reality. Furthermore, I have suggested that this self-assertion manifests an artistic streak that is central to the genre of reportage, understood as intentional eyewitness account. In the analyzed texts the human making of reality is necessarily based on embodied human experience, mediated and made meaningful in thought and transmitted in written language. For instance, David Foster Wallace pitches self-awareness against isolation, George Saunders raises the profile of feeling, and Mac McClelland and Rachel Kaadzi Ghansah detail how physical difference decisively affects meaning, as we have seen most prominently expressed in what I have termed the areas of *experience* and *interpretation*. Mark Johnson has argued that this insistence upon the centrality of the inevitable embodiment of human experience corresponds to the drive to enact modes of human experience at the core of art:

> We care about the arts and find them important, on the occasions we do, not merely because they entertain us, but more importantly because they enact worlds – or at least modes of experience that show us the breadth and depth of possibilities for human meaning.[1]

When viewed from this perspective, art is not merely a human product, but rather a particular way of paying attention to the means by which humans produce experience. The detailed accounts of the ways in which human memory, imagination, and attention shape meaning in the texts under consideration consequently have broader political implications.

---

1   Johnson, *The Aesthetics of Meaning and Thought*, 25.

Essentially, they are human responses to the technological mediation of experience. This rather abstract claim certainly needs further elaboration. After all, no text raises the issue of media technology's challenge to human experience explicitly. Therefore, the following questions need more systematic treatment than I have provided so far: Against whom do reporters affirm themselves as humans more precisely? Why? What political implications does this self-affirmation carry?

I have repeatedly suggested that, to use Lyotard's term, the *inhuman other*, which is addressed by reporters' self-affirmation, could superficially be identified as various explicitly mentioned technological media. The writers of the texts analyzed confront concrete technological media directly and in quite a few instances. David Foster Wallace, for instance, contrasts the exclusively visual mediation of cameras with the complex interplay of senses found in human perception. John Jeremiah Sullivan observes reality TV's revealing fakeness. George Saunders mistrusts online news reports about a meditating boy. Michael Paterniti laments the isolating effects of live broadcasts. Rachel Kaadzi Ghansah notes the role of online forums in inciting the genesis of a racist mass shooting.

Art and Critique in a Collision of World-Views

However, I have sought to identify a more profound concern and engagement with the technological mediation of reality that can primarily be identified by way of the exhibited authorial consciousness manifested in the very prominent role of self-reflection in the analyzed texts. This points to a bigger concern with a larger underlying technological shift, an ideological conflict between media in which world-views collide.[2] As Neil Postman has argued, this conflict takes places on an existential level because the technological changes such as the ones referred to by mediatization are ecological. Because they are so fundamental, they cannot be limited to human activities.[3] "New technologies", Postman has insisted, "alter the structure of our interests: the things we think *about*. They alter the character of our symbols: the things we think *with*. And they alter the nature of community: the arena in which thoughts develop."[4] Therefore,

---

2   Postman, *Technopoly: The Surrender of Culture to Technology*, 16.
3   Postman, 18.
4   Postman, 20.

the complex ways in which media technology has come to shape the human experience of reality in Western societies, such as the U.S., deserves further elaboration. In 1984, Fredric Jameson argued that the *other* in these societies was indeed no longer nature—as in precapitalist societies—but technology as the manifestation of developed and globalized capital.[5] For Jameson, computers—"machines of reproduction rather than production"—were the most dominant technology in the new era of a capitalism dominated by media.[6] Jameson viewed their capacity to represent this new reality as limited, as machines of reproduction rather than production.[7]

More specifically, computers, as machines that can integrate other media technologies such as the camera or the written type, mark the latest development of electronic media. These have been argued—as in the early case of the telegraph— to have fundamentally altered the conditions of human representation of reality, given that they destabilize that relationship between signifier and signified or word and world. In 1999, Scott Lash described what he termed *reflexive modernity* as decisively shaped by the computer as a new medium. Late modern culture, he argued:

> rightly understood in terms of "the media," can never represent without sending, without transmitting or communicating. Indeed, contemporary "economies of signs and space," especially in their capacity as information, have a lot more to do with transmission than with representation. That is, in contemporary culture the primacy of transmission has displaced the primacy of representation.[8]

In Jameson's view, this primacy of transmission over representation or reproduction over production challenged the traditional arts. In 1991, he claimed that they were "mediatized", which meant that:

> they now come to consciousness of themselves as various media within a mediatic system in which their own internal production also constitutes a

---

5   Jameson, "Postmodernism, or The Cultural Logic of Late Capitalism," 77–78.
6   Jameson, 79.
7   Jameson, 79.
8   Lash, *Another Modernity, a Different Rationality: Space, Society, Experience, Judgment, Objects*, 276.

symbolic message and the taking of a position on the status of the medium in question.⁹

In other words, Jameson argued that it was precisely the primacy and ubiquity of superficial reproduction over representation that prompted traditional modes of artistic representation to address their own modes of production more thoroughly.

For the purposes of this study, this shift might be best understood with regard to yet another different dichotomy. This one is based on Lev Manovich's theorization of "new media" from 2001 that distinguishes between media technologies and communication technologies.¹⁰ Unlike communication technologies such as gesture, speech, or telephony that transmit messages without their storage, media technologies such as writing or photography also inscribe whatever they transmit by capturing or storing the respective content.¹¹ New media such as the computer, then, Bruce Clarke has pointed out: "are figured as the *technological* deconstruction through conglomeration of this very distinction between communication and representation".¹² By simultaneously transmitting and storing, digital platforms: "mimic or travesty the human subject, while doubling once again in binary informatics the prior doubling of the world in communicative representations."¹³ The crucial technological development is the integration of the computer's function in terms of these materials, both literally—the capturing and storing of content—and symbolically—the transmission of content as messages.

That this mimicking of the human subject might provoke an emotional response has been argued for a while. The media theorist Marshall McLuhan had anticipated the challenge of media technology and the human subject's reflexive reaction decades before Jameson performed his analysis of the postmodern. "Today technologies and their consequent environments succeed each other so rapidly that one environment makes us aware of the next", McLuhan wrote in 1965.¹⁴ McLuhan located these consequences by way of

---

9   Jameson, *Postmodernism, or, The Cultural Logic of Late Capitalism*, 13.
10 Manovich, *The Language of New Media*.
11 Clarke, "Communication," 136.
12 Clarke, 136.
13 Clarke, 136.
14 McLuhan, *Understanding Media: The Extensions of Man*, 1965, viii.

his interpretation of media as extensions of our human bodies, and of electronic media specifically as extensions of the human nervous system and consciousness that carried considerable consequences for the human psyche. Any accepted use of an extension of ourselves, among them electronic media, equaled its embrace for McLuhan. At the same time, however, in the case of the extended nervous system, this embrace also necessitated the blocking of perception, or numbness, to handle its electrified amplification. "Technologies begin to perform the function of art in making us aware of the psychic and social consequences of technology",[15] McLuhan therefore argued. For him, the compression of time and space caused by electronic media necessarily came with increased senses of both apathy and unconsciousness as well as connection, commitment, involvement, and participation.[16] "The aspiration of our time for wholeness, empathy and depth of awareness is a natural adjunct of electric technology",[17] he claimed.

Importantly, McLuhan deemed the reflexive human reaction to technology to be more decisive than the technology itself and understood art as a possible cure thereto. He claimed that the: "counter-irritant usually proves a greater plague than the initial irritant, like a drug habit."[18] "In experimental art," he stated, "men are given the exact specifications of coming violence to their own psyches from their own counter-irritants or technology."[19] "The artist", McLuhan further wrote, "grasps the implications of his actions and of new knowledge in his own time" and "is the man of integral awareness."[20] According to McLuhan, artists: "can correct sense ratios before the blow of new technology has numbed conscious procedures... before numbness and subliminal groping and reaction begin."[21]

Understood by way of this functional meaning of art, the writer's self-reflection insists on a distinction between human experience and technological mediation. It addresses the tension between apathy and participation caused by technology. More specifically, self-reflection itself is one such expression of

---

15 McLuhan, viii.
16 McLuhan, *Understanding Media: The Extensions of Man*, 1994, 3–4.
17 McLuhan, 5.
18 McLuhan, 66.
19 McLuhan, 66.
20 McLuhan, 65.
21 McLuhan, 65–66.

human experience that deals with the problem of the anesthetic human reaction to the nervous system's extension. It is the existential affirmation of the literal and figurative human sense confronted with its existential challenge by technology.

Thus, authorial self-reflection more generally takes on the function of critique, rather than confirmation, and works as what Luc Boltanski has termed an *existential test*. *Existential tests* emphasize possibility, unlike *truth tests* which are employed by confirming instances such as in computers and which, according to Boltanski: "strive to deploy in stylized fashion, with a view to consistency and saturation, a certain pre-established state of the relationship between symbolic forms and states of affairs."[22] They are based on lived human experience that serves to contradict both confirmed and unquestioned relations as well as the existing *reality tests* that are already in place.[23] Thus, the existential test: "unmasks the incompleteness of reality and even its contingency, by drawing examples from the flux of life that make its bases unstable and challenge it".[24]

Now, according to Boltanski, this critique can have two main trajectories. Importantly, it:

> cannot be determined solely by its opposition to the established order of reality, considered in its opaque generality, but also, or above all, by its reference to possibilities, already identifiable in the experience of the world, of which suffering and desire are the manifestation in the flux of life.[25]

On the one hand, then, the author's main reliance on deeply subjective experience and interpretation of reality affirms the validity and significance of physical human mediation, as irreproducible knowledge production vis-à-vis technical media's ways of seemingly objective and reproducible mediation. On the other hand, however, the persistent integration of the material and symbolic making of reality by the human medium that is promoted in the texts counter to experiences of alienation, disconnection, or fragmentation in society and culture, emphasizes the existing possibilities of human cooperation for potential change.

---

22 Boltanski, *On Critique: A Sociology of Emancipation*, 103.
23 Boltanski, 110.
24 Boltanski, 113.
25 Boltanski, 113.

This embodiment not only serves to confront self-affirmation with the corresponding conglomeration of media in the computer, but it also carries a more explicitly political significance. The key is that, as is the case in several of the texts analyzed, this embodiment blurs or even erases the distinction between subject and object. As Mitchum Huehls has shown, by using the work of Bruno Latour, it has precisely been this opposition that has allowed capitalistic ideology to appropriate and render traditional modes of critique useless.[26] The most recent expression of capitalistic ideology is arguably neoliberalism, in which humans are "configured exhaustively as *homo œconomicus*" and "all dimensions of human life are cast in terms of a market rationality".[27] Under neoliberalism, as Huehls has argued, *homo oeconomicus* becomes the embodiment of simultaneously subject and object of *laissez-faire* that absorbs both the critique of objective facts as well as that of subjective values.[28] To counter this force with critical literary value, Huehls has identified an ontological production of meaning in which words: "neither reduce nor stand apart from the world" and in which representation: "is not ontologically distinct from the world it describes".[29] This insight might be particularly significant for the analysis of fictional literature. For nonfictional literature, it helps at least to reiterate the critical potential of reportage as the genre of a decidedly human medium against the backdrop of identical concerns.

Irreproducible Mediation

From my material perspective, I have sought to analyze reportage as a specific instantiation of a hybrid medium that can itself be analyzed as a kind of technology. This approach opens up several possibilities for a more pronounced analysis of the kind of power that is at stake. As Peter-Paul Verbeek has argued, using the concept of a "material hermeneutics of technology", this power is exerted both materially and symbolically, as "technologies have an influence on people's actions and practices on the one hand, and on people's perceptions and frameworks of interpretation on the other".[30] On the material micro-level,

---

26 Huehls, *After Critique: Twenty-First-Century Fiction in a Neoliberal Age*, 13–15.
27 Brown, "Neo-Liberalism and the End of Liberal Democracy," 40.
28 Huehls, *After Critique: Twenty-First-Century Fiction in a Neoliberal Age*, 14–15.
29 Huehls, 25.
30 Verbeek, "Politicizing Postphenomenology," 143.

I have already pointed to the writers' perspective onto the productive artist who rebels against reproducibility. Importantly, this idea also includes a conceptualization of the reader as a kind of complicit co-producer who does not consume the writer's material and symbolic offering in the manner of a passive consumer. The texts analyzed essentially perform the political project of de-fetishizing their experience of reality as object, thereby exposing the social process of the production of meaning.[31]

This micro-perspective transports political implications onto the macro-level because it reveals technologies, particularly new media, as clear agents of capital. This observation heightens the importance of issues of control and ownership of media technology in mediatized societies because it suggests that new media technology also mediates the very frameworks of people's interpretation of reality. This matters. "When technologies do not only mediate human actions and perceptions, but also the interpretive frameworks on the basis of which we make decisions", Peter-Paul Verbeek has argued, "there is no opt-out, and no 'outside' from which we could decide whether we want to use a technology or not."[32] Verbeek does not look for a way out of this technological dominance, but seeks a democratic perspective "from within". He finds it in Isaiah Berlin's suggestion to replace the idea of negative freedom, which means the absence of constraints on individual acts, with the idea of positive freedom that means the ability to pursue one's aims.[33]

The political aspect of the writers' self-reflection also shows itself in their endorsement of this positive freedom. More importantly, it is precisely their insistence on their own human capacities that enables them to be free in precisely this way. They use sense not merely against the machine, but *over and against* the machine as they depict themselves as subjects that find freedom *precisely in their very own human nature*. If the self-reflection in reportage, which I have examined, expresses the reflexive modern subject's resistance to capitalism's attempts to objectify human experience by way of technology, then the human subject's embrace of self-reflection equals an insistence on the powers of this human subject of flesh, blood, and nerves. As my analyses have shown, one of the core features of self-reflection in this struggle is the singularity and specificity of the respective author's mediation, because it resists its own re-

---

31   Bradshaw, "The Politics of Consumption," 520.
32   Verbeek, "Politicizing Postphenomenology," 145.
33   Berlin, "Two Concepts of Liberty."

producibility and simultaneously exerts the freedom to make itself anew on its own terms.

This singularity is expressed in four main areas throughout the texts analyzed. First, and perhaps most obviously, this works on both the levels of thematic content and knowledge. In every text, the specificity of the writer's experience of reality, signified decisively by self-reflection, unmasks existing interpretive narratives of reality as untenable. In the first section of texts, writers critically replaced the narratives of pre-fabricated touristic experience that meant to ascertain the experience's meaning. In the second section, writers positioned stories of human agency and self-transformation against larger ideas of a de-mystified, unitary, and stable subject shaped mainly by external forces. In the third section, writers unveiled existing interpretations that depicted violence as natural or inevitable as false by way of emphasizing its own specific mediate qualities and rootedness in concrete human action. Importantly, these writers' narratives all counter existing modes of material and symbolic meaning-making that suggest inevitability or pre-determination and that correspond to the interpretive logics of both the computer and neoliberalism.

Second, the singularity and specificity of the respective authors' experiences and mediations affect functions in the area of *work*. The writers effectively resist any absorption of their work as industrialized journalism produced via a defined set of professional standards and methods, as they mark their experiences as intentional and yet personal. Relational concerns appear tied to the thematic subject at hand and are more important than seemingly reproducible journalistic practices. In the first section of texts on touristic experience, writers relate to the role of the tourist as ordinary guy and primarily delineate themselves by way of their supposedly (un)-professional behavior, even while acknowledging the economic incentives of the experience produced. In the second set of texts, authors define their roles more actively in distinction from their main characters as believer, viewer, or writer. In the third section, writers consider the collective ethics of violence as they affiliate themselves more actively (in Saunders's case, however, ironically) with impacted communities.

Third, the ways in which sensory perception and thought are described to interact in the areas of *experience* and *interpretation* suggest an interplay that is operatively similar to the ways in which computers work, but which remains irreproducible. For instance, John Johnston has argued that: "both living creatures and the new machines operate primarily by means of self-control and regulation, which is achieved by means of the communication and feedback of electro-chemical or electronic signals now referred to as information."[34] What makes these internal workings irreproducible by a computer, however, is their embedding in a human body that uses its own singular capacities to both remember and imagine in order to make sense of sensory impressions. In most instances where this interplay is considered, then, it is not the singularity of the sensory impression (i.e., a view or a smell) that authors describe as specific, but its very personal meaning in the memories that it triggers or in the future possibilities it suggests.

Like the computer, the human body integrates both the capacity to store sensory impressions as well as to communicate their meaning. Fundamentally different from the computer, however, the writers' criteria for their selection of the sensory experience produced is highly contingent, idiosyncratic, and full of surprises. Furthermore, as both David Foster Wallace and Michael Paterniti in specific emphasize, the human capacity to experience can be at odds with the respective ability to remember. Unlike technological media, which works by using automated selection criteria, writers' principles of selection are constantly re-negotiated according to reflexive ethical and moral considerations.

Fourth, the authors' depiction of *transmission* suggests a process defined by uncertain human reception in a social context. As such, it is always necessarily relative to the interaction between the specific writer and reader. This interaction, in turn, depends on many different factors, such as the thematic content or the reader's trust. In the first section of texts about touristic experience, for instance, writers seek to establish a trustful relationship infused with humility and sincerity over and against grandiose meta-tales of belief, promise, and equality. In this relationship, they depict the reader as an active participant in an ongoing dialogue about the meaning of the experiences being described. In the second set of reportage that was analyzed concerning other human media, writers emphasize the inherent performativity and difference that affect their relationship with readers. However, they depict the resulting intersubjective gaps as loci of possibility, rather than of separation. In the final group of texts, writers address readers on equal footing as imagined fellow members of privileged, inattentive, responsible, or hated communities.

All in all, their processes of transmission are described as highly contingent exercises between social actors. Due to their deeply uncertain outcomes, they decisively contradict models of automated information transmission or

---

34 Johnston, "Technology," 200.

supposedly effective intersubjective communication.[35] An important piece of this depiction is the idea of a certain plasticity of text or writing that allows for vast possibilities of expression. As depicted time and again, in these pieces of reportage, text is precisely not characterized as aiming at the reliable transportation of unambiguous meaning but always as the mere instrument of a human in exchange with another. In these instances, the conditions of understanding and meaning are not predefined, but are at the very most anticipated, which offers vast opportunities for a kind of (self-referential) play that is absolutely impossible with computers.

The Ethics of Everything

Still, as I have also sought to work out, critical concerns with technological mediation are generally present as a backdrop. Such concerns are a kind of secondary effect of self-reflection. It can be identified in distinction to the acknowledgment of media's tendency to "make something legible, audible, visible, perceivable, while simultaneously erasing itself and its constitutive involvement in this sensuality, thus becoming unperceivable, anesthetic",[36] as Lorenz Engell and Joseph Vogl have put it. It is only against this tendency of media to make themselves obsolete that authorial self-reflection in reportage effectively works as a kind of critique that suggests the falsity of this impression, given that it emphasizes the fundamental mediate quality of all communicated experience to produce the impression of seamless immediacy. Importantly, in John Jeremiah Sullivan's somewhat provocative words, this: "increased awareness in the complicity of the falseness of it all"[37] does not suggest the opposite of a kind of true mediation or seamless transmission, but a shift. As my study suggests, meaning-making under these circumstances, and in neoliberal mediatized societies, is not primarily an epistemological undertaking, but much more pointedly is an ethical undertaking.

As McLuhan has indicated, it is not paradoxical that this shift is attributable to the ubiquity of technological mediation in modern Western

---

35 For critical analyses of these concepts of transmission or communication, see Chang, *Deconstructing Communication: Representation, Subject, and Economies of Exchange*; Clarke, "Communication."
36 Engell and Vogl, "Vorwort," 10.
37 Sullivan, "Getting Down To What Is Really Real," 98.

societies and cultures, such as the U.S. But it is also worth noting that this shift, which corresponds to the corporeal turn in scholarly interest on a larger level, insists on the human body's agency as a universal knowledge container. As such, it stabilizes: "the world, putting bounds and limits to things that might otherwise run out of control" and ultimately anchors our existence.[38]

Like any other knowledge container, the human body can never be completely adequate. Siri Hustvedt asks why, as writers, we choose to tell the particular story that we end up telling and why, as readers, we relate to some stories and not to others in her essay "Why One Story and Not Another?" "The story's truth or falseness", Hustvedt writes, "lies in a resonance that is not easily articulated, but it is one that lives between reader and text – and that resonance is at once sensual, rhythmic, emotional, and intellectual."[39]

Perhaps the human body that communicates through letters on pages and screens does not have to be completely adequate as a knowledge container. Perhaps this authentic inadequacy is a substantial reason why humans who experience their shared existential reflexivity themselves relate to each other as modest and therefore trusting producers, carriers, and communicators of knowledge to make common sense. And perhaps this is especially true in the face of such an imposing medium as the computer, which claims unprecedented adequacy as container and communicator of knowledge. In relating to one another primarily as humans then, humans make their own links and connections between bodies of flesh and blood; between the only ones that ultimately matter.

---

[38] Cmiel and Peters, *Promiscuous Knowledge: Information, Image, and Other Truth Games in History*, 256.

[39] Hustvedt, "Why One Story and Not Another?," 399.

Bibliography

Abercrombie, Nick, and Brian Longhurst. *Audiences: A Sociological Theory of Performance and Imagination.* London: Sage, 1998.
Anderson, Chris, ed. *Literary Nonfiction: Theory, Criticism, Pedagogy.* Carbondale and Edwardsville: Southern Illinois University Press, 1989.
———. *Style as Argument: Contemporary American Nonfiction.* Carbondale and Edwardsville: Southern Illinois University Press, 1987.
Anonymous. "The Confessions of 'a Literary Journalist.'" *Bookman*, no. 26 (December 1907): 370–76.
Aristotle. *Poetics.* Translated by John Warrington. London: Dent, 1963.
Arnold, Matthew. "Up to Easter." *The Nineteenth Century* 21, no. 123 (1887): 629–43.
Ashuri, Tamar, and Amit Pinchevski. "Witnessing as Field." In *Media Witnessing: Testimony in the Age of Mass Communication*, edited by Paul Frosh and Amit Pinchevski. New York: Palgrave MacMillan, 2009.
Bak, John S., and Bill Reynolds, eds. *Literary Journalism across the Globe: Journalistic Traditions and Transnational Influences.* Amherst and Boston: University of Massachusetts Press, 2011.
Barthes, Roland. "The Death of the Author." In *The Rustle of Language*, translated by Richard Howard, 49–55. New York: Hill and Wang, 1986.
Baudrillard, Jean. *Symbolic Exchange and Death.* London: SAGE, 1993.
———. *The Consumer Society: Myths and Structures.* London: SAGE, 1998.
Bearman, Joshuah. *Journeys with George (Saunders), or Why Magazines Should Hire More Fiction Writers, Part 2*, 2009. http://therumpus.net/2009/11/journeys-with-george-saunders/.
Benjamin, Walter. "An Outsider Makes His Mark." In *Selected Writings Volume 2, Part 1, 1927–1930*, edited by Michael W. Jennings. Cambridge and London: The Belknap Press of Harvard University Press, 1999.

———. "The Author as Producer." In *The Work of Art in the Age of Its Technological Reproducibility and Other Writings on Media*, edited by Michael W. Jennings, Brigid Doherty, and Thomas Y. Levin, 79–95. Cambridge and London: The Belknap Press of Harvard University Press, 2008.

———. "The Work of Art in the Age of Its Technological Reproducibility: Second Version." In *The Work of Art in the Age of Its Technological Reproducibility and Other Writings on Media*, edited by Michael W. Jennings, Brigid Doherty, and Thomas Y. Levin, 19–55. Cambridge and London: The Belknap Press of Harvard University Press, 2008.

Berlin, Isaiah. "Two Concepts of Liberty." In *Four Essays on Liberty*, 118–72. Oxford: Oxford University Press, 1979.

Bly, Nellie. *Ten Days in a Mad-House*. New York: Ian L. Munro, 1887.

Boddy, Kasia. "'A Job to Do': George Saunders on, and at, Work." In *George Saunders: Critical Essays*, edited by Philip Coleman and Steve Gronert Ellerhoff, 1–22. American Literature Readings in the 21st Century. Cham: Springer International Publishing, 2017.

Boltanski, Luc. *On Critique: A Sociology of Emancipation*. Translated by Gregory Elliott. Cambridge and Malden: Polity Press, 2011.

Boorstin, Daniel J. *The Image: A Guide to Pseudo-Events in America*. New York: Vintage, 1992.

Boswell, Marshall. *Understanding David Foster Wallace*. Columbia: University of South Carolina Press, 2003.

Bradshaw, Alan. "The Politics of Consumption." In *The SAGE Handbook of Consumer Culture*, edited by Olga Kravets, Pauline Maclaran, Steven Miles, and Alladi Venkatesh, 516–29. SAGE Reference. London: SAGE Publications, 2018.

Brockus, Susan. "Coming to You 'Live': Exclusive Witnessing and the Battlefield Reporter." *Journal of Communication Inquiry* 33, no. 1 (January 1, 2009): 27–42.

Brown, Wendy. "Neo-Liberalism and the End of Liberal Democracy." In *Edgework: Critical Essays on Knowledge and Politics*, 37–59. Princeton: Princeton University Press, 2005.

Burnett III, Zaron. "The Dark Secrets of Nepal's Famous Buddha Boy." *Mel Magazine*, January 21, 2019. https://melmagazine.com/en-us/story/the-dark-secrets-of-nepals-famous-buddha-boy.

Bushman, Brad J. "Narcissism, Fame Seeking, and Mass Shootings." *American Behavioral Scientist* 62, no. 2 (February 1, 2018): 229–41.

Butler, Judith. *Gender Trouble: Feminism and the Subversion of Identity*. New York: Routledge, 1990.

Campbell, Kate. "W.E. Gladstone, W.T. Stead, Matthew Arnold and a New Journalism: Cultural Politics in the 1880s." *Victorian Periodicals Review* 36, no. 1 (Spring 2003): 20–40.

Carey, James W. "Time, Space, and the Telegraph." In *Communication in History: Technology, Culture, Society*, edited by David Crowley and Paul Heyer, 150–55. Boston: Pearson, 2007.

Carey, John. "Introduction." In *The Faber Book of Reportage*, edited by John Carey, xxix–xxxviii. London: Faber and Faber, 1987.

Caton, Carol L. M. *The Open Door: Homelessness and Severe Mental Illness in the Era of Community Treatment*. New York: Oxford University Press, 2017.

Celis Bueno, Claudio. *The Attention Economy: Labour, Time and Power in Cognitive Capitalism*. London: Rowman & Littlefield International, 2017.

Chaffee, Daniel. "Reflexive Identities." In *Routledge Handbook of Identity Studies*, edited by Anthony Elliott, Second Edition, 118–29. London and New York: Routledge, 2019.

Chang, Briankle. *Deconstructing Communication: Representation, Subject, and Economies of Exchange*. Minneapolis: University of Minnesota Press, 1996.

Clark, Andy, and David Chalmers. "The Extended Mind." *Analysis* 58, no. 1 (January 1998): 7–19.

Clarke, Bruce. "Communication." In *Critical Terms for Media Studies*, edited by W. J. T. Mitchell and Mark B. N. Hansen, 131–44. Chicago and London: University of Chicago Press, 2010.

Clifford, James. "On Ethnographic Allegory." In *Writing Culture: The Poetics and Politics of Ethnography*, 98–121. Berkeley: University of California Press, 1986.

Cmiel, Kenneth, and John Durham Peters. *Promiscuous Knowledge: Information, Image, and Other Truth Games in History*. Chicago and London: The University of Chicago Press, 2020.

Cohn, Dorrit. *The Distinction of Fiction*. Baltimore: Johns Hopkins University Press, 1999.

Connery, Thomas B. "Discovering a Literary Form." In *A Sourcebook of American Literary Journalism: Representative Writers in an Emerging Genre*, edited by Thomas B. Connery. Westport: Greenwood Press, 1992.

Couldry, Nick, and Andreas Hepp. *The Mediated Construction of Reality*. Cambridge and Malden: Polity Press, 2017.

Crane, Stephen. "An Experiment in Misery." In *Maggie: A Girl of the Streets*, edited by Adrian Hunter, 137–146. Peterborough: Broadview Press, 2006.

Cuddon, John Anthony, and Claire Preston, eds. "Post-Structuralism." In *A Dictionary of Literary Terms and Literary Theory*, 4th ed., 690–93. Oxford: Blackwell, 1998.

——, eds. "Reader-Response Theory." In *A Dictionary of Literary Terms and Literary Theory*, 4th ed., 726–28. Oxford: Blackwell, 1998.

De Man, Paul. "The Rhetoric of Temporality." In *Blindness and Insight: Essays in the Rhetoric of Contemporary Criticism*, 187–228. London: Routledge, 1993.

DeFoster, Ruth. *Terrorizing the Masses: Identity, Mass Shootings, and the Media Construction of "Terror."* New York: Peter Lang, 2017.

Derbyshire, Jonathan. "John Jeremiah Sullivan." *New Statesman* 141, no. 5120 (2012): 41.

Deutscher, Penelope. *How to Read Derrida*. London: Granta Books, 2005.

Dingledine, Don. "'Feel the Fact': The 1930s Reportage of Joseph North, John L. Spivak and Meridel Le Sueur." In *The Routledge Companion to American Literary Journalism*, edited by William Dow and Roberta Maguire, 110–29. New York: Routledge, 2020.

Dow, William. "Reading Otherwise: Literary Journalism as an Aesthetic Narrative Cosmopolitanism." *Literary Journalism Studies* 8, no. 2 (2016): 118–37.

Dunn, Robert. *The Shameless Diary of an Explorer*. New York: The Outing Publishing Co., 1907.

Eason, David. "The New Journalism and the Image-World." In *Literary Journalism in the Twentieth Century*, edited by Norman Sims, 191–205. Evanston: Northwestern University Press, 2008.

Ellis, John. *Seeing Things: Television in the Age of Uncertainty*. London: I.B. Tauris & Co., 2000.

Engell, Lorenz, and Joseph Vogl. "Vorwort." In *Kursbuch Medienkultur: Die massgeblichen Theorien von Brecht bis Baudrillard*, edited by Claus Pias, Joseph Vogl, and Lorenz Engell, 8–11. Stuttgart: Deutsche Verlags-Anstalt, 1999.

Featherstone, Mike. *Consumer Culture and Postmodernism*. London, 2007.

Feldman, Gerald D. *The Great Disorder: Politics, Economics, and Society in the German Inflation, 1914–1924*. New York and Oxford: Oxford University Press, 1993.

Fish, Stanley E. "Interpreting the 'Variorum.'" *Critical Inquiry* 2, no. 3 (1976): 465–85.

Fitzgerald, Jonathan D. "Setting the Record Straight: Women Literary Journalists Writing Against the Mainstream." Dissertation, Northeastern University, 2018.

Flanagan, Kieran. "Religion and Modern Personal Identity." In *The Many Faces of Individualism*, edited by Anton van Harskamp and Albert W. Musschenga, 239–66. Leuven: Peeters, 2001.

Flis, Leonora. *Factual Fictions: Narrative Truth and the Contemporary American Documentary Novel*. Newcastle Upon Tyne: Cambridge Scholars Publishing, 2010.

Foley, Barbara. *Telling the Truth: The Theory and Practice of Documentary Fiction*. Ithaca and London: Cornell University Press, 1986.

Ford, Edwin H. *A Bibliography of Literary Journalism in America*. Minneapolis: Burgess, 1937.

Fore, Devin. "Introduction." *October* 118, special issue, Soviet Factography (Fall 2006): 3–10.

Fosler-Jones, Elizabeth. "Author Michael Paterniti Talks Process, Travel and Journalism." *The Bowdoin Orient*, April 6, 2018. https://bowdoinorient.com/2018/04/06/author-michael-paterniti-talks-process-travel-and-journalism/.

Foster Wallace, David. "A Supposedly Fun Thing I'll Never Do Again." In *A Supposedly Fun Thing I'll Never Do Again: Essays and Arguments*, 256–353. London: Abacus, 1997.

———. *A Supposedly Fun Thing I'll Never Do Again: Essays and Arguments*. London: Abacus, 1997.

———. "Deciderization 2007 – A Special Report." In *The Best American Essays 2007*, xii–xxiv. Boston: Houghton Mifflin, 2007.

———. *Infinite Jest*. Boston: Little, Brown, 1996.

———, ed. *The Best American Essays 2007*. Boston: Houghton Mifflin, 2007.

Franck, Georg. "The Economy of Attention in the Age of Neoliberalism." In *Communication in the Era of Attention Scarcity*, edited by Claudia Roda, 1–19. Heidelberg: Springer, 2017.

Friedman, Ann. "On Being a Badass." *The Cut* (blog), March 1, 2015. https://www.thecut.com/2015/02/on-being-a-badass.html.

Frus, Phyllis. *The Politics and Poetics of Journalistic Narrative: The Timely and the Timeless*. Cambridge: Cambridge University Press, 1994.

Frye, Northrop. *Anatomy of Criticism*. Princeton: Princeton University Press, 1971.

Galtung, Johan. "Twenty-Five Years of Peace Research: Ten Challenges and Some Responses." *Journal of Peace Research* 22, no. 2 (1985): 141–58.

Gardell, Mattias. *Lone Wolf Race Warriors and White Genocide*. Elements in Religion and Violence. Cambridge: Cambridge University Press, 2021.

Garver, Newton. "What Violence Is." In *Philosophy for a New Generation*, edited by A. K. Bierman and James A. Gould, 256–266. New York: Macmillan, 1973.

Geertz, Clifford. *The Interpretation of Cultures*. New York: Basic Books, 1977.

Geisler, Michael. *Die Literarische Reportage in Deutschland: Möglichkeiten und Grenzen eines Operativen Genres*. Königstein/Ts.: Scriptor, 1982.

Ghansah, Rachel Kaadzi. "A Most American Terrorist: The Making of Dylann Roof." *GQ Magazine*, August 21, 2017. https://www.gq.com/story/dylann-roof-making-of-an-american-terrorist.

Giddens, Anthony. *Modernity and Self-Identity: Self and Society in the Late Modern Age*. Cambridge: Polity Press, 1991.

Giffard, Pierre. *Le Sieur de Va-Partout*. Paris: M. Dreyfous, 1880.

Goffman, Erving. *The Presentation of Self in Everday Life*. Harmondsworth: Penguin Books, 1959.

Gordon, Ian. "Love in the Time of PTSD: Mac McClelland's Irritable Heart." *Mother Jones*, February 13, 2015. https://www.motherjones.com/media/2015/02/mac-mcclelland-interview-ptsd-irritable-hearts/.

Gravitz, Lauren. "Mac McClelland Tails Extreme Birders Through Cuba." *The OPEN Notebook*, January 24, 2017. https://www.theopennotebook.com/2017/01/24/mac-mcclelland-tails-extreme-birders-through-cuba/.

Greenwood, James. "A Night in a Workhouse." In *Into Unknown England, 1866–1913*, edited by Peter Keating, 33–54. Manchester: Manchester University Press, 1976.

Habermas, Jürgen. *The Philosophical Discourse of Modernity: Twelve Lectures*. Translated by Frederick Lawrence. Cambridge: MIT Press, 1987.

Hansen, Mark B. N. "New Media." In *Critical Terms for Media Studies*, 172–85. Chicago and London: University of Chicago Press, 2010.

Hapgood, Hutchins. "A New Form of Literature." *The Bookman* 21 (1905): 424–27.

Hartog, François. "The Presence of the Witness." In *Testimony/Bearing Witness: Epistemology, Ethics, History and Culture*, edited by Sybille Krämer and Sigrid Weigel, 3–16. London and New York: Rowman & Littlefield International, 2017.

Hartsock, John C. *A History of American Literary Journalism: The Emergence of a Modern Narrative Form*. Amherst: University of Massachusetts Press, 2000.

———. "Exploring the Referentiality of Narrative Literary Journalism." In *The Routledge Companion to American Literary Journalism*, edited by William Dow and Roberta Maguire, 325–44. New York: Routledge, 2020.

———. *Literary Journalism and the Aesthetics of Experience*. Amherst: University of Massachusetts Press, 2016.

Hellmann, John. *Fables of Fact: The New Journalism as New Fiction*. Urbana: University of Illinois Press, 1981.

———. "Postmodern Journalism." In *Postmodern Fiction: A Bio-Bibliographic Guide*, edited by Lawrence McCaffery, 51–61. Westport: Greenwood Press, 1987.

Hepp, Andreas, and Friedrich Krotz. "Mediated Worlds – Understanding Everyday Mediatization." In *Mediatized Worlds: Culture and Society in a Media Age*, edited by Andreas Hepp and Friedrich Krotz, 1–15. New York: Palgrave MacMillan, 2014.

Herzig, Rebecca M. *Suffering for Science: Reason and Sacrifice in Modern America*. New Brunswick, N.J: Rutgers University Press, 2005.

Hicks, Wilson. "What Is Photojournalism?" In *Photographic Communication: Principles, Problems and Challenges of Photojournalism*, edited by Raymond Smith Schuneman, 19–56. New York: Hastings House, 1972.

Hill, Alec. "A Conversation with John Jeremiah Sullivan." *The Sewanee Review* 126, no. 1 (2018): 28–56. https://doi.org/10.1353/sew.2018.0005.

Hill, Annette. *Reality TV*. New York: Routledge, 2015.

Hill, Peter C., Kenneth II. Pargament, Ralph W. Hood, Jr. McCullough Michael E., James P. Swyers, David B. Larson, and Brian J. Zinnbauer. "Conceptualizing Religion and Spirituality: Points of Commonality, Points of Departure." *Journal for the Theory of Social Behaviour* 30, no. 1 (March 1, 2000): 51–77. https://doi.org/10.1111/1468-5914.00119.

Hochschild, Arlie Russell. *The Managed Heart: Commercialization of Human Feeling*. Berkeley: University of California Press, 1983.

Hoffmann, Lukas. *Postirony: The Nonfictional Literature of David Foster Wallace and Dave Eggers*. Bielefeld: transcript, 2016.

Holland, Mary K. *The Moral Worlds of Contemporary Realism*. New York: Bloomsbury, 2020.

Hollowell, John. *Fact and Fiction: The New Journalism and the Nonfiction Novel*. Chapel Hill: University of North Carolina Press, 1977.

Homberg, Michael. *Reporter-Streifzüge: Metropolitane Nachrichtenkultur und die Wahrnehmung der Welt 1870–1918*. Göttingen: Vandenhoeck & Ruprecht, 2017.

Huehls, Mitchum. *After Critique: Twenty-First-Century Fiction in a Neoliberal Age*. Oxford Studies in American Literary History. New York: Oxford University Press, 2016.

Hustvedt, Siri. "Why One Story and Not Another?" In *A Woman Looking at Men Looking at Women: Essays on Art, Sex, and the Mind*, 382–99. New York: Simon & Schuster, 2016.

Hutcheon, Linda. "Telling Stories: Fiction and History." In *Modernism/Postmodernism*, edited by Peter Brooker, 232–41. New York: Longman, 1992.

International Association of Literary Journalism Studies. "About Us." International Association of Literary Journalism Studies. Accessed April 30, 2018. http://ialjs.org/about-us/.

Jack, Ian. "Introduction." In *The Granta Book of Reportage*, 3rd ed., v–xiii. London: Granta Books, 2006.

Jacob, Didier. "Interview with David Foster Wallace." In *Conversations with David Foster Wallace*, edited by Stephen J. Burn, 152–57. Jackson: University Press of Mississippi, 2012.

Jameson, Fredric. "Postmodernism, or The Cultural Logic of Late Capitalism." *New Left Review* I, no. 146 (August 1984): 53–92.

———. *Postmodernism, or, The Cultural Logic of Late Capitalism*. Durham: Duke University Press, 1991.

Johnson, Greg, and Gregory Hood. *Dark Right: Batman Viewed From the Right*. San Francisco: Counter-Currents Publishing Ltd., 2018.

Johnson, Mark. *The Aesthetics of Meaning and Thought*. Chicago & London: University of Chicago Press, 2018.

Johnston, John. "Technology." In *Critical Terms for Media Studies*, edited by W. J. T. Mitchell and Mark B. N. Hansen, 199–214. Chicago and London: University of Chicago Press, 2010.

Joseph, Sue, and Richard Keeble. *Profile Pieces: Journalism and the "Human Interest" Bias*. Routledge Research in Journalism; 13. New York: Routledge, 2016. https://doi.org/10.4324/9781315675893.

Jünke, Claudia. "Selbstschwächung und Selbstbehauptung – Zur Dialektik moderner Subjektivität." In *Von Rousseau zum Hypertext: Subjektivität in Theorie und Literatur der Moderne*, edited by Paul Geyer and Claudia Jünke, 9–18. Würzburg: Königshausen & Neumann, 2001.

Kahana, Jonathan. *Intelligence Work: The Politics of American Documentary*. New York: Columbia University Press, 2008.

Kamali, Sara. *Homegrown Hate: Why White Nationalists and Militant Islamists Are Waging War Against the United States*. University of California Press, 2021. https://doi.org/10.1525/9780520976115.

Keeble, Richard Lance. "Literary Journalism." In *Oxford Research Encyclopedia of Communication*. Oxford University Press, 2018.

———. "Literary Journalism." In *Oxford Research Encyclopedia of Communication*, 2018.
Keeble, Richard, and John Tulloch, eds. *Global Literary Journalism: Exploring the Journalistic Tradition*. Vol. 2. New York: Peter Lang, 2014.
———, eds. "Introduction: Mind the Gaps, On the Fuzzy Boundaries between the Literary and the Journalistic." In *Global Literary Journalism: Exploring the Journalistic Tradition*, 1:1–19. New York: Peter Lang, 2012.
Kelly, Adam. "Language Between Lyricism and Corporatism: George Saunders's New Sincerity." In *George Saunders: Critical Essays*, edited by Philip Coleman and Steve Gronert Ellerhoff, 41–58. Cham: Springer International Publishing, 2017.
———. "The New Sincerity." In *New American Canon: Postmodern/Postwar and After: Rethinking American Literature*, edited by Jason Gladstone, Andrew Hoberek, and Daniel Worden, 197–208. Iowa City: University of Iowa Press, 2016.
Keohane, Joe. "Hurting for Words." *Columbia Journalism Review*, April 2015. https://www.cjr.org/criticism/hurting_for_words.php.
Kerrane, Kevin, and Ben Yagoda, eds. *The Art of Fact: A Historical Anthology of Literary Journalism*. New York: Scribner, 1997.
Kilby, Jane, and Antony Rowland, eds. *The Future of Testimony: Interdisciplinary Perspectives on Witnessing*. New York and London: Routledge, 2014.
Kisch, Egon Erwin. *Der rasende Reporter*. Berlin: Erich Weiss Verlag, 1925.
———. "Die sozialistischen Typen des Reporters Emile Zola." In *Mein Leben für die Zeitung 1926–1947: Journalistische Texte 2*, 55–64. Berlin und Weimar: Aufbau Verlag, 1983.
———. "John Reed, Ein Reporter auf der Barrikade." In *Mein Leben für die Zeitung 1926–1947: Journalistische Texte 2*, 91–104. Berlin und Weimar: Aufbau Verlag, 1983.
———, ed. *Klassischer Journalismus: Die Meisterwerke der Zeitung*. München: Rogner & Bernhard, 1974.
———. "Reportage als Kunstform und als Kampfform." In *Reporter und Reportagen: Texte zur Theorie und Praxis der Reportage der Zwanziger Jahre.*, edited by Erhard Schütz, 45–51. Giessen: Achenbach, 1974.
———. "Soziale Aufgaben der Reportage." In *Mein Leben für die Zeitung 1926–1947: Journalistische Texte 2*, 9–12. Berlin und Weimar: Aufbau Verlag, 1983.

———. "Was Reporter verschweigen müssen." In *Mein Leben für die Zeitung 1926–1947: Journalistische Texte 2*, 114–16. Berlin und Weimar: Aufbau Verlag, 1983.

———. "Wesen des Reporters." In *Reporter und Reportagen: Texte zur Theorie und Praxis der Reportage der Zwanziger Jahre.*, edited by Erhard Schütz, 40–44. Giessen: Andreas Achenbach, 1974.

Klein, Amanda Ann. "'This Is the True Story . . .': The Real World and MTV's Turn to Identity (1992 –)." In *Millennials Killed the Video Star: MTV's Transition to Reality Programming*, 57–88. MTV's Transition to Reality Programming. Duke University Press, 2021.

Knudsen, Daniel. "Afterword: Authenticity and Life." In *Authenticity & Tourism: Materialities, Perceptions, Experiences*, by Jillian Rickly and Elizabeth Vidon, 253–59. Bingley: Emerald Publishing, 2018.

Kovach, Bill, and Tom Rosenstiel. *The Elements of Journalism. What Newspeople Should Know and the Public Should Expect*. 3rd ed. New York: Three Rivers Press, 2014.

Kracauer, Siegfried. *The Salaried Masses: Duty and Distraction in Weimar Germany*. Translated by Quintin Hoare. London: Verso, 1998.

Kramer, Mark. "Breakable Rules for Literary Journalists." Nieman Foundation, 1995. http://nieman.harvard.edu/stories/breakable-rules-for-literary-journalists/.

Krämer, Sybille. *Medium, Messenger, Transmission: An Approach to Media Philosophy*. Amsterdam: Amsterdam University Press, 2015.

Krämer, Sybille, and Sigrid Weigel. "Introduction." In *Testimony/Bearing Witness: Epistemology, Ethics, History and Culture*, edited by Sybille Krämer and Sigrid Weigel, ix–xli. London and New York: Rowman & Littlefield International, 2017.

Kraus, Gideon-Lewis. "Examining Pop Culture's Heroes, and Himself." *The New York Times Sunday Book Review*, 2011. https://www.nytimes.com/2011/10/30/books/review/pulphead-by-john-jeremiah-sullivan-book-review.html.

———. "Viewer Discretion: The Trajectory of Writer-Worrier David Foster Wallace." Bookforum, 2012. http://www.bookforum.com/inprint/019_03/10012.

Kreiswirth, Martin. "Merely Telling Stories? Narrative and Knowledge in the Human Sciences." *Poetics Today* 21, no. 2 (Summer 2000): 293–318.

Kristeva, Julia. "Word, Dialogue and Novel." In *The Kristeva Reader*, edited by Toril Moi, 34–61. New York: Columbia University Press, 1986.

Krotz, Friedrich. "Media, Mediatization and Mediatized Worlds: A Discussion of the Basic Concepts." In *Mediatized Worlds: Culture and Society in a Media Age*, 72–87. New York: Palgrave MacMillan, 2014.

———. "Mediatization: A Concept With Which to Grasp Media and Societal Change." In *Mediatization: Concept, Changes, Consequences*, edited by Knut Lundby, 22–40. New York: Peter Lang, 2009.

Krug, Etienne G., Linda L. Dahlberg, James A. Mercy, Anthony B. Zwi, and Rafael Lozano. "World Report on Violence and Health." Geneva: World Health Organization, 2002. http://www.who.int/violence_injury_prevent ion/violence/world_report/en/.

Lania, Leo. "Reportage als soziale Funktion." *Die literarische Welt* 26 (1926): 5.

Lash, Scott. *Another Modernity, a Different Rationality: Space, Society, Experience, Judgment, Objects*. Oxford: Blackwell, 1999.

Lemert, Charles. "A history of identity" In *Routledge Handbook of Identity Studies*, edited by Anthony Elliott, Second Edition, 18–45. London and New York: Routledge, 2019.

Lindner, Rolf. *The Reportage of Urban Culture*. Cambridge: Cambridge University Press, 1996.

Linsky, Max. "Longform Podcast 93: Michael Paterniti," May 21, 2014. https://lo ngform.org/posts/longform-podcast-93-michael-paterniti.

———. "Longform Podcast 260: Rachel Kaadzi Ghansah," July 4, 2018. https:// longform.org/posts/longform-podcast-260-rachel-kaadzi-ghansah.

Lippert, Florian, Marcel Schmid, Djoeke Dijksterhuis, and Marlen Stöhr, eds. "Read Thyself: Cultural Self-Reflection and the Relevance of Literary 'Self'-Labels." In *Self-Reflection in Literature*, 1–16. Time, Astronomy, and Calendars; Volume 08. Leiden: Brill Rodopi, 2020.

Loon, Joost van. *Media Technology: Critical Perspectives*. Maidenhead: Open University Press, 2008.

Lopate, Phillip. *To Show and To Tell: The Craft of Literary Nonfiction*. New York: Free Press, 2013.

Lorentzen, Christian. "The Rewriting of David Foster Wallace." Vulture, 2015. http://www.vulture.com/2015/06/rewriting-of-david-foster-wallace.html.

Lounsberry, Barbara. *The Art of Fact: Contemporary Artists of Nonfiction*. Westport: Greenwood Press, 1990.

Lovell, Joel. "George Saunders Has Written The Best Book You'll Read This Year," 2013. http://www.nytimes.com/2013/01/06/magazine/george-saun ders-just-wrote-the-best-book-youll-read-this-year.html?pagewanted=a ll&_r=0.

Lyon-Callo, Vincent. "Homelessness, Employment, and Structural Violence: Exploring Constraints on Collective Mobilizations against Systemic Inequality." In *The New Poverty Studies: The Ethnography of Power, Politics, and Impoverished People in the United States*, edited by Judith Goode and Jeff Maskovsky, 293–320. New York and London: New York University Press, 2001.

———. *Inequality, Poverty, and Neoliberal Governance: Activist Ethnography in the Homeless Sheltering Industry*. Peterborough: Broadview, 2004.

Lyotard, Jean-François. "Note on the Meaning of Post-." In *The Postmodern Explained*, translated by Don Barry, Bernadette Maher, Julian Pefanis, Virginia Spate, and Morgan Thomas, 75–80. Minneapolis: University of Minnesota Press, 1992.

———. *The Inhuman: Reflections on Time*. Translated by Geoffrey Bennington and Rachel Bowlby. Cambridge: Polity Press, 1991.

———. *The Postmodern Explained*. Translated by Don Barry, Bernadette Maher, Julian Pefanis, Virginia Spate, and Morgan Thomas. Minneapolis: University of Minnesota Press, 1993.

Mac, Gabriel. "About." Gabriel Mac, n.d. http://gabrielmac.com/about.

———. "The End of Straight." *GQ*, July 29, 2019. https://www.gq.com/story/the-end-of-straight.

MacCannell, Dean. *The Tourist: A New Theory of the Leisure Class*. New York: Schocken Books, 1999.

MacKenzie, Matthew. "Reflexivity, Subjectivity, and the Constructed Self: A Buddhist Model." *Asian Philosophy* 25, no. 3 (July 3, 2015): 275–92.

Malpas, Simon. *The Postmodern*. New York: Routledge, 2005.

Manovich, Lev. *The Language of New Media*. Cambridge: MIT Press, 2001.

Marcus, James, ed. *Second Read: Writers Look Back at Classic Works of Reportage*. Columbia Journalism Review Books. New York: Columbia University Press, 2012.

Marder, Michael. *The Event of the Thing: Derrida's Post-Deconstructive Realism*. Toronto: University of Toronto Press, 2009.

Martin, Marc. *Les Grands Reporters: Les Débuts du Journalisme Moderne*. Paris: L. Audibert, 2005.

Mayer, Dieter. "Die Epoche der Weimarer Republik." In *Geschichte der deutschen Literatur vom 18. Jahrhundert bis zur Gegenwart*, edited by Viktor Žmegač, Bernd Balzer, Kurt Bartsch, and Dieter Borchmeyer. Königstein: Athenäum Verlag, 1984.

McCaffery, Lawrence. "An Interview with David Foster Wallace." *Review of Contemporary Fiction* 13, no. 2 (1993): 127–50.

McClelland, Mac. "Bio." Mac McClelland, n.d. http://mac-mcclelland.com/about.

———. "Can the Ivory-Billed Woodpecker Be Found in Cuba?" Audubon Magazine, 2016. http://www.audubon.org/magazine/may-june-2016/can-ivory-billed-woodpecker-be-found-cuba.

———. "Delusion Is the Thing with Feathers." In *Best American Magazine Writing 2017*, 3–22. Columbia University Press, 2017.

McLuhan, and Quentin Fiore. *War and Peace in the Global Village: An Inventory of Some of the Current Spastic Situations That Could Be Eliminated by More Feedforward*. McGraw-Hill, 1968.

McLuhan, Marshall. *Understanding Media: The Extensions of Man*. New York: McGraw-Hill, 1965.

———. *Understanding Media: The Extensions of Man*. Cambridge: MIT Press, 1994.

Mead, George Herbert. *Mind, Self, and Society*. Chicago and London: University of Chicago Press, 1934.

Mersch, Dieter. "Wort, Bild, Ton, Zahl: Eine Einleitung in Die Medienphilosophie." In *Kunst Und Medien: Zwei Vorlesungen*, 131–249. Kiel: Muthesius-Hochschule, 2002.

Milam, Erika Lorraine, and Robert A. Nye. "An Introduction to Scientific Masculinities." *Osiris* 30, no. 1 (2015): 1–14.

Millen, Alex. "Affective Fictions: George Saunders and the Wonderful-Sounding Words of Neoliberalism." *Critique – Bolingbroke Society* 59, no. 2 (2018): 127–41. https://doi.org/10.1080/00111619.2017.1378610.

Miller, Toby. *Violence*. London and New York: Routledge, 2021.

Mitchell, William John Thomas. "Addressing Media." *Media Tropes* 1 (2008): 1–18.

Mooney, Timothy. "Derrida's Empirical Realism." *Philosophy & Social Criticism* 25, no. 5 (September 1, 1999): 33–56.

Morris, Pam. *Realism*. The New Critical Idiom. London and New York: Routledge, 2003.

Mosser, Jason. *The Participatory Journalism of Michael Herr, Norman Mailer, Hunter S. Thompson, and Joan Didion: Creating New Reporting Styles*. Lewiston: Edwin Mellen Press, 2012.

Murphy Paul, Annie. *The Extended Mind: The Power of Thinking Outside the Brain*. Boston & New York: Houghton Mifflin Harcourt, 2021.

Norridge, Zoe. "Professional Witnessing in Rwanda: Human Rights and Creative Responses to Genocide." In *The Future of Testimony: Interdisciplinary Perspectives on Witnessing, edited by Jane Kilby and Antony Rowland, 129–43. New York and London: Routledge, 2014.

Norris, Christopher. "Truth in Derrida." In *A Companion to Derrida*, edited by Zeynep Direk and Leonard Lawlor, 23–41. Chichester: Wiley Blackwell, 2014.

North, Joseph. "Preface to 'Reportage.'" In *Proletarian Literature in the United States: An Anthology*, edited by Granville Hicks, Michael Gold, Isidor Schneider, Joseph North, Paul Peters, and Alan Calmer, 211–12. New York: International Publishers, 1935.

———. "Reportage." In *American Writer's Congress*, edited by Henry Hart. New York: International, 1935.

Ong, Walter J. *Orality and Literacy: The Technologizing of the Word*. London and New York: Routledge, 2012.

Pastoor, Colleen, Kellee Caton, Yaniv Belhassen, Billy Collins, and Mark Rowell Wallin. "Rock of Our Salvation: Ideological Production at the Christian Youth Music Festival." *Annals of Leisure Research* 21, no. 4 (2018): 440–61. https://doi.org/10.1080/11745398.2016.1239542.

Paterniti, Michael. *Love and Other Ways of Dying: Essays*. New York: Dial Press, 2015.

———. "Should We Get Used to Mass Shootings?" *GQ Magazine*, April 29, 2016. https://www.gq.com/story/gun-violence-and-mass-shootings-in-america.

———. "The Long Fall of One-Eleven Heavy." *Esquire Magazine*, June 1, 2009. https://www.esquire.com/news-politics/a1115/long-fall-one-eleven-heavy-0700/.

Peiró Sempere, Julio. *The Influence of Mikhail Bakhtin on the Formation and Development of the Yale School of Deconstruction*. Newcastle upon Tyne: Cambridge Scholars Publishing, 2014.

Peters, John Durham. "Like a Thief in the Night." In *Testimony/Bearing Witness: Epistemology, History and Culture*, edited by Sybille Krämer and Sigrid Weigel, 189–207. London and New York: Rowman & Littlefield International, 2017.

———. *Speaking into the Air: A History of the Idea of Communication*. Chicago and London: The University of Chicago Press, 1999.

———. "Witnessing." *Media, Culture & Society* 23, no. 6 (November 1, 2001): 707–23.

———. "Witnessing." In *Media Witnessing: Testimony in the Age of Mass Communication*, edited by Paul Frosh and Amit Pinchevski, 23–41. New York: Palgrave MacMillan, 2009.

Peukert, Detlev. *The Weimar Republic: The Crisis of Classical Modernity*. Translated by Richard Deveson. New York: Hill and Wang, 1992.

Phelan, James. *Somebody Telling Somebody Else: A Rhetorical Poetics of Narrative*. Columbus: Ohio State University Press, 2017.

Phelan, James, and Peter J. Rabinowitz. "Narrative as Rhetoric." In *Narrative Theory. Core Concepts and Critical Debates.*, edited by David Herman, James Phelan, Peter J. Rabinowitz, Brian Richardson, and Robyn Warhol, 3–8. Columbus: Ohio State University Press, 2012.

Porter, Theodore. *Trust in Numbers: The Pursuit of Objectivity in Science and Public Life*. Princeton: Princeton University Press, 1995.

Postman, Neil. *Amusing Ourselves to Death: Public Discourse in the Age of Show Business*. New York: Viking Penguin, 1985.

———. *Technopoly: The Surrender of Culture to Technology*. New York: Alfred A. Knopf, 1992.

Potolsky, Matthew. *Mimesis*. New York and London: Routledge, 2006.

Rando, David. "George Saunders and the Postmodern Working Class." *Contemporary Literature* 53, no. 3 (2012): 437–60.

Reidy, Michael S. "Mountaineering, Masculinity, and the Male Body in Mid-Victorian Britain." *Osiris* 30, no. 1 (2015): 158–81.

Renz, Ursula. "Introduction." In *Self-Knowledge: A History*, edited by Ursula Renz, 1–18. New York: Oxford University Press, 2017.

Oxford English Dictionary. "Report." Accessed October 5, 2018. http://www.oed.com/view/Entry/162918?

Rickly, Jillian, and Elizabeth Vidon. "Introduction: From Pseudo-Events to Authentic Experiences." In *Authenticity & Tourism: Materialities, Perceptions, Experiences*, 1–14. Bingley: Emerald Publishing, 2018.

Ricoeur, Paul. "Narrative Time." In *On Narration*, edited by W. J. T. Mitchell, 165–86. Chicago: University of Chicago Press, 1981.

Roberts, David. *Human Insecurity: Global Structures of Violence*. Zed Books, 2008.

Robinson, Michael. "Manliness and Exploration: The Discovery of the North Pole." *Osiris* 30, no. 1 (2015): 89–109.

Roiland, Joshua. "By Any Other Name: The Case for Literary Journalism." *Literary Journalism Studies* 7, no. 2 (2015): 60–89.

———. "Derivative Sport: The Journalistic Legacy of David Foster Wallace." Longreads, December 2017. https://longreads.com/2017/12/07/derivative-sport/.

———. "Getting Away From It All: The Literary Journalism of David Foster Wallace and Nietzsche's Concept of Oblivion." In *The Legacy of David Foster Wallace*, edited by Samuel Cohen and Lee Konstantinou, 25–52. Iowa City: University of Iowa Press, 2012.

———. "The Fine Print: Uncovering the True Story of David Foster Wallace and the 'Reality Boundary.'" *Literary Journalism Studies* 5, no. 2 (2013): 148–61.

Rosenblatt, Josh. *Elements of Style*, 2007. https://www.texasobserver.org/2612-elements-of-style/.

Roy, Joaquin. "Reportage." In *Encyclopedia of the Essay*, edited by Tracy Chevalier, 696. London and Chicago: Fitzroy Dearborn, 1997.

Sandler, Sergeiy. "Habermas, Derrida, and the Genre Distinction between Fiction and Argument." *International Studies in Philosophy* 39, no. 4 (2007): 103–19.

Saunders, George. "Buddha Boy." In *The Braindead Megaphone. Essays*, 211–50. New York: Riverhead Books, 2007.

———. *Tent City, U.S.A.*, 2009. http://www.gq.com/story/homeless-tent-city-george-saunders-fresno.

———. "The New Mecca." In *The Braindead Megaphone: Essays*, 21–56. New York: Riverhead Books, 2007.

Savchuk, Katia. "Annotation Tuesday! Mac McClelland and 'Delusion Is the Thing With Feathers.'" Nieman Storyboard, June 13, 2017. https://nieman.harvard.edu/stories/annotation-tuesday-mac-mcclelland-and-delusion-is-the-thing-with-feathers/.

Schoene, Berthold. "Contemporary American Literature as World Literature: Cruel Cosmopolitanism, Cosmopoetics, and the Search for a Worldlier American Novel." *Anglia (Tübingen)* 135, no. 1 (2017): 86–104.

Schopenhauer, Arthur. "On Writing and Style." In *Schopenhauer: Parerga and Paralipomena: Short Philosophical Essays*, edited by Adrian Del Caro and Christopher Janaway, 2:450–95. The Cambridge Edition of the Works of Schopenhauer. Cambridge University Press, 2015.

Schreiber, Holly E. "Journalistic Critique through Parody in Stephen Crane's 'An Experiment in Misery'." *Literary Journalism Studies* 6, no. 1 (Spring 2014): 31–46.

Schudson, Michael. *Discovering the News: A Social History of American Newspapers*. New York: Basic Books, 1978.

Schutt, Russell K. *Homelessness, Housing, and Mental Illness*. Cambridge and London: Harvard University Press, 2011.

Schütz, Erhard. *Kritik der literarischen Reportage*. Munich: Wilhelm Fink Verlag, 1977.

Seguin, Robert. "Form, Voice, and Utopia in David Foster Wallace." *Criticism* 62, no. 2 (Spring 2020): 219–41.

Shaw, Donald L. "News Bias and the Telegraph: A Study of Historical Change." *Journalism Quarterly* 44, no. Spring 1967 (1967): 3–12, 31.

Sidney, Sir Philip. *An Apology for Poetry, or The Defence of Poesy*. Edited by Robert W. Maslen. 3rd ed. Manchester: Manchester University Press, 2002.

Sigg, Pascal. "The Disclosure of Difference." In *The Routledge Companion to American Literary Journalism*, edited by William Dow and Roberta Maguire, 498–508. New York: Routledge, 2020.

Silvers, Robert B, ed. *The New York Review Abroad: Fifty Years of International Reportage*. New York: New York Review Books, 2013.

Sims, Norman, ed. *The Literary Journalists: The New Art of Personal Reportage*. New York: Ballantine Books, 1984.

———. *True Stories: A Century of Literary Journalism*. Evanston: Northwestern University Press, 2007.

Skeggs, Beverley, and Helen Wood. *Reacting to Reality Television: Performance, Audience and Value*. London and New York: Routledge, 2012.

Sklair, Leslie. "Iconic Architecture and the Culture-Ideology of Consumerism." *Theory, Culture & Society* 27, no. 5 (2010): 135–59.

Smythe, Ted Curtis. "The Reporter, 1880–1900. Working Conditions and Their Influence on the News." *Journalism History* 7, no. 1 (Spring 1980): 1–10.

Spellman, Robert L. "Journalist or Witness? Reporters and War Crimes Tribunals." *Gazette: The International Journal for Communication Studies* 67, no. 2 (2005): 123–39.

Spradley, James P. *Participant Observation*. New York: Holt, Rinehart and Winston, 1980.

"State of Homelessness: 2021 Edition." National Alliance to End Homelessness, 2021. https://endhomelessness.org/homelessness-in-america/homelessness-statistics/state-of-homelessness-2021/.

Studdert, David, and Valerie Walkerdine. *Rethinking Community Research: Inter-Relationality, Communal Being and Commonality*. London: Palgrave MacMillan, 2016.

Sullivan, John Jeremiah. "Getting Down To What Is Really Real." In *Pulphead. Dispatches From the Other Side of America*, 89–108. London: Vintage, 2012.

———. "Too Much Information," 2011. http://www.gq.com/story/david-foster-wallace-the-pale-king-john-jeremiah-sullivan.
———. "Upon This Rock." In *Pulphead. Dispatches from the Other Side of America*, 3–42. London: Vintage, 2012.
The Pulitzer Prizes. "Rachel Kaadzi Ghansah, Freelance Reporter, GQ." The 2018 Pulitzer Prize Winner in Feature Writing, n.d. https://www.pulitzer.org/winners/rachel-kaadzi-ghansah-freelance-reporter-gq.
Thompson, Hunter S. *Hells Angels: A Strange and Terrible Saga*. New York: Random House, 1967.
Turkle, Sherry. *Life on the Screen: Identity in the Age of the Internet*. New York: Simon & Schuster, 1995.
Usher, Nikki. "News Cartography and Epistemic Authority in the Era of Big Data: Journalists as Map-Makers, Map-Users, and Map-Subjects." *New Media & Society* 22, no. 2 (2020): 247–63.
Vattimo, Gianni. *The Transparent Society*. Translated by David Webb. Baltimore: Johns Hopkins University Press, 1992.
Vendler, Helen. "314." In *Dickinson*, 118–20. Cambridge and London: The Belknap Press of Harvard University Press, 2010.
Verbeek, Peter-Paul. "Politicizing Postphenomenology." In *Reimagining Philosophy and Technology, Reinventing Ihde*, edited by Glen. Miller and Ashley Shew. Philosophy of Engineering and Technology, 33. Cham: Springer International Publishing, 2020.
Vries, Hent de. "Violence and Testimony." In *Violence, Identity, and Self-Determination*, edited by Hent de Vries and Samuel Weber, 14–43. Stanford: Stanford University Press, 1997.
Vries, Hent de, and Samuel Weber. "Introduction." In *Violence, Identity, and Self-Determination*, edited by Hent de Vries and Samuel Weber, 1–13. Stanford: Stanford University Press, 1997.
Wallace, Lewis Raven. *The View From Somewhere: Undoing the Myth of Journalistic Objectivity*. Chicago and London: University of Chicago Press, 2019.
Wang, Ning. "Rethinking Authenticity in Tourism Experience." *Annals of Tourism Research* 26, no. 2 (1999): 349–70.
Weber, Ronald. *The Literature of Fact: Literary Nonfiction in American Writing*. Athens: Ohio University Press, 1980.
Wellek, René, and Austin Warren. *Theory of Literature*. New York: Harcourt, Brace and Company, 1949.

White, Hayden. "Historical Text as Literary Artifact." In *Tropics of Discourse: Essays in Cultural Criticism*, 81–100. Baltimore: Johns Hopkins University Press, 1978.

Williams, Keith. "'History as I Saw It': Inter-War New Reportage." *Literature and History* 1, no. 2 (1992): 39–54.

———. "The Will to Objectivity: Egon Erwin Kisch's 'Der Rasende Reporter.'" *The Modern Language Review* 85, no. 1 (1990): 92–107.

Williams, Raymond. "Means of Communication as Means of Production." In *Culture and Materialism: Selected Essays*. London and New York: Verso, 2005.

Wilson, Chris. "Chapter 1: Introduction and First Principles." Reading Narrative Journalism: An Introduction for Students, 2020. https://mediakron.bc.edu/readingnarrativejournalism/table-of-contents/chapter-1-introduction-new.

———. "Immersion and Second-Order Narrative." In *The Routledge Companion to American Literary Journalism*, edited by William Dow and Roberta Maguire, 345–59. New York: Routledge, 2020.

———. "The Chronicler: George Packer's The Unwinding (2013)." Post45, 2017. http://post45.research.yale.edu/2017/05/the-chronicler-george-packers-the-unwinding-2013/.

Winterowd, W. Ross. *The Rhetoric of the "Other" Literature*. Carbondale: Southern Illinois University Press, 1990.

Wolfe, Tom. *The New Journalism*. Vol. 1973. London: Picador, 1996.

Wood, James. "Reality Effects: John Jeremiah Sullivan's Essays." *The New Yorker*, 2011. https://www.newyorker.com/magazine/2011/12/19/reality-effects.

Wu, Tim. *The Attention Merchants*. London: Atlantic Books, 2017.

Yeats, William Butler. *The Second Coming*, 1920. https://www.poetryfoundation.org/poems-and-poets/poems/detail/43290.

Young, Iris Marion. "Lived Body vs. Gender: Reflections on Social Structure and Subjectivity." *Ratio* 15, no. 4 (December 1, 2002): 410–28. https://doi.org/10.1111/1467-9329.00200.

Zavarzadeh, Mas'ud. *The Mythopoeic Reality: The Postwar American Nonfiction Novel*. Urbana: University of Illinois Press, 1976.

Zima, Peter Václav. *Subjectivity and Identity: Between Modernity and Postmodernity*. Bloomsbury Studies in Philosophy. London: Bloomsbury, 2015. https://doi.org/10.5040/9781474218641.

Zola, Emile. "The Experimental Novel." In *Documents of Modern Literary Realism*, edited by George J. Becker, 162–96. Princeton: Princeton University Press, 1963.